CRITICAL THINKING

Critical Thinking

An Introduction to the Basic Skills

second edition

WILLIAM HUGHES

broadview press

Canadian Cataloguing in Publication Data
Hughes, William (William II.), 1936-
    Critical thinking: an introduction to the basic skills, 2nd. ed.
ISBN 1-55111-084-9
1. Logic. 2. Critical thinking. I. Title.
BC177.H84 1996 160 C95-932827-0

Broadview Press Ltd., is an independent, international publishing house, incorporated in 1985.
North America:
Post Office Box 1243, Peterborough, Ontario, Canada K9J 7H5
3576 California Road, Orchard Park, NY 14127
TEL: (705) 743-8990; FAX: (705) 743-8353;
E-MAIL: 75322.44@compuserve.com
United Kingdom:
Turpin Distribution Services Ltd., Blackhorse Rd., Letchworth, Hertfordshire SG6 1HN
TEL: (1462) 672555; FAX: (1462) 480947; E-MAIL: turpin@rsc.org

Broadview Press gratefully acknowledges the support of the Ontario Arts Council, and the Ministry of Canadian Heritage. We acknowledge the financial support of the Government of Canada through the Book Publishing Industry Development Program for our publishing activities.

Excerpt from "The Love Song of J. Alfred Prufrock" on page 38 is taken from *Collected Poems* by T.S. Eliot, © Faber and Faber Limited; reprinted by permission.
Excerpts from the *University of Guelph Graduate Calendar 1994/1996* and the *University of Guelph Undergraduate Calendar 1995-1996* © University of Guelph; reprinted by permission.

Book design by George Kirkpatrick
Cover photograph by Olga Tracey

PRINTED IN CANADA

Contents

PART III ASSESSING ARGUMENTS

APPENDICES

Appendix I Paradoxes and Puzzles   280

Appendix II Answers to Self-Tests   293

Acknowledgements

Many people have helped me during the process of writing and revising this book. I am grateful to Dr. Jack Macdonald, Vice President Academic of the University of Guelph, for support from the New Initiatives Fund, which enabled me to produce the first draft of this book. I am also grateful to all the University of Guelph students in 74-210 who, through their questions and comments, gave me a better understanding of what is (and what is not) needed in a critical thinking course. I am especially grateful to those students who have changed my mind about so many matters by successfully *arguing back* (see Chapter 12), thereby demonstrating directly that there is something of practical importance to be learned from mastering critical thinking skills.

The following colleagues and students deserve special mention for their generosity with their time and their helpful suggestions: John-Paul Boyd, Brian Calvert, Tobias Chapman, Paul Genest, Jeff Hurdman, Susan-Judith Hoffmann, Hugh Lehman, Rob Ridley, and Brian Wetstein. I am also indebted to numerous instructors who have drawn to my attention several errors in the first edition.

Finally, I want to acknowledge a special debt of gratitude to my family: to my wife, Daphne, for her general support as well as her efforts to clean up my prose and help me achieve a measure of clarity; and to my children, Miranda, Jeremy, Jonathan, and Anna, for putting up with so much over the years while providing grist for the mill. To them all, I dedicate this book.

PART I

INTRODUCTION

Chapter 1

Reasoning and Critical Thinking

1.1 Reasoning

The ablility to reason is the fundamental characteristic of human beings. It has long been held that the capacity to reason is unique to human beings, but even if it is not – if it turns out, for example, that reasoning is a quality we share with dolphins or apes, or even computers – the capacity to reason is nevertheless central to what we are and how we think of ourselves. Virtually every conscious human activity involves reasoning: we reason whenever we solve problems, make decisions, assess character, explain events, write poems, balance chequebooks, predict elections, make discoveries, interpret works of art, or repair carburetors. We reason about everything from the meaning of life to what to have for dinner.

Of course, much of the time we are not engaged in conscious reasoning: often we simply listen to what others say, take note of things around us, experience feelings, daydream, listen to concerts, tell stories, or watch television. These activities need not involve conscious reasoning, but to the extent that we understand what is going on around or inside us we are not entirely passive. Some reasoning must be taking place even if it is at a pre-conscious level. To understand reasoning properly, however, we need to understand how it differs from mere thinking. When we are merely thinking our thoughts simply come to us, one after another: when we reason we actively link thoughts together in such a way that we believe one thought provides support for another thought. This active process of reasoning is termed **inference**. Inference involves a special relationship between different thoughts: when we infer B from A, we move from A to B because we believe that A *supports* or *justifies* or *makes it reasonable to believe* in the truth of B.

The difference between mere thinking and reasoning or inference is easy to understand through examples. Consider the following pairs of sentences:

Alan is broke, and he is unhappy.
Alan is broke, therefore he is unhappy.

Anne was in a car accident last week, and she deserves an extension on her essay.
Anne was in a car accident last week, so she deserves an extension on her essay.

This triangle has equal sides and equal angles.
This triangle has equal sides; hence it has equal angles.

Notice that the first sentence in each pair simply asserts two thoughts but says nothing about any relationship between them, while the second sentence asserts a relationship between two thoughts. This relationship is signalled by the words *therefore, so,* and *hence.* These are called **inference indicators**: words that indicate that one thought is intended to support (i.e., to justify, provide a reason for, provide evidence for, or entail) another thought. Other common inference indicators are:

since
thus
implies
consequently
because
it follows that
given that

It is important to note that sometimes the inference indicator is missing; this can occur when a speaker thinks the inference is quite obvious. For example:

It's raining; I'd better take my umbrella.

The actual presence of an inference indicator is not important. What is important is the relationship of support between the thoughts of the speaker. This relationship is a defining condition of an inference: if two thoughts are linked by such a relationship they constitute an inference, otherwise they do not.

When we express an inference in words, we do so by means of statements. A **statement** is a sentence (i.e., a set of words) that is used to make a claim that is capable of being true or false. If a sentence is not capable of being true or false, then it is not a statement. Questions (*Are you awake?*) and commands (*Wake up!*) are not capable of being true or false, and hence are not statements. Only statements can be true or false. When an inference is expressed in statements it is called an argument. An **argument** is a set of statements that claims that one or more of those statements, called the **premises**, support another of them, called the **conclusion**. Thus, every argument claims that its premises support its conclusion, or that the conclusion is supported by the premises.

1.2 The Concept of Logical Strength

Since a statement makes a claim that can be true or false, any statement can be assessed by asking whether it is true or false. Is Alan really unhappy? Was Anne actually in a car accident? When we assess the truth or falsity of a statement, it makes no difference whether or not it is part of an argument. A statement that is part of an argument is assessed in the same way as one that is not. The truth or falsity of the statement that Alan is unhappy does not depend upon whether or not it is part of an argument. To discover the truth or falsity of statements we examine the statement itself, and look for evidence that will show us whether it is true or false.

Assessing an argument is quite different. Since an argument always includes a claim that its premises support its conclusion, assessing an argument means assessing this claim. Do the premises really support the conclusion, and if so, how much support do they provide? In other words, how *strong* is the argument? We say that an argument has **logical strength** when its premises, *if true*, actually provide support for its conclusion.

The concept of logical strength is central in critical thinking and has two important features that need to be stressed. First, the logical strength of an argument is independent of the truth or falsity of its premises: we do not need to know that the premises of an argument are true in order to assess its logical strength. When we assess the logical strength of an argument we are really asking, *If the premises are true would we be justified in accepting the conclusion?* and we can answer this question without knowing whether or not the premises actually are true. Consider the following example:

> *The population of Chatham is 27,000.*
> *The population of Orillia is 26,000.*
> *Therefore, Chatham has a larger population than Orillia.*

Even if we don't know the populations of Chatham and Orillia we can still see that the argument is a strong one. If both premises are true, then obviously the conclusion would have to be true as well. The fact that either or both premises might be false does not affect the logical strength of the argument. For similar reasons, an argument with premises and conclusion that are known to be true may be a very weak argument. For example:

> *Toronto is the capital of Ontario.*
> *Ottawa is in Ontario.*
> *Therefore, Ottawa is the capital of Canada.*

In this example the premises and the conclusion are all true, but the facts that Toronto is the capital of Ontario and that Ottawa is in Ontario provide no support for the statement that Ottawa is the capital of Canada. The inference is therefore a bad or weak one. Only if the information contained in the premises really provides a good reason for holding that the conclusion is true can we say the inference is a strong one.

Second, the logical strength of an argument is often a matter of degree. Some arguments are so strong that the truth of the premises guarantees the truth of the conclusion. Such arguments are called **deductive arguments**, and they constitute strict proofs. But most arguments are not as strong as this; usually, the truth of the premises makes it reasonable to hold that the conclusion is also true, but does not provide an absolute guarantee. Such arguments are called **inductive arguments**. For example:

> *Arthur has been a moderate social drinker for twenty years.*
> *No-one has ever known him to get drunk.*
> *Therefore, he won't get drunk at the party tonight.*

This is a strong argument, since if the premises are true it is reasonable to conclude that the conclusion will also be true. Nevertheless, Arthur might get drunk tonight. Given the truth of the premises this might astonish us, but it is not impossible.

Understanding the concept of logical strength is the key to developing critical thinking skills. The fact that the logical strength of an argument is independent of the truth of its premises means that in order to assess an argument we must do more than merely determine whether its premises are true. And the fact that logical strength may be a matter of degree means that we must be sensitive to the various features of arguments that affect its degree of strength. If we lack critical thinking skills we can easily be fooled into thinking that an argument is strong when the premises actually provide little or no support for the conclusion. Consider the following inferences:

> *The Liberals won a majority of seats in the 1993 election.*
> *So, they must have received more votes than any other party.*

> *My sister always got better marks in school than I did.*
> *That proves that she's smarter than I am.*

> *Eighty per cent of those who tried Painaway said they would take it the next time they had a headache.*
> *Therefore, Painaway is a better headache remedy.*

> *The city council is unfair to city employees.*
> *Jones is a city councillor.*
> *Hence, Jones is unfair to city employees.*

> *By definition, God is a perfect being.*
> *A being who does not exist is not perfect.*
> *Therefore, God must exist.*

> *Whenever there is high unemployment interest rates increase.*
> *So, high unemployment causes high interest rates.*

These are all weak arguments: the conclusions are not adequately supported by their premises. This does not mean that the conclusions are false or even likely to be false. It only means that the evidence presented in the premises, even if true, does not entitle us to draw the conclusion. The premises do not, in other words, adequately support the conclusion.

1.3 Truth, Logical Strength and Soundness

In section 1.2 we drew a distinction between assessing the truth or falsity of a statement and assessing the logical strength of an argument. Although these are quite different tasks, both are important if we want to arrive at the truth. Remember that a strong argument is one whose premises really do support its conclusion. In other words, its premises, *if true*, provide a justification for believing the conclusion to be true. But a logically strong argument, as we saw, may have false premises. So if we want to know whether the conclusion of an argument is likely to be true we need to know *both* that the argument is a strong one *and* that its premises are true. What we want, in other words, are logically strong arguments with true premises. An argument that has both logical strength and true premises is called a **sound argument**.

It is very important to be aware of the differences among these three properties. *Truth* is a property of statements and never of arguments. *Logical strength* and *soundness* are properties of arguments and never of statements. *Logical strength* refers to the connection between the premises and conclusion of an argument. *Soundness* is a property of an argument as a whole. Always keep the question of strength separate from the question of truth when dealing with any argument. Never ask simply, *Is this a good argument?* Ask two questions instead:

(1) *Is this a logically strong argument?* and
(2) *Are its premises true?*

The order in which these questions are asked is not important. What is crucial is that they be asked separately. Only when both have been answered are we in a position to know whether an argument is sound – whether we have a good reason to accept its conclusion.

Sometimes, however, it is inappropriate to ask whether the premises are true. We may, for example, want to explore the consequences of an assumption whose truth or falsity we cannot determine. For example:

No-one knows for certain whether Martin Bormann died in 1945. If he did not, then he probably escaped through Switzerland and Italy to South America. That is what Adolf Eichmann and a number of other high-ranking Nazis did.

There are even times when we want to develop an argument with premises that we know or assume to be false. Such arguments are called **counterfactual arguments**. For example, we may want to explore the consequences of the supposition that some historical event never happened. For example:

If Hitler had invaded Britain in 1940 he would have succeeded, because at that time the Germans had military superiority.

Or we may want to explore the consequences of the occurrence of some hypothetical situation. For example:

If the provincial sales tax were reduced to 5 per cent, there would not be a corresponding decrease in government revenues. This is because part of the decrease would be offset by an increase in sales as a result of the sales tax reduction.

We should also note a special kind of counterfactual argument called the **reductio ad absurdum**. In a reductio argument, a statement is proven to be true by assuming it to be false and then deriving a contradiction from that assumption. For example:

It is preposterous to claim, as some people have, that Gorbachev engineered the August 1991 coup attempt by Communist hard-liners in order to strengthen his position and stop the secessionist movements in the republics. If he engineered the coup then we would have to conclude that he is an exceptionally stupid man, for not only did the coup weaken his personal position and strengthen the position of Yeltsin, his chief rival, but it unleashed a wave of secessionism that destroyed the Soviet Union. Gorbachev may not be the smartest man in the world, but no-one could have become political leader of the Soviet Union and been that stupid.

In all these kinds of cases we want our arguments to be strong, but we cannot even pretend that these arguments are sound, since we know or assume that at least one of the premises is false.

Counterfactual arguments, however, are the exception to the rule. In almost all cases our main concern is with sound arguments. If we start with true premises, and use only logically strong arguments, we are entitled to rely on the conclusions we reach. Sound arguments expand our knowledge and increase our understanding. This is why developing the ability to recognize sound arguments is so important.

1.4 Critical Thinking Skills

The primary focus of critical thinking skills is on determining whether arguments are sound, i.e., whether they have true premises and logical strength. But determining the soundness of arguments is not a simple matter, for three reasons.

First, before we can assess an argument we must determine its precise meaning. It would be convenient if the meaning of arguments were always clear, but unfortunately this is often not so. An argument may be unclear because the meaning of one or more of its statements is unclear, or because the nature of the connection that is being asserted between the premises and conclusion is unclear. This means we have to learn how to interpret statements and arguments in a way that makes their meaning as clear as possible. The skills needed for this task are interpretive skills. Chapters 2 to 4 are aimed at developing these skills.

Second, determining the truth or falsity of statements is often a difficult task. Even when we are sure we know precisely what a statement means we may be unsure about its truth, and may even be unsure how to go about determining whether it is true or false. As we shall see, there are several different types of statements, and each type has its own method for determining truth and falsity. The skills needed for this task are verification skills. We shall deal with these skills in Chapter 6.

Third, assessing arguments is complex because there are several different types of inferences, and each type requires a different kind of assessment. It is necessary to learn how to recognize these different types of inferences and to become familiar with these different methods of assessment. For this purpose reasoning skills are needed. These skills are dealt with in Chapters 7 to 14.

These three types of skills – interpretive skills, verification skills, and reasoning skills – constitute what are usually referred to as critical thinking skills. Developing a mastery of them is important for several practical reasons.

First, we are inundated with information of all sorts, but this information is useless unless we know how to use it in our thinking to draw out its implications and consequences. Much of it is incomplete and one-sided in ways that are often not apparent, and if we are not on our guard we may be misled.

Second, we are constantly presented with arguments designed to get us to accept some conclusion that we would otherwise not accept. Politicians, preachers, advertisers, editorial writers, and special-interest groups of all sorts spend a great deal of time, thought, and money attempting to persuade us to believe the things they want us to believe, and it is important to be on guard against arguments that fail to meet the appropriate logical criteria. This is partly a matter of our own self-interest, for when others seek to make us believe things that are in their interest it is possible, or even likely, that our interests are not being well served.

Third, mastering critical thinking skills is also a matter of intellectual self-respect. We all have the capacity to learn how to distinguish good arguments from bad ones and to work out for ourselves what we ought and ought not to believe, and it diminishes us as persons if we let others do our thinking for us. If we are not prepared to think for ourselves, and to make the effort to learn how do this well, we will always be in danger of becoming slaves to the ideas and values of others and to our own ignorance.

And finally, critical thinking skills can make it easier for us to persuade others to change their beliefs. Many beliefs are based more on emotion than on reason, although those holding them usually believe they are based on reason. In fact, it is rare to find a person, even a complete bigot, who does not believe that his or her beliefs have a rational basis. Critical thinking skills can often be effective in dislodging such beliefs, and persuading others to change their views.

This last point raises a number of moral questions. Like any skill, critical thinking skills can be used for good or ill. There are many ways in which they can be abused. They can be used to make a bad argument look much stronger than it really is, and to make an opponent's position look much weaker than it really is. They can be used to make ourselves look wise, and to make others look foolish. They can be used to avoid having to respond to legitimate criticisms, and to persuade others to change their beliefs for inadequate reasons. Every day we find ourselves in situations in which we could use our critical thinking skills for such purposes, and sometimes we may be tempted to do so. Yielding to the temptation, however, is dishonest and hypocritical. It is analogous to a medical doctor who uses his or her medical training not to help people, but to torture them more effectively.

There are other, more difficult, moral questions that can arise. How far should we go in revealing the weaknesses we see in our arguments to our opponents? Is it always right to attack the weaknesses in the views of others? How are we to be fair to our opponents? How far should we go in our attempts not to distort others' views when discussing them? How forceful should we be in attempting to persuade others to agree with our views? As we shall see, there are no easy answers to such questions. They need to be approached with an equal regard for the truth and for the feelings of others, and with a proper sense of our own fallibility.

1.5 Critical Thinking and the Science of Logic

Reasoning skills involve the application of principles of logic. Logic is the science that studies the relationships between premises and conclusions with a view to determining when and to what extent the premises actually support the conclusion. Logic was first recognized as a science in the fourth century BC by Aristotle, who described what he believed were the basic principles of correct reasoning. These principles were elaborated and developed by a number of medieval logicians, but the basic nature of logic remained essentially Aristotelian until the late nineteenth century. About a hundred years ago, logic entered a period of radical change when mathematicians began using logic to solve certain problems regarding the foundations of mathematics. More recently, developments in computer science and in artificial intelligence have contributed to further developments in logic. As a result, logic has become a highly complex and sophisticated discipline of considerable theoretical importance. The power and sophistication of modern logic, however, have been purchased at the price of increasing abstractness. The principles of modern logic have been abstracted from ordinary language and are considered as purely formal principles, devoid of content.

Many of the critical thinking skills described in this book are drawn from logic. Our interest in them, however, is not in their theoretical foundations or theoretical significance but in their practical application. In particular, we are interested in the way in which the principles of logic function when used in natural language. When any logical principle is used in a real-life setting we face a host of special problems that take us beyond the domain of formal logic. Throughout this book these problems of practical application will engage most of our attention. The principles of formal logic have their own interest and intellectual challenge, but they lie beyond the scope of this book.

1.6 Self-Test No. 1

I. Which of the following passages are arguments? For those that are arguments, identify the premise(s) and the conclusion.

1. You should go home next weekend because you promised your parents you would.

2. You should go home next weekend and have a good time with your friends.

3. Ted won the Intercollegiate ten thousand metres last year and has been training hard ever since, so he should win easily this year.

4. I will be able to visit you next month after all. The doctor just told me that a second operation won't be necessary and that I'll be able to go home this Friday.

5. His car skidded on the ice and hit a van in the middle of the intersection. The car was a write-off and the van suffered three thousand dollars in damage.

6. It is obvious that no great leader ever suffered from low self-esteem.

7. The company laid off 250 assembly line workers last week. I think they were justified because their sales had declined by 23 per cent in the past three months.

8. Many people think that thunder is caused by lightning. This is a mistake.

9. Most evenings I go for a walk after dinner. Usually, I walk to the park and back, which is about three kilometres, but last night I only went as far as the library.

10. You're crazy if you think you can take a full course load while working twenty hours a week, and pass your semester. Don't you remember what happened to Alex and Doreen last year?

II. Using your common-sense knowledge, which of the following are sound arguments, and which are merely logically strong arguments?

1. Guelph is in Ontario. Ontario is in Canada. Therefore, Guelph is in Canada.

2. Toronto is larger than Guelph. Guelph is larger than Vancouver. Therefore, Toronto is larger than Vancouver.

3. Jimmy is taller than Jane. Jane is taller than June. Therefore, June is shorter than Jimmy.

4. No-one under the age of eighteen is legally an adult. Katherine is only seventeen years old. Therefore, Katherine is not legally an adult.

5. Hockey is Canada's national sport. A country's national sport is likely to be very popular in that country. Therefore, hockey is likely to be very popular in Canada.

6. Barrie is north of Toronto. Parry Sound is north of Barrie. Therefore, Parry Sound is north of Toronto.

7. A cat makes a good house pet. A tiger is a cat. Therefore, a tiger makes a good house pet.

8. No human being is immortal. Even the Prime Minister is a human being. Therefore, the Prime Minister is not immortal.

9. Everybody loves a winner. Robin is a winner. Therefore, everybody loves Robin.

10. At this moment, I am reading a book. If I am reading a book I must be awake. Therefore, I must be awake.

1.7 Questions for Discussion

In section 1.1, an argument was defined as a set of statements that *claims* that its premises support its conclusion. Sometimes it is not clear whether a speaker intends to make such a claim. In these cases we have to rely upon whatever clues the context provides to decide whether it is reasonable to interpret what the speaker has said as being an argument rather than something else. For each of the following passages, briefly describe a context that makes it reasonable to interpret it as either an argument, or not an argument.

1. The expressway was closed for three hours this afternoon because of the train derailment on the overpass.

2. When George finished speaking Frances sat quietly for several minutes, her brow furrowed in intense concentration. Suddenly, she leapt up and ran to her room, rummaged through her desk, found a sheet of paper, and scrawled a few words on it. She crammed it in an envelope, addressed and stamped the envelope, ran out of the house, and thrust it into the mailbox. "That's done," she said. "Now I am committed, and my life will never be the same again."

3. The company laid off 250 assembly line workers last week because their sales had declined by 23 per cent in the past three months. The company seems to have had no choice.

4. Mike refuses to vote because he thinks all political parties are the same.

5. I went for a walk last evening, but when I got to London Road it started to rain so I turned around and came home.

6. Hey, it's seven o'clock; it's time to go.

7. To get rid of hiccoughs, breathe into a paper bag for a few minutes.

8. By the end of the war in 1945, Churchill realized that, although Britain had won the war against the Axis powers, it was an economically devastated nation that would need massive foreign aid if it was to recover.

9. This is an important decision, obviously, and I don't want to decide in haste. I suppose, all things considered, that the best thing to do would be to resign, but I would like to have until tomorrow to think about it.

10. It is a beautiful day out, and a walk in the park will make you feel better.

PART II

MEANING

Chapter 2

Meaning and Definition

Reasoning, we have said, involves thinking. Thinking, in turn, involves language, for without language we could not express (and probably not even have) any thoughts. In order to understand reasoning, therefore, it is necessary to pay careful attention to the relationship between thought and language. The relationship seems to be straightforward: thought is expressed in and through language. But this claim, while true, is an oversimplification. People often fail to say what they mean. Everyone has had the experience of having their words misunderstood by others. And we all use words not merely to express our thoughts, but also to shape them. Developing our critical thinking skills, therefore, requires an understanding of the ways in which words can (and can fail to) express our thoughts.

2.1 The Complexity of Language

Language is an extremely complex phenomenon. The number of different words in any language is finite, but these words can be used to generate an infinite number of different sentences with different meanings. Many of the ordinary things we say every day have never been said before by anyone. For example:

> *Professor Sutherland reminds me of my Uncle Tony; they both have the habit of running their fingers through their hair when they are thinking hard.*

It is likely that when this sentence was first written it had never before been said. And it is not just the precise wording that is unique: it is unlikely that anyone has ever had the same thought. In fact, there is no limit to the number of new sentences with new meanings that could be created. Conversely, there are often different ways of saying the same thing. For example:

Anne is older than everyone else in the room.
Everyone else in the room is younger than Anne.

In addition, there are often many different sentences that mean more or less the same thing. One lexicographer has recorded over twenty-two hundred synonyms for the word *drunk*.

Written and spoken language, although closely connected, are nevertheless not identical: spoken language is more flexible (and hence more complex) than written language, for we can change the meaning of words and sentences through our gestures, tone of voice, and facial expressions. Note the different meanings that arise when the underlined word is emphasized in the following sentences:

You shouldn't steal library books. (But it may be acceptable for others to do so.)
You shouldn't steal library books. (But I won't be surprised if you do.)
You shouldn't steal library books. (But defacing books is acceptable.)
You shouldn't steal library books. (But stealing books from the bookstore is acceptable.)
You shouldn't steal library books. (But stealing magazines from the library is acceptable.)

Understanding spoken language, therefore, requires much more than knowing the written language. In fact, the close connection between written and spoken language that exists in European languages is sometimes absent in other languages. Chinese spoken dialects (which are as different from one another as English and German) all use the same written language, so that people who speak different dialects can communicate through writing even though they may not understand each other's speech.

Language is always in a state of gradual change, in ways that are in large part unpredictable even in principle. A single language can, in a few centuries, evolve into two languages so different from one another that those who speak one will find the other incomprehensible. Surprisingly, when languages evolve they do not evolve into more complex forms, for the complexity of all natural languages seems to remain more or less constant. So-called primitive languages may have somewhat smaller vocabularies than modern languages (although we need to remember that the Inuit have eleven different words for the different kinds of snow), but in other respects they are just as complex. "Primitive" languages are not really primitive at all.

Given this complexity, it is astonishing that we learn almost everything we will ever know about language before we are old enough to go to school. We are all intimately familiar with at least one language, and we therefore understand what language is, at least in the sense of knowing how to use language. But at a deeper level most of us have only the most elementary understanding of what language is and how it works. Even linguistic theorists are uncertain about many features of language. They do not know, for example, whether the basic structure of language (i.e., its underlying grammar) reflects certain characteristics of the human mind, or is merely conventional in nature. Nor do they fully understand the relationship between language and thinking: we normally use a language when we think, but is language necessary for human thought? And if it is, do people who think in different languages think differently? When we translate a speech from Russian into English can we be sure that we understand exactly what it meant to the original speaker or what it means to a Russian audience? The relationship between language and reality is also problematic. Does language describe the world as it really is, or do we use language to impose a structure on our experience, experience that would otherwise be chaotic and meaningless?

2.2 The Meaning of Language

Usually it is not difficult to explain what a particular word or sentence means. But there is much that is puzzling about the nature of meaning itself. How do words get their meaning, and how do meanings change? Is the meaning that words have different from the meaning of sentences? In order to enhance our understanding of the nature and complexity of meaning, we will look briefly at three theories of meaning. The first two are common-sense views that have been held by many people, including many philosophers and linguistic theorists. Unfortunately, both are open to serious objections, and many philosophers now regard them as untenable. The third theory avoids the weakness of the first two, and is the one we will rely upon in this book.

The reference theory of meaning was first expounded by Aristotle in the fourth century BC. According to this view the meaning of a word consists in what it refers to. The word *dog* refers to all the dogs in the world, so it seems plausible to hold that the meaning of *dog* is all the dogs in the world. After all, if we know what *dog* refers to we obviously know what the word means. Similarly, the meaning of *tree* is every tree in the world, the meaning of *automobile* is every automobile, the meaning of *joke* is every joke, and so on. The meaning of a term thus consists of its reference class, that is, the class of objects to which the word refers. At first glance, the reference theory is a plausible account of meaning, and its plausibility is enhanced by the fact that pointing to the reference class is often a good way of explaining the meaning of a word. If you don't know what *antimacassar* means I can easily explain its meaning by pointing to an antimacassar, and explaining that other antimacassars vary in size and design but are essentially the same as this one.

There are, however, serious difficulties with the reference theory. At the heart of the theory there seems to be a confusion between understanding the meaning of a word, and having knowledge of what the word refers to. When we understand the meaning of the word *dog*, we usually have knowledge of only a small proportion of the dogs that exist, and this is puzzling if the meaning of *dog* is the reference class of the term. The fact that even small children can understand the meaning of *dog* on the basis of direct knowledge of only a few dogs cannot be explained by the reference theory. The theory encounters even more serious difficulties, however, when we consider words that have no reference class. What do the following words refer to: *unless, after, yes, unlikely, the, nevertheless, was, if, where*? Does it even make sense to suggest that the meaning of *unless* is the class of unlesses? In addition, there are certain phrases whose meaning is easily understood but whose reference is unknown. For example, we all understand the meaning of the phrase *the oldest man in the world*, even when we don't know to whom it refers. If the meaning *is* the reference, then we shouldn't be able to understand what the phrase means unless we know who is the oldest man in the world. The reference theory of meaning, therefore, has to be rejected.

2.2.2 THE IDEA THEORY OF MEANING

The idea theory of meaning was developed by John Locke in the seventeenth century. He held that the meaning of a word consists of the idea or mental image that is associated with the word. When we think of the word *dog*, it seems that we have a mental image we associate with the word, and it is plausible to hold that the meaning of *dog* is this image in our minds. This theory seems to be able to deal with phrases like *the oldest man in the world*, since it is plausible to suggest that we have a mental image we associate with this phrase.

But the idea theory also encounters several difficulties. Just as the class of unlesses seems to make no sense, the mental image of *unless* also seems to make no sense. But in addition, the image or idea we associate with a word like *dog* turns out on reflection to be very unclear. If we attempt to describe our image of a dog, we can only describe a typical dog: one that is black, short-haired, about eighteen inches high, with a short tail, etc. Of course, we know that many dogs are not black, that some are long-haired, that some are very small and some are very large, and so forth. But we cannot have an image of a dog which is both black and not black, both long-haired and short-haired, and both tall and short. It is impossible for our image of a dog to include all those characteristics that we know dogs have. How, then, can our image *be* the meaning of the word?

Another difficulty with the idea theory is that it has the consequence that we can never know what another person means by certain words. You can never see my mental images and I can never see yours. If the mental image is the meaning, how can I know what you mean by *dog* and how can you know what I mean by *dog*? One reply to this objection is that we can describe our mental images in words that others can understand, and in this way we can know what others mean by a word. This reply is adequate for some words, but not for all. The mental images we have for simple properties (for example, properties such as *red, hot, sour,* etc.) can never be stated. We simply cannot describe the meaning of the word *red* by using other words. If we could, then someone who has been blind since birth would know what *red* means merely by hearing a description of our mental image, which is impossible. Words fail us at this point. So the idea theory must also be rejected.

A new approach to meaning was developed in this century by Ludwig Wittgenstein (1889-1951) and John Austin (1911-1960). They recognized that many words do refer to things, and that many words have a mental image or idea associated with them, but they held that the primary bearers of meaning are not words but sentences. Words have meaning only when they are used in sentences: without such a context they have no meaning. When we ask what some particular word means, we seem to be asking for *the* meaning of the word itself, as if it had a meaning apart from the way it is used in sentences. In fact, the only meaning a word can have is the meaning it gains from the meanings of the sentences in which the word is typically used. Notice how the different meanings of a word are expressed by using that word in different sentences:

> *I gave him a **hand** with his baggage.* (i.e., help)
> *The crowd gave him a **hand**.* (i.e., applause)
> *Please **hand** me the scissors.* (i.e., give)

> *She is a **green** lawyer.* (i.e., inexperienced)
> *He is looking **green**.* (i.e., nauseous)
> *We had a **green** Christmas last year.* (i.e., without snow)

> *Don't **strike** that child.* (i.e., hit)
> *The **strike** was over wages.* (i.e., refusal to work)
> ***Strike** three!* (i.e., the batter is "out")

But if the meaning of sentences is primary and the meaning of words is derivative – if we cannot derive the meaning of a sentence from the meanings of the words it contains – how are we to account for the meaning of sentences? Wittgenstein and Austin held that the meaning of sentences is to be found in their use. Language is a tool, and just as we don't really know what a hammer is until we know what its use is, so we don't know what language means until we know what it is being used to do. In order to know what a particular sentence means we need to ask, *What is this speaker, in this particular context, using this sentence to do?* If someone says *Hold it*, we cannot know what the sentence means until we know what the speaker means, and we cannot know what the speaker means until we know what he or she is using the sentence to do. Did the speaker say *Hold it* to get someone to stop doing something, or to instruct someone to grasp hold of an object? Only when we have answered this question will we know what the sentence means.

It is important to pay attention to the context, for the context typically gives us the clues we need to determine what the speaker is using a sentence to do, and thus what the sentence means. There are various contextual features we can make use of, such as the social setting, the speaker's personal goals, the nature and expectations of the audience, and what has just been said by other speakers. Changing the context of a sentence can sometimes dramatically affect its meaning. For example:

> *The queen is in a vulnerable position:* (a) when said by a spectator at a chess match and (b) when said by a teacher in a lecture on the role of the monarchy in Britain.

> *The President has been shot and died a few minutes ago:* (a) when said by a character in a film and (b) when said by a radio announcer in a news broadcast.

> *Let me go:* (a) when said by a person whose arm has been grabbed by someone and (b) when said by a child whose teacher has asked for a volunteer to run an errand.

More commonly, however, context affects meaning in less dramatic but equally important ways. Usually, there are only a few possible uses of a sentence in any particular context, and we can make a reasonable judgement of its primary or intended use. It is important, therefore, to understand the various uses or functions of language.

2.3 The Main Functions of Language

Whenever we use language we do so for some purpose, and if we consider these purposes we can see that there are several different types. Language, in other words, has several functions. Language is often characterized as a means of communication, and although this view is correct, it is not very informative. When we use language we almost always communicate something to someone, but usually our purpose is much more specific, and frequently we are not primarily concerned with communicating information at all. Our purpose is usually not merely to communicate, but to communicate for a specific purpose. What we mean often reflects these purposes. Consequently, how we interpret, and therefore react to, what others say depends upon what we take their purpose to be. It is therefore important to be aware of the main purposes for which language is used and how these purposes affect meaning. Each of these purposes reflects a different function of language.

1. **Descriptive** One very important function of language is to describe (i.e., to convey factual information about) something. Whenever we describe something – an object, a situation, or a feeling – we are stating facts, or what we believe to be facts. For example:

> *This coffee is cold.*
> *I don't have any change for the coffee machine.*
> *A cup of coffee would calm my nerves.*

Almost every time we use language we convey factual information, even though this may not be our primary purpose.

2. **Evaluative** Often we use language not (or not merely) to describe something but to make a value judgement about it, that is, to evaluate it. For example:

> *Ellen is the best student in the class.*

This is different from a mere factual description, for it presents a value judgement about Ellen. There are several different types of evaluations: aesthetic, moral, economic, technological, and even scientific. For example:

> *That was the worst movie I've seen in years.*
> *He is an irresponsible person.*
> *The best way to get rich is by investing in real estate.*
> *The safest way of disposing of uranium waste is to bury it in old coal mines.*
> *The theory of evolution provides the best account of the origin of biological species.*

3. **Emotive Language** is sometimes used to express emotions, and thus has an emotive function. When you hit your thumb with a hammer, you probably say something. If you say, *My thumb hurts,* you are

describing your feelings. If you say, *This is a terrible hammer,* you are evaluating the hammer. But if, like most people, you say, *Damn!* (or worse), you are not describing or evaluating anything but are simply expressing your feelings or emotions. Almost any emotion can be expressed in words. For example:

> *I love you.*
> *You are a loathsome creature; go away.*
> *I shall die of unrequited love.*
> *Thank heavens that's over.*

Note that these sentences also convey factual information about the speakers' feelings, but in most contexts this function would be secondary.

4. **Evocative Language** can also used for the purpose of evoking certain emotions in an audience. If we want someone to feel sad about something we can try to evoke that emotion through the careful choice of words and images. Poets are especially concerned with this function of language. Consider, for example, the line from T.S. Eliot's "The Love Song of J. Alfred Prufrock," which beautifully evokes the feeling of a meaningless life:

> *I have measured out my life with coffee spoons.*

Again, W.B. Yeats, in "The Lake Isle of Innisfree," evokes a feeling of peacefulness:

> *And I shall have some peace there, for peace comes dropping slow.*

Advertisers frequently use language to evoke certain feelings. For example:

> *At Speedy you're a Somebody.*

And everyone from time to time wants to evoke certain emotions in their audience. We want others to feel pity for someone, to feel anger at some situation, or to approve of something, and we use language for this purpose. Threats are usually intended to evoke fear in the victim. Political speeches are often aimed at making voters feel that a government is trustworthy, or untrustworthy. Sermons often are designed to make us feel ashamed of the mean things we do.

5. **Persuasive**   One of the most widespread uses of language is to persuade people to accept something or to act in a certain way. For example:

You shouldn't take astrology seriously. There is no scientific basis for it.

I know you don't like parties, but I hope you'll come anyway. There will be several people there that you have been wanting to meet. I know you will enjoy yourself once you get there.

We try to persuade people to recycle waste, that the government's budget is likely to increase unemployment, that the police officer should not give us a speeding ticket, or that lotteries are a waste of money. Every argument is an example of the persuasive use of language. There are two ways language can be used to persuade. Sometimes our purpose is to persuade by means of rational arguments, even if we often fail to achieve our purpose. But often we abandon this restriction and use anything we think might succeed in persuading our audience. This is the case with propaganda and most advertising.

6. **Interrogative**   In order to elicit information we usually need to ask for it. Most often this is done by asking a question. For example:

What is the due date for the essay?

But asking questions is not the only way to elicit information. For example:

Tell me your age.
I won't lend you twenty dollars unless you explain why you need it.

Whatever form of words we use, we are not describing, evaluating, expressing, or evoking anything, or attempting to persuade, but seeking to gain information.

7. **Directive**   We sometimes use language to tell others to do something. For example:

Go to the principal's office immediately.
Take these pills twice a day.

These sentences would normally be used to tell someone to do something. They do not describe or evaluate anything, express or evoke an emotion, seek information, nor, usually, do they attempt to persuade us of anything. They simply tell us what to do. The directive use of language covers ordering, commanding, directing, advising, requesting, and similar types of actions.

8. **Performative**   There is a small but interesting class of sentences that are known as performative utterances, i.e., utterances that are not descriptions, evaluations, directives, and so on, but are themselves to be regarded as actions. They are actions that consist of saying certain words. If a question arises of whether someone actually performed such an action, the only relevant evidence would consist of showing that the person uttered certain words under appropriate circumstances. For example:

I find the accused guilty of murder.

If these words are uttered by Judge Bean at the conclusion of a trial they constitute the action of finding someone guilty of murder. If someone asks for proof that Judge Bean found the accused guilty of murder it would be sufficient to quote the judge's words. It would make no sense to suggest that Judge Bean might have been mistaken or lying. If he said the words at the conclusion of the trial then he did find the accused guilty of murder. On the other hand, if I say,

Judge Bean found the accused guilty of murder,

I could not appeal to the fact that I said it as proof that it is true, since I might be mistaken or lying. It is not a performative utterance, but a description: it is true only if it correctly states or describes a fact. Similarly, if after the trial Judge Bean says,

I found the accused guilty of murder,

this would not be a performative utterance, for we could not appeal to the fact that Judge Bean uttered this sentence as proof that it is true, since he might be mistaken or lying. Here are two more examples of performative utterances:

I now pronounce you husband and wife.
I resign, here and now.

When uttered under the appropriate circumstances, each would constitute an action.

9. **Recreational** Finally, we should not overlook the fact that language is often used to amuse ourselves and others. We tell jokes and stories, write novels, invent puns, do crossword puzzles, play guessing games, make up limericks, sing nursery rhymes, and write rude things on washroom walls. When language is used in any of these ways it serves a recreational function. People who tell jokes, write stories, or sing nursery rhymes usually do so out of simple enjoyment.

There are other functions of language, but these are the main ones, and all others can be fitted in at least one of the above categories. For example, we sometimes use language to hurt others' feelings, but this can be regarded as an evocative use of language. It is important to understand that these categories are not mutually exclusive: most of the time language serves more than one function. Often we intend to use a sentence for two or more purposes. We tell a joke in order to make someone relax (i.e., we amuse in order to evoke a feeling). We describe an automobile accident in hopes of persuading someone to drive more carefully. We evaluate a murder so as to express our abhorrence. We order someone to do something in order to evoke in them a feeling of respect for our authority.

The functions of language can be viewed from both a subjective and an objective point of view. From the subjective point of view we regard the speaker's intention or purpose as primary. Did Sally intend to express her feelings or to convey information? Did Todd really intend to say something funny or was he just trying to be helpful? Was the doctor just describing the options or was she trying to persuade me to have the operation? From this point of view what is important is the speaker's intentions. From the objective point of view, on the other hand, we disregard the speaker's intentions and consider how the audience is affected by what is said. From the objective point of view every utterance always has several functions, even when the speaker has only one purpose. The other functions go beyond what the speaker intends. For example, we always convey some information to our audience whenever we speak, even when conveying information is not our purpose. Again, it is sometimes difficult, or even impossible, to describe certain things in a way that avoids expressing our emotions. (Try to describe a rape in a way that expresses nothing of your feelings.) Sometimes when we intend to describe something we inadvertently amuse others, as in *We had chork pops for dinner*. Frequently, there is an unacknowledged persuasive or evaluative function in what people say. From the objective point of view we can often draw out levels of meaning in what someone says that the speaker is unaware of, and may even refuse to admit are present.

The difference between these two points of view is important. To understand the meaning of what someone says, we must give priority to the subjective point of view. As we shall see later, when we assess an argument it is important to pay careful attention to what the speaker *means*, i.e., to the subjective meaning.

2.4 Self-Test No. 2

Using the contextual clues provided, what is the most likely primary purpose of the speakers of the following sentences?

1. If you want to succeed in life you need a good education. (Said by a father to his seventeen-year-old daughter who has just told him she wants to drop out of school.)

2. Retail clothing stores can increase sales by about 30 per cent through advertising in local media. (Said by a teacher in a business class at a community college.)

3. You can increase your sales by 30 per cent through advertising in local media. (Said by an advertising salesperson from a local TV station when talking to the manager of a clothing store.)

4. I love you more than anyone else I've ever known. (Said by a young woman to a young man.)

5. She loves him more than anyone she's ever known. (Said by a father about his daughter and her boyfriend.)

6. Peter Piper picked a peck of pickled peppers. (Said by a father to his four-year-old daughter.)

7. Your essay must be at least fifteen hundred words and must include a full bibliography. (Said by a professor to a class.)

8. I now declare this building officially open. (Said by a politician when cutting the ribbon at the opening of a new school building.)

9. Pedestrians Cross Here. (A sign at a crosswalk.)

10. Reading an old copy of a Dickens novel is like spending an afternoon in the attic of an old house: the feel of the old paper, the look of the dated typeface, and the musty smell all take you back to the days when even your grandparents were still children. (From an article by a literary critic entitled *Why Reading Literature is Important.*)

2.5 Questions for Discussion

Unlike the self-test questions above, the contextual clues provided here allow of more than one reasonable answer. Suggest additional contextual detail that would support attributing at least two plausible purposes to the speakers.

1. Why can't you pay attention? (Said by a Grade 6 teacher to a student who frequently daydreams.)

2. The next car I buy will definitely be a Volvo. (Said by someone in a TV ad for Volvo.)

3. Military intelligence is a contradiction in terms. (Said by a historian in a course on the history of World War II.)

4. Frankly, Scarlett, I don't give a damn. (Said by Clark Gable in the film *Gone With The Wind*.)

5. Like, wow, man, what a blast. (Said by a teenager after a rock concert.)

6. Can you imagine what it must have been like, having to care for two small children in a Nazi concentration camp? (Said by a woman about her grandmother.)

7. Your time is now up. (Said by a teacher at the end of an examination.)

8. Most of the time he's a real jerk. (Said by a girl about her brother.)

9. I have often wondered what became of him. (Said by a middle-aged woman about a childhood friend.)

10. The best way to remove chewing gum from a carpet is to rub it with an ice cube for a minute or so. (An excerpt from a book of household hints.)

2.6 Definition

In section 2.2.3 we noted that words often have more than one use or meaning. It is important to understand that not all the different uses of a word need have anything in common; for some words there may be a common element, but for many there is not. As long as we know how to use a word for some particular purpose, we know what the word means when used in that sense. Indeed, it is often difficult to enumerate all the different accepted uses of a word. But this is not a problem for the meaning-as-use theory, for it denies that words must have a single meaning. Since words typically have several different uses, it follows that there will be several different meanings, and as long as we understand a particular use (i.e., know how to use the word for that purpose) we understand the meaning of the word when used in that way.

We have seen that the meaning of language depends upon its use and context, and that it is often difficult to say precisely what a word means if we ignore its use and context. Normally this is not a serious difficulty, for we can usually get by with a rough idea of what words mean as long as they are being used in ordinary contexts. But sometimes this casual approach is inadequate, and it becomes important to focus on the precise meanings of a word. When a lawyer explains what constitutes an assault, or a sales clerk says the microwave oven has a warranty, or a scientist talks about energy, we run the risk of misunderstanding if we fail to pay careful attention to the precise meanings of their words. These are the kinds of occasions when definitions are important; without them we may misunderstand what is being said. Of course, we also need definitions when we come across a word we are unfamiliar with, or when a familiar word is being used in an unfamiliar way. In these cases, it is not misunderstanding that we want to avoid, but not understanding at all.

To understand how definitions work we need to note the distinction between the **sense** of a term (sometimes called its **connotation** or **intension**) and its **reference** (or **denotation** or **extension**). The sense of a word is what we understand when we understand its meaning, and the reference is the class of things to which the word refers. The sense of the term *bachelor*, for example, is the concept of an unmarried male, and the reference of the term is the class of all bachelors in the universe, not only those who now exist but those who have existed in the past and may exist in the future. All words must have a sense, although some words, as we saw in section 2.2.1, have no reference. Words with no reference, however, are quite rare and, as we saw, pose special difficulties.

2.7 The Purposes of Definition

In order to understand how definitions work, we need to be aware of the different purposes for which definitions may be put forward. There are three main types.

2.7.1 REPORTIVE DEFINITIONS

The most common purpose of definitions is to convey the information needed to use a word correctly. The correct use of a word consists of its standard usage – how the word is in fact used by those who make regular use of it. When we want to know the meaning of a word in its standard usage, we need a reportive definition, i.e., one that reports its standard usage. Dictionaries always give reportive definitions.

Reportive definitions can sometimes be troublesome because it may not be clear whether or not a particular use can be regarded as part of the standard usage. For example, fifty years ago the word *cohort* was standardly used only to refer to a group of persons banded together. (This reflected its original meaning in Latin, where it referred to a military unit roughly akin to a platoon.) Now, however, it is usually used to refer to a friend or associate. The sentence *Fred arrived with his cohort*, if used to mean that Fred arrived with his friend, would have been incorrect fifty years ago, but is now usually accepted as correct. This shift in meaning was probably brought about by people who did not understand the old usage, and who were therefore using the word incorrectly, but the mistake has become so widespread that it is no longer regarded as incorrect. Only dedicated linguistic reactionaries continue to regard the new usage as incorrect. Except for cases where a meaning shift has not yet been accepted as standard usage, however, reportive definitions are usually quite straightforward.

2.7.2 STIPULATIVE DEFINITIONS

Sometimes it is useful to be able to fix a particular meaning for a word. Someone who is writing a report on land use in Ontario would find it necessary to define the categories of land use that are being employed. The report would therefore stipulate how the words *agricultural, residential, industrial, recreational,* and so forth are being used. When we do this we are not attempting to report the standard usage, although it would clearly be foolish to depart radically from it. For many specific purposes, such as doing research or enacting legislation, it makes good sense to stipulate the precise meaning that is to be attached to key words. As long as this stipulated meaning is explicitly stated, there is no risk of misunderstanding, and there is an obvious gain in clarity and precision.

There is nothing to prevent us from inventing a new word by using a stipulative definition. For example, we might invent the word *spinge* to refer to the deposit that builds up between the bristles on a toothbrush, or the word *tele-rape* to refer to obscene telephone calls. We can also stipulate a new meaning for an old word: for example, using *bubble* to refer to a promise made by a politician. There is, however, no guarantee that these new words or uses will become part of the standard usage. This is likely to happen only when there is a need (or a perceived need) for the new term. If enough people think it is important to be able to talk about a new object or phenomenon or to refer to something in a new way, then a new word will usually be forthcoming, and will soon become part of standard usage. Until this happens, however, new words depend for their meaning upon stipulative definitions.

Some words – such as *justice, truth, love, religion, freedom, deity, death, law, peace, health*, and *science* – refer to things or qualities that have considerable importance. When we ask *What is justice?* we are not asking for a reportive definition, since such a definition might reflect a widespread misconception about the essential nature of justice. Nor would we be asking for a stipulative definition, since we can invent these for ourselves as easily as the next person. We are asking for a definition that reveals the essential nature of justice.

The correctness of an essentialist definition cannot be determined merely by an appeal to standard usage, like a reportive definition, nor by an appeal to its usefulness, like a stipulative definition. Essentialist definitions really need to be understood as compressed theories; they attempt to express in succinct form a theory about the nature of what is being defined. Thus, assessing an essentialist definition involves assessing a theory, and this goes far beyond questions about the meaning of words.

These three purposes of definition are important since when we want to determine whether a definition is acceptable we must first decide its purpose. Good stipulative definitions and good essentialist definitions are usually inadequate reportive definitions, and good reportive definitions are usually unsatisfactory essentialist definitions.

2.8 Methods of Definition

There are several different methods that can be used to define words. These methods can be used for reportive, stipulative, and essentialist definitions.

1.   **Genus–Species**   The most common method of defining a word is to refer to a class (i.e., a genus) of which the term is a member and to specify how it is different from other members of the class (i.e., the species). For example:

A sea-plane is an airplane that is adapted for landing on and taking off from a body of water.

The definition states that a sea-plane is a member of the class of airplanes (i.e., it is a type of airplane) that is distinguished from other airplanes by being adapted for landing on and taking off from a body of water.

Most words can be defined using the genus-species method. Some, however, cannot because they lack a genus of which they are a member. A sea-plane is a member of the class of airplanes; an airplane is a member of the class of machines; a machine is a member of the class of...? At this point we have to look hard to find an appropriate class. We might use the class of systems:

> A machine is a system of interacting parts.

But then what is the appropriate class for systems? At some point, the process of finding a genus-class must end, and at this point we can no longer use the genus-species method.

2. **Ostensive** Sometimes the meaning of a word can easily be conveyed by giving examples, either verbally or by pointing. If someone wants to know what a bassoon is, it may be sufficient to hold one up and say,

> Here is a bassoon.

Or we may point one out by saying,

> The bald guy in the third row of the orchestra is playing a bassoon.

Sometimes it is necessary to give several examples in order to ensure that the meaning is clear. If we try to define *vehicle* ostensively, we will need to point to more than cars: we will also need to point to vans, trucks, busses, tractors, motorcycles, bicycles, and so on. If the range of examples given is too limited, we will have conveyed only part of the meaning of the term.

Using ostensive definitions for general terms can be problematic. If we attempt to define ostensively terms such as *fairness* or *truth*, it may be difficult for someone to grasp what the different examples have in common. For some words it is difficult to point to or give examples: for example, *neutron, space,* or *history*. And words that have no reference (for example, *very, where,* and *forever*) simply cannot be defined ostensively because there is nothing to point to.

3. **By Synonym**   Often all that is needed to define a word is to give a synonym. For example:

> Effulgent *means the same as* radiant.

Obviously, this method only works for words that have more or less exact synonyms. Words that lack a synonym have to be defined using one of the other methods. And, of course, such definitions will only be helpful for someone who understands the meaning of the synonym.

4. **Contextual**   Some words can best be defined by using the word in a standard context and providing a different sentence that does not use the word but has the same meaning. For example, the concept of *logical strength* used in this book can be defined as follows:

> This argument has logical strength *means the same as* The premises of this argument, if true, provide a justification for believing that its conclusion is true.

5. **Operational**   Sometimes it is important that terms be defined very precisely. In science, for example, it is essential that each concept be defined in a way that specifies exactly when it can be applied and when it cannot. One way of achieving such precision is to establish a rule that the term is to be applied only when a specified test or operation yields a certain result. For example:

> *A genius is anyone who scores over 140 on a standard I.Q. test.*

Operational definitions are commonly used outside science when defining terms that are used to distinguish things that form a continuum, such as the quality of meat, student performance, or degree of drunkenness. Thus we have operational definitions for such terms as *Grade A beef, honours standing,* and *legal intoxication.* Operational definitions often arise initially as stipulative definitions, but may become part of the standard usage.

2.9 Assessing Reportive Definitions

A good stipulative definition is one that fixes a precise meaning of a term in a way that will be useful for some specific purpose. A good essentialist definition is one that reflects a true or reasonable theory about the essential nature of the phenomenon to which the term refers. But what is a good reportive definition? The short answer to this question is that a good reportive definition of a word is one that tells us what others mean when they use the word and what others will understand us to mean when we use it. In other words, it will accurately describe the actual standard usage of the term. There are several ways in which a reportive definition can fail to be a good definition.

2.9.1 TOO BROAD

A definition is too broad when the defining phrase refers to some things that are not included in the reference of the term being defined. The definition

A typewriter is a means of writing

fails as a definition because the defining phrase (*a means of writing*) refers not only to typewriters but also to chalk, pens, and pencils, among other things. The definition is too broad because it includes more than it should. Here are some other examples of definitions that are too broad:

Soccer is a game played with a ball.
A beaver is an amphibious rodent, native to northeastern North America.
A sofa is a piece of furniture designed for sitting.

If we regard these not as definitions, but as statements, they are all true. Soccer is, obviously, a game played with a ball. In a sense, therefore, definitions that are too broad do not say anything that is actually false. It is when such statements are put forward as definitions that problems may arise.

2.9.2 TOO NARROW

A definition is too narrow when the defining phrase fails to refer to some things that are included in the reference of the term being defined. The definition

A school is an institution that aims at teaching children how to read and write

is a bad definition because the defining phrase fails to refer to schools that do not aim at teaching children how to read and write, such as medical schools and dance schools. It is too narrow; it excludes these other kinds of schools. Here are some other examples of definitions that are too narrow:

A parent is a person's mother or father.
A farm is a place where crops are grown.
A bigamist is a man who is married to two women at the same time.

As with definitions that are too broad, definitions that are too narrow do not necessarily say anything that is false. A true statement may be a bad definition.

2.9.3 TOO BROAD AND TOO NARROW

A definition can sometimes be too broad and too narrow at the same time. This happens when the defining phrase refers to some things to which the term does not (too broad) and also fails to refer to some things to which the term does (too narrow). For example:

A pen is an instrument designed for writing words.

This definition is too broad because it includes pencils and typewriters as well as pens, and it is too narrow because it fails to include pens that are designed for drawing pictures.

In order to determine whether a definition is too broad or too narrow, it is necessary to compare the reference of the term being defined with the reference of the defining phrase. Two questions need to be asked: (1) does the reference of the defining phrase include things that are not included in the reference of the term being defined? If it does, then the definition is too broad. And (2) does the reference of the defining phrase exclude things that are included in the reference of the term? If it does, then the definition is too narrow.

Here are some examples of definitions that are both too broad and too narrow:

Hockey is a game played on ice in Canada.
A doctor is a person who treats physical ailments.
A professor is a teacher who does research.

2.9.4 CIRCULAR

A circular definition is one that includes the term being defined (or its cognate) in the definition. For example:

A golf ball is a small spherical object used in the game of golf.

The problem here is obvious: anyone who does not already know what golf is, is not going to be enlightened by the definition. Circular definitions are therefore usually useless.

When a definition uses a cognate of the term being defined the circularity may be less obvious. For example:

A surgeon is a person who practises surgery.

This definition is circular because *surgeon* and *surgery* are cognates (i.e., they come from the same root.) Circular definitions involving cognates may not always be useless, however, since a person may know the meaning of one and not the other.

People do not often put forward circular definitions that are as blatant as these examples. But sometimes a pair of definitions, neither of which is itself circular, can lead to a kind of circularity when taken together. If someone defines *freedom* as *the absence of coercion*, and then defines *coercion* as *the absence of freedom*, the definitions taken together are circular and therefore likely to be useless.

A definition can also be useless when it fails, through the use of vague, obscure, or metaphorical language, to express clearly the meaning of the term being defined. Consider the following definitions:

> *A marathon is a long foot-race.*
> *A grampus is a kind of blowing, spouting, blunt-headed, dolphin-like cetacean.*
> *A fact is anything that rubs the corners off our prejudices.*

The first of these definitions uses a vague expression (*long*) that leaves the meaning of the term somewhat obscure. The second uses a scientific term (*cetacean*) that is likely to be unenlightening (to non-biologists, at least.) The third is likely to be uninformative because it uses a metaphor (*rubs the corners off*). In most circumstances these definitions will be unsatisfactory. However, a definition that uses an obscure technical term may nevertheless be correct (for example, the second of the above definitions), and if we want to have a precise understanding of the term we will have to look for a definition of the obscure term and hope that it is not equally obscure.

2.10 Assessing Stipulative and Essentialist Definitions

The errors in section 2.9 describe five different ways in which a definition can fail to convey adequately the standard usage of a term. Stipulative and essentialist definitions, however, are not intended to convey the standard usage of a term. As we saw in section 2.7.2, stipulative definitions are intended to establish a new or restricted meaning for a term and cannot, therefore, be criticized for failing to convey adequately the standard usage of the term. Essentialist definitions are intended to describe the essential nature of something, and since there is no guarantee that the standard usage of a term will reflect a correct understanding of its essence, we cannot criticize an essentialist definition for failing to convey the standard usage of the term. How, then, are such definitions to be assessed?

Stipulative and essentialist definitions are always put forward for a specific purpose. Whatever their purpose, they must enable the audience to know how to use the term in accordance with its stipulated or essential meaning, and this means that they should not be obscure or circular. For example, if a report defined an offensive weapon as

anything that can be used to inflict harm on another person

we could criticize it for being vague, even though we recognize that it is intended as a stipulative definition. Similarly, the definition

love is essentially a mutual loving dependency between two people

is clearly circular. Except in contexts where a definition has a humorous purpose, obscurity and circularity will be grounds for criticism.

A more serious problem can arise when a stipulative or essentialist definition of a term is significantly different from the standard usage of the term. The fact that the two meanings are different is not by itself a problem, but it can lead to misunderstanding and confusion. It might be reasonable for some purposes to stipulate the meaning of heat wave as a period of at least three successive days in which the high temperature exceeds 30 degrees Celsius. But if the high temperatures over the past week were 29, 35, 35, 29, 35, 35, and 29, we would be puzzled if someone denied we were in a heat wave. Anyone who uses such a stipulative definition should remind us of this fact; for example, by saying, Technically, this doesn't count as a heat wave.

The possibilities for misunderstanding are increased when the term being given a stipulative or essentialist definition lacks a clear and precise usage, since the discrepancy between the ordinary usage and the defined meaning may not be immediately apparent. Worse, terms whose ordinary meaning is somewhat vague often stand in the greatest need of a more precise definition; for example, *conflict of interest, sexual harassment, potentially violent offender, dangerous level of PCBs, mental abnormality, pollutant,* and *national security.* For bureaucratic or legal reasons, such terms may need to have a precise meaning assigned, and it is extremely important to be aware of the possible meaning shifts that may deliberately or inadvertently be involved.

These meaning shifts can best be described by reference to the concepts of too broad and too narrow. We have seen that in order to determine whether a reportive definition is too broad or too narrow we compare the reference classes of the defining phrase and the term being defined. This same comparison allows us to determine whether the reference of a stipulative or essentialist definition of a term is broader or narrower than the standard usage of the term. Consider the following stipulative definition, taken from section 2 of the Narcotic Control Act of Canada.

"Narcotic addict" means a person who, through the use of narcotics, (a) has developed a desire or need to continue to take a narcotic, or, (b) has developed a psychological or physical dependence on the effect of a narcotic.

This definition is broader than the standard usage of the term, since it regards a person who has developed a desire to continue to take a narcotic as an addict. We must be careful, however, in making claims about standard usage. Do those who commonly use these terms in fact agree that someone who, through the use of narcotics, has developed a desire to continue to take a narcotic, would not be called a narcotic addict? Most people would probably want to say that such a person is in danger of becoming an addict, but if the desire is not a strong one and is easily and regularly overcome they would likely deny that such a person is an addict. If this is the standard usage of the term *narcotic addict*, we can conclude that the definition contained in the Narcotic Control Act is a broad one.

If we want to criticize such a definition, however, we must do more than point out that it is broader or narrower than the standard usage. The question is whether the broader or narrower definition has desirable or undesirable consequences. In some cases it may be desirable to broaden or narrow the scope of a term, and in other cases not. There is nothing sacred about standard usage, so such questions are always debatable. These debates sometimes raise important questions of social policy. More commonly, however, it is only necessary to remember that a stipulative or essentialist definition of a term gives a *different* (i.e., broader or narrower) meaning than the term has in its standard usage. For example, when the theologian Paul Tillich defines *atheist* as a person who lacks what he calls *ultimate concern*, it is important for the reader to be aware that Tillich's definition is significantly different from the ordinary usage of the term.

2.11 A Warning

Defining words is an art. It requires good judgement to know what kind of definition is appropriate in any particular context. Compilers of dictionaries attempt to provide definitions that can serve in a very broad range of contexts, but even they make no claim to give a full and complete account of the meanings of words. They do not, for example, attempt to cover slang, dialect, or metaphorical uses.

Most of us are not writers of dictionaries, and we only attempt to provide definitions when a particular need arises. Sometimes we are asked what a word means. A friend asks what the difference is between *disinterested* and *uninterested*. A German tourist asks what *street* means. A child asks what *obstetrician* means. In such circumstances, there is no need to give a full definition: we need only provide enough information to remove the questioner's ignorance. The friend may only need to be told that *disinterested* means the same as *impartial*. The German tourist only needs to be informed that *street* means *strasse*. The child will be content if told that *obstetrician* means *baby-doctor*. The appropriate kind of answer is one that meets the needs of the questioner, and this is usually less than a full reportive definition.

Sometimes, however, we need to define a word because we want to increase or deepen our understanding. This is likely to arise with terms that are abstract or stand for a complex object or phenomenon; we often have a general idea of what they mean and can point to examples, but find it very difficult to say precisely what they mean. For most people, the following terms fall into this category: *energy, classical, crime, psychiatry, nation, pornography, religion, imagination, evil, illness, cause,* and *trust*. These are important matters, and if we want to increase our understanding of them we must attempt to ensure that we have a clear understanding of the words. But even here we do not usually want a full reportive definition. Often we are interested in only one sense of the word (for example, *energy* as a scientific term), and sometimes we want only to be able to distinguish between similar things (for example, between *psychiatry* and *psychology*).

2.12 Self-Test No. 3

What errors are committed by the following definitions? (Assume a context in which they have been put forward as reportive definitions.)

1. Parliament is the supreme legislative body of Canada.

2. Poetry is an art form that uses words to communicate ideas and images.

3. A snowplough is an implement designed to remove snow.

4. Restoration is the process or activity of restoring something to its former condition.

5. A tritone is the musical interval of an augmented fourth, or a diminished fifth.

6. A stapler is a device for fastening pages together.

7. A nurse is a woman who is trained to look after the sick.

8. A bungalow is a one-storey building.

9. The United Nations is an organization aimed at fostering co-operation and peace between nations.

10. A sport is any activity involving competition between individuals or groups of individuals.

2.13 Questions for Discussion

Comment upon the following definitions:

1. A psychological disorder is any personal way of perceiving or interpreting events which is used repeatedly in spite of its consistent failure (from G.A. Kelly, *Personality Theory and Research* [Toronto: John Wiley and Sons, 1970], p. 240).

2. The term suicide is applied to all cases of death resulting directly or indirectly from a positive or negative act of the victim himself, which he knows will produce his death (from Émile Durkheim, *Suicide: A Study in Sociology*, tr. Spalding and Simpson [New York: Free Press, 1966], p. 44).

3. No person is criminally responsible for an act committed or an omission made while suffering from a mental disorder that rendered the person in-

capable of appreciating the nature and quality of the act or omission or of knowing that it was wrong (from the *Criminal Code of Canada*, section 16.(1)).

4. **Socialism**. Principle that individual freedom should be completely subordinated to interests of community, with any deductions that may be correctly or incorrectly drawn from it, e.g. substitution of co-operative for competitive production, national ownership of land & capital, State distribution of produce, free education & feeding of children... (from *Concise Oxford Dictionary*, 1934 edition).

5. **Full-time Student**: A full-time student is one who (i) is geographically available and visits the campus regularly, (ii) is not regularly employed, save in the most exceptional circumstances, for more than an average of 10 hours per week during any period in which the student is registered as a full-time graduate student, and (iii) is not employed outside the University except by the Advisor's permission; and in light of the foregoing is designated as a full-time graduate student (from *University of Guelph, Graduate Calendar, 1994-1996*, p. 161).

6. Poetry is the spontaneous overflow of powerful feelings...recollected in tranquillity (from William Wordsworth, *Preface to Lyrical Ballads*, 1800).

7. A cynic is a person who knows the price of everything and the value of nothing (attributed to Oscar Wilde).

8. Liberty is the right to do whatever the law permits.

Chapter 3

Clarifying Meaning

The failure to understand the meaning of what others say, and the failure to understand how others can misunderstand the meaning of what we say, are the seeds of much frustration, resentment, and discord. In this chapter we examine some of the ways in which misunderstanding can result from a lack of clarity in the language we use. Our purpose here is to develop the ability to recognize obscurity in what others say, and to learn how to say clearly what we mean.

3.1 The Principle of Charity

Often we are confronted by a choice between two or more interpretations of what someone has said, and sometimes these interpretations have different degrees of plausibility. If we adopt the least plausible interpretation it is often easy to show that the statement is false. On the other hand, if we adopt the most plausible interpretation it is usually more difficult to show that the statement is false. It is tempting, therefore, when faced with a statement we disagree with, to adopt the least plausible interpretation of it. After all, if we can get away with foisting an implausible view on our opponents it makes it easier to show that they are wrong (or stupid, irrational, foolish, etc.) It is especially tempting to do this when the most implausible interpretation is the literal one. For example:

> The worst thing that can happen to a worker in this province is to fall into the clutches of the Workers' Compensation Board.

> The only difference between an amateur and a professional musician is that the amateur performs for personal satisfaction while the professional performs for money.

> Doctors who perform abortions are guilty of first-degree murder.

We all recognize that the literal interpretation of such statements is unlikely to be what the speaker intended. They are exaggerations or overstatements. If the speaker is present we may want to have a bit of fun by pointing out the absurdity of what was actually said. Sometimes this is legitimate; for example, when debating in parliament. However, when there is an important issue at stake we should not let our desire to poke fun at our opponents prevent us from listening to what they are really trying to say. When our opponents are not present and cannot clarify what they have said we ought to be prepared to do so on their behalf. It is up to us to find the fairest interpretation of their words, the one that best represents their presumed intentions.

Thus, in any discussion we have a moral obligation to treat our opponents fairly. When they are present we ought to give them the opportunity to clarify what they have said. When they are not present, we have a moral obligation to follow the **principle of charity**, that is, to adopt the most charitable interpretation of their words. The most charitable interpretation is the one that makes our opponent's views as reasonable, plausible, or defensible as possible. According to the principle of charity, whenever two interpretations are possible we should always adopt the more reasonable.

Why should we be charitable to our opponents? After all, it might be argued that if the purpose of engaging in a debate is to win, the principle of charity will make our task more difficult. But winning is not the primary purpose of rational discussion. The primary purpose should always be to discover the truth and to develop views and positions that are as reasonable and defensible as they can be. It is always possible that our opponents are right and we are wrong, or that our opponents are partly right and our position needs to be amended in some way; in either case we stand to benefit from discussion. Even if our opponents are totally wrong it is a useful test of the strength of our own position to be able to show their errors. In any case we owe it to our opponents as persons to interpret their words in the most reasonable manner. Anyone who has ever been involved in a discussion with an opponent who persistently violates the principle of charity will understand the unfairness of such treatment and will appreciate the importance of observing the principle.

The principle of charity should be followed not only when we are interpreting single statements, but also when we are interpreting longer passages and even entire books. Throughout this book we shall often find it necessary to invoke the principle of charity. Being charitable to our opponents should eventually become second nature.

3.2 Linguistic Ambiguity

3.2.1 AMBIGUITY AND VAGUENESS

Some sentences are ambiguous. Some sentences are vague. But ambiguity and vagueness are not the same. An **ambiguous sentence** is one that has two or more different but usually quite precise meanings. A **vague sentence** is one that lacks a precise meaning. Ambiguous sentences should be avoided whenever there is a risk of misinterpretation – whenever there is a risk that the hearer will select the wrong meaning. Vague sentences, however, are necessary if we are trying to express a vague thought or feeling. For example:

I don't care much for Beethoven's early string quartets.
That was a noisy party they had last night, and it went on until all hours.
Lots of people own two television sets.
Margaret Laurence's novels have a disquieting effect upon the reader.

These sentences are vague but they are not ambiguous. In most contexts there is no need for greater precision about such matters. If challenged we could easily be a little more precise, but it would be very difficult (and usually pointless) to attempt to remove the vagueness altogether. There is nothing wrong with vagueness when we want to express a vague thought or when there is no need for precision.

In contexts in which precision is needed, however, we sometimes come across sentences that look quite precise, but that turn out to be extremely vague. For example:

Applicants must hold a diploma in early childhood education or have equivalent work experience.

The phrase *equivalent work experience* sounds quite precise, but without further information it is impossible to tell what kinds of work experience are going to count as equivalent. Does raising three children of one's own count? What about occasional baby-sitting over a period of six years? A half-time job as a helper in a nursery school for three years?

Two years' experience as a kindergarten teacher? Potential applicants need a precise statement of the minimum qualifications for the position, but the sentence fails to provide it.

Those who use vague sentences when precision is needed or who use vague sentences that look precise, should be challenged. Sometimes it is quite easy to see precisely what needs to be challenged. For example:

> *The fact that the Liberals won more seats than any other party in the 1993 federal election shows that the voters want a Liberal government.*

The vagueness here arises with the phrase *the voters*. We need to ask *How many voters?* We know that *the voters* cannot refer to all the voters, since other parties also received votes. Does it mean most of the voters? This may well be the speaker's intent, but if so the claim is false since in fact less than half of the votes cast were for Liberal candidates. The Liberal victory resulted from the multi-party system, not from the support of most of the electorate. This example shows the importance of asking for quantifiers: *Do you mean all, most, or just some?* and *Do you mean always, usually, or just sometimes?*

In other cases, however, the vagueness arises from the use of terms that are inherently vague. The cabinet minister who says,

> *My officials are monitoring this situation very closely, and I can promise that we shall take all appropriate measures to ensure that the situation is resolved in a way that is fair to all the parties involved,*

should be challenged on grounds of vagueness. Despite the appearance of having promised to do something specific, the minister has not really promised to do anything at all. What are *appropriate measures*? They could be anything or nothing. What does *fair to all the parties* mean? We have no clear idea. Such phrases are inherently vague, and can mean almost anything. People who use them should be challenged to say more precisely what they mean.

It is important to understand that ambiguity and vagueness are properties of sentences and not of the words themselves. This is because, as we saw in section 2.2.3, words typically have more than one meaning, and the context in which they are used usually tells us which meaning is the intended one. It is the context that makes sentences vague, and it is when the context lets us down that sentences become ambiguous. Of course, the ambiguity or vagueness of a sentence often rests upon the meaning of a word or phrase, but the ambiguity or vagueness arises only at the level of the sentence.

Here are some other sentences that should be challenged on grounds of vagueness, at least in normal contexts:

Essays for this course should be long enough to deal adequately with the assigned topic.

You should sign our petition to protest against the violation of our rights by the government.

If you persist in this course of action, all hell is going to break loose.

3.2.2 REFERENTIAL AMBIGUITY

Referential ambiguity arises when a word or phrase could, in the context of a particular sentence, refer to two or more properties or things. Usually the context tells us which meaning is intended, but when it doesn't we may choose the wrong meaning. If we are not sure which reference is intended by the speaker, we will misunderstand the speaker's meaning if we assign the wrong (i.e., the unintended) meaning to the word. If someone tells you that Pavarotti is a big opera star, you will have to guess whether *big* refers to *fat* or to *famous*. Sometimes, however, it is the context that creates the ambiguity. If someone is comparing the merits of two universities and says, *It is quite a good university*, the context may not tell us which university is being referred to.

Referential ambiguities are usually easy to spot and, once recognized, are easily avoided. This is especially true in conversation, since we can ask for clarification: *Do you mean that Pavarotti is fat or famous?* Or, if we select the wrong meaning, it will not be long before we discover our mistake: *Oh, I thought you meant he was famous!* There is, however, one type of referential ambiguity that deserves special mention: that between the collective and the distributive use of a term. Most nouns refer to a class of individual objects: *dog*, for example, refers to the class consisting of all dogs and *book* refers to the class of all books. Usually when we use such nouns we do so in order to say something about each and every member of the class. When we use a term in this way it is being used **distributively**. But sometimes we use terms to say something not about each and every member of the class but about the class as such. When we use a term in this way it is being used **collectively**. Consider the following:

Our university has a large wrestling team.

If we interpret *wrestling team* distributively, the statement means that the individual members of the team are large. If we interpret the term collectively, the statement means that the team has a large number of members. Usually the context makes it clear whether a term should be interpreted distributively or collectively, but sometimes it does not and we can mistakenly assume the wrong interpretation.

It is useful to develop the ability to recognize referential ambiguities even when they are unlikely to cause misunderstandings, for then we are less likely to assume a wrong interpretation inadvertently. Here are some more examples of sentences containing referential ambiguities:

Tom gave Ted's skis to his sister.
Harold told me that he would do it next week.
Americans make more telephone calls than Canadians.
The government has provided constant funding for post-secondary education over the last three years.

3.2.3 GRAMMATICAL AMBIGUITY

Grammatical ambiguity arises when the grammatical structure of a sentence allows two interpretations, each of which gives rise to a different meaning. A few years ago a British newspaper reported that

Lord Denning spoke against the artificial insemination of women in the House of Lords.

The grammar makes it unclear whether it was the speech or the insemination that took place in the House of Lords. This is because the phrase *in the House of Lords* could modify either *insemination* or *spoke*. Here are a few examples:

He promised to pay Patrick and Michael fifty dollars to clear all the junk out of the basement and take it to the dump.
Ashley strode out of the studio with Nikki following her, saying, "I'll never give him up."
Olga decided to quit smoking while driving to Toronto.

Jim and I have suffered tremendously; often I wake up in the morning and wish I were dead and I know Jim does too.

Sometimes we come across sentences that are clearly ambiguous, but where it is hard to determine whether the ambiguity is referential or grammatical. Consider the sentence *Let me go.* If someone grabs your arm in the midst of an argument you might say, *Let me go*, meaning that you want the person to let go of your arm. If your spouse says that someone is going to have to go out to get some milk for breakfast and you say, *Let me go*, you are obviously volunteering to go and get some milk. Whether this is a grammatical or referential ambiguity is not important, however, as long as we can recognize that it is ambiguous.

3.2.4 USE AND MENTION

Another type of linguistic ambiguity arises through the failure to distinguish between using and mentioning a word or phrase. Consider the following sentences:

Tom said I was angry.
Tom said, "I was angry."

Clearly these sentences have different meanings, even though the words are identical. The difference in meaning arises because the phrase *I was angry* is being *used* in the first sentence but is only *mentioned* in the second. Quotation marks or italics are commonly used to mark the difference. But direct quotation is not the only occasion when we want to mention a word and in these cases we should also use italics or quotation marks to make our meaning clear. For example:

Paddy is Irish.

As it stands, this sentence means that a particular person, called Paddy, is an Irishman. But if we put quotation marks around "Paddy" it would mean that "Paddy" is an Irish name. Here are some more examples of sentences whose meaning would change if the word or phrase which is mentioned (as indicated by Capitalized Words or quotation marks) were being used instead:

The Music of the Renaissance is extremely demanding.
The word "itself" is hard to define.
"John Smith" was placed on the ballot.
The Joy of Sex costs $24.95.

The ability to detect linguistic ambiguities is an important skill, for undetected ambiguities can create misunderstandings that lead to those frustrating discussions in which everyone seems to be at cross purposes. On the other hand, people who delight in finding linguistic ambiguities that do not in fact mislead anyone may be amusing for a time but can become extremely annoying. Since our interest is in clarifying meaning, we are concerned only with ambiguities that do or may mislead.

3.3 Self-Test No. 4

Describe the ambiguities in the following sentences.

1. Billy gave his sisters a box of candy for Christmas.

2. He's a chicken.

3. Melissa only has one dress.

4. General Loses Battle With Nurses. (A newspaper headline)

5. Conversational German is extremely difficult.

6. Children need discipline to become responsible adults.

7. If, after you think it over, you still decide to drop out of school, I promise I won't say another word to you.

8. In multi-section courses the instructors should be free to choose the text.

9. Eighty percent of the stores tested illegally sell cigarettes to minors with no questions asked.

10. She arrived at the theatre in a white limousine with a bright red hood.

3.4 Analytic, Contradictory, and Synthetic Statements

Usually, when we know what a statement means we still do not know whether it is true or false. If I say, *I was born on October 22*, you understand the meaning of what I have said, but you do not know whether what I have said is true or false. There are, however, certain statements whose truth or falsity is determined by their meaning. Consider the following statements:

All bachelors are unmarried adult males.
Some bachelors are married.

Once we understand the meaning of these statements, we know that the first is true and the second is false. They are true, or false, by definition. We do not need to investigate the facts in order to know whether they are true or false. Someone who tries to discover their truth or falsity by sending a questionnaire to a group of bachelors asking whether or not they were married obviously does not understand the meaning of the statements.

A statement that is true by definition is called an **analytic** statement. A statement that is false by definition is called a **contradictory** statement. A statement whose truth or falsity is not solely dependent upon the meanings of the words in it is called a **synthetic** statement. All statements can be placed in one of these three categories.

These distinctions are useful in clarifying the meaning of certain statements whose meaning is imprecise. When a statement seems false, we can ask whether it is a false synthetic or a contradictory statement. When a statement seems true, we can ask whether it is a true synthetic or an analytic statement. For example, if someone claims that every successful person is wealthy it is useful to know whether they are interpreting the word successful as meaning financially successful. If so, their claim becomes analytic, for it really means that all wealthy people are wealthy. It is usually a waste of time arguing against an analytic statement. In practice, however, people do not usually approach discussions with precise definitions of the key terms. It is when they are challenged – for example, when someone says, *I know several very successful poets and artists who are not wealthy* – that the temptation arises to define words in a way that makes their claim analytic. Since analytic statements are true by definition, such a move seems to ensure victory in the debate.

But such victories are usually hollow, for analytic statements are always in a sense trivial. Obviously, all successful people are wealthy – if by *successful* you mean *wealthy*. But why should anyone think it interesting to claim that all wealthy people are wealthy? It is true, but trivially true. The interesting question in such a debate is whether one should regard financial success as the only kind of success, and this cannot be determined merely by defining words. In practice, people who attempt to win a debate by making their claim analytic usually shift back and forth between analytic and synthetic interpretations in the course of the debate. To show that their claim is true they adopt the analytic interpretation; to show that it is important they adopt the synthetic interpretation. In this way they convince themselves that their claim is both true and important; but the true meaning is trivial and the important meaning is unproven and possibly false.

Sometimes a claim is made into an analytic one in ways that are indirect, and it may take some perseverance to uncover these moves. Usually, these indirect moves arise from arguments that are used to defend a claim. The claim that a free-enterprise system is superior to a socialist system, in its most plausible interpretation, is a synthetic statement. But suppose the following argument were put forward to support this claim:

(1) *In a free-enterprise system market forces determine how resources are allocated within the society.*
(2) *It is more efficient to allocate resources through market forces than through decisions by government officials.*
(3) *An efficient system is superior to an inefficient system.*
(4) *Therefore, a free-enterprise system is superior to a socialist system.*

This is a logically strong argument, in the sense that if the first three statements are true then the conclusion must also be true. The danger arises when attempting to show that premises (2) and (3) are true. It is all too easy to assume their truth by regarding them as analytic. Premise (2) becomes analytic if it is assumed that an efficient allocation of resources is by definition one that is produced by market forces. Premise (3) becomes analytic if it is interpreted to mean that an economically efficient system is economically superior to an economically inefficient system. But if the premises are interpreted in this way, then the conclusion needs to be re-interpreted to mean that a system that allocates resources efficiently is more efficient than one that does not allocate resources efficiently. In this way the conclusion itself becomes analytic. It is true, but trivially so, since its truth depends not on the facts but only on the way the key terms are defined. The real argument will, of course, resurface as an argument about the truth or adequacy of the interpretations of premises (2) and (3).

3.5 Self-Test No. 5

State whether the following sentences are analytic, synthetic, or contradictory.

1.   A full deck of playing cards contains fifty-two cards.

2.   A centimetre is longer than a millimetre.

3.   It is better to be free and unhappy than to be a contented slave.

4.   No-one has ever run the marathon in less than two hours.

5.   Death comes for us all, in the end.

6.   I'm not saying that postal workers should not have the legal right to strike, but the postal service is so vital to the economy, and postal strikes cause so much personal inconvenience to so many people, that I think the government should enact legislation banning strikes in the post office.

7.   In the southern hemisphere, the sun rises in the west and sets in the east.

8.   All parents love their children, when they are new born.

9.   A rose by any other name would smell as sweet.

10.   A rose is a rose is a rose.

3.6 Descriptive and Evaluative Meaning

In section 2.3 we characterized the main uses of language. The first two of these − the descriptive and the evaluative − are probably the most common uses of language, and probably also the most fundamental. As a result, we find that many words have come to have meanings that are both descriptive and evaluative. When someone says that Fritz Kreisler was a renowned violinist, the word *renowned* has a double meaning. First, it means that Kreisler was well known as a violinist. Second, it means that he was an excellent violinist. The first meaning is descriptive, since it refers to the fact that Kreisler was well known. If there is a disagreement about this fact it can be settled by looking for historical evidence regarding how widely known he was during his lifetime. The second meaning, however, is evaluative; the speaker is giving his or her opinion that Kreisler was an excellent violinist. This opinion is not factual, since if there is a disagreement over whether Kreisler was an excellent violinist it cannot be settled by consulting the facts. Someone who thinks that Kreisler was not an excellent violinist would be able to accept the descriptive meaning but would have to reject the evaluative meaning of our statement.

There are many descriptive words and phrases that also have an evaluative meaning. It is common to find two or more words or phrases that have more or less the same descriptive meaning but different evaluative meanings. We have seen that *renowned* and *well known* have the same descriptive meaning, but the former has a positive evaluative meaning that the latter lacks. The word *notorious* has the same descriptive meaning, but has a negative evaluative meaning. The evaluative meanings of *renowned* and *notorious* convey an evaluation of the person as being good or bad, whereas *well-known* conveys nothing about the speaker's evaluation. Notice the shift in the evaluative meanings in the following pairs of sentences while the descriptive meaning remains more or less unchanged:

He is very self-confident.
He is arrogant.

She is sexually liberated.
She is promiscuous.

He is a dedicated conservative.
He is a fanatical conservative.

They are freedom fighters.
They are terrorists.

It is important to be aware of such differences in meaning, since we can sometimes be led to accept a particular evaluation through a failure to distinguish descriptive and evaluative meanings. The facts that would show that someone is very self-confident and the facts that would show that someone is arrogant are very similar, and a skilled arguer can easily create the impression that someone who is self-confident is really arrogant (or vice versa). But the same facts can only be used to justify two statements with different evaluative meanings if the evaluative meaning is ignored and they are regarded as purely descriptive statements. The evaluative part of the meaning requires a separate justification.

3.7 Self-Test No. 6

The italicized word or phrase in each of the following sentences has both a descriptive and an evaluative meaning. Indicate whether its evaluative meaning is positive or negative, and briefly describe its descriptive meaning in non-evaluative terms. Suggest a descriptive synonym or equivalent phrase that has a neutral (or no) evaluative meaning, but preserves the descriptive meaning of the sentence.

1. There is *vicious* competition among students at the Julliard School of Music.

2. Jennifer is a *compulsively* tidy person.

3. This year Mark has been a very *responsible* student.

4. During the last thirty years the moral standards of ordinary people have *declined*.

5. Simon is one of those people whose main motivation in life is *greed*.

6. The Minister announced that the budget for social services would be *slashed* by 12 per cent over the next three years.

7. I think your doctor is being *excessively* cautious in his approach to treating your illness.

8. Jon was *suckered* by the salesman into buying the car.

9. Beethoven's Ninth Symphony was composed during his *mature* years.

10. So we have a deal, then. I'll get my *girl* to type it up and send it to you for signing.

3.8 Necessary and Sufficient Conditions

A special kind of ambiguity can arise when talking about the conditions that have to be met in order for something to occur. Referring to such conditions is common when we are talking about the causes (i.e., the causal conditions) of certain events: for example, *Under what conditions would a major economic depression occur again?* It is also common when we are talking about entitlements or justifications for certain actions: for example, *What are the conditions for graduating with distinction?* It seems that all we need to do to answer such questions is to list the conditions that, if they existed, would lead to a depression or to graduating with distinction. Unfortunately, the relationships between conditions and what they are conditions for are often a great deal more complex than they seem, and in order to clarify these relationships philosophers and scientists have developed a distinction between two types of conditions, necessary conditions and sufficient conditions. Much confusion and ambiguity can result when these two types of conditions are not clearly distinguished.

To understand the ambiguity that results when the two types of conditions are not distinguished, consider the following:

(1) Being at least eighteen years of age is a condition for being eligible to vote in federal elections in Canada.

This could mean either of the following:

(2) Anyone who is at least eighteen years of age is eligible to vote in federal elections in Canada, or

(3) Anyone who is not at least eighteen years of age is not eligible to vote in federal elections in Canada.

These sentences have different meanings. We can see the difference by asking what each says about a particular case, for example, a twenty-seven-year-old prison inmate. According to (2) such a person is eligible to vote, but (3) says nothing about whether such a person is eligible to vote. In fact the correct interpretation of (1) is (3). By law, every eligible voter must be at least eighteen years of age – that is, if you are not eighteen you can't vote – but the law also states that judges, persons serving prison sentences, and insane persons are not eligible to vote. This means that not everyone who is eighteen years of age is eligible to vote, which means that (2) is false. Being at least eighteen years of age is *a* condition, but it is not the only condition that has to be satisfied for someone to be an eligible voter. To avoid this ambiguity we should revise (1) to read:

(4) Being at least eighteen years of age is a necessary condition for being eligible to vote in federal elections in Canada.

A **necessary condition** is defined as follows: X is a necessary condition for Y if, and only if, when X is false Y must also be false (or, when X is absent Y cannot occur). In other words, a necessary condition for Y is something whose falsity or absence prevents Y, but whose truth or presence does not guarantee Y. This yields a simple test for the truth of a necessary-condition statement: look for an instance of Y that is not also an X. If we can find one such case then the statement must be false, since we have discovered an instance where X is not a necessary condition for Y. If we cannot find such a case then we should accept the statement.

A sufficient condition is quite different from a necessary condition. Consider the following:

(1) Holding a B.A. from the University is a condition for being a member of the University Alumni Association.

This is ambiguous between:

(2) Anyone holding a B.A. from the University is a member of the University Alumni Association, and
(3) Anyone not holding a B.A. from the University is not a member of the University Alumni Association.

Obviously, (2) is the most likely interpretation of (1). Notice the structural difference from our first example, where (3) was the correct interpretation. This is because here we are dealing with a sufficient condition. A person who holds a B.A. from the University does not need to meet any additional conditions in order to be a member of the University Alumni Association, although obviously holding a B.A. is not the only way one can become a member of the University Alumni Association. To remove the ambiguity we need to revise (1) to read:

(4) Holding a B.A. from the University is a sufficient condition for being a member of the University Alumni Association.

A **sufficient condition** is defined as follows: X is a sufficient condition for Y if, and only if, when X is true Y must also be true (or, when X is present Y must occur). In other words, a sufficient condition for Y is something whose truth or presence guarantees Y, but whose falsity or absence does not prevent Y. This yields a simple test for the truth of a sufficient-condition statement: look for an instance of an X that is not also a Y. If we can find one such case then the statement must be false, since we have discovered an instance where X is not a sufficient condition for Y. If we can find no such case then we should accept the statement.

The essential difference between a necessary and a sufficient condition for some Y is that a necessary condition is something whose falsity or absence guarantees that Y is false or won't occur, and a sufficient condition is something whose truth or presence guarantees that Y is true or will occur.

Sometimes, a condition can be both necessary and sufficient at the same time. Consider the following:

It is a condition for a candidate being declared the winner in an election for the Ontario legislature that the candidate received more votes than any other candidate in the election.

In this example, receiving more votes than any other candidate is a sufficient condition for being declared the winner (since any one who receives more votes than any other candidate must be declared the winner); and it is also a necessary condition (since every candidate who is declared the winner must have received more votes than any other candidate.) Another example of this sort is the relationship between *Today is Tuesday* and *Tomorrow is Wednesday*. Each of these statements is both a necessary and sufficient condition for the other.

Now, just to make things more complicated, we need to note what can happen when two or more conditions for the same thing are joined together. Being at least eighteen years of age is not the only necessary condition for being eligible to vote in federal elections in Canada; we have already noted that one must *not* be a judge, a person serving a prison sentence, or an insane person, but in addition one must also be a Canadian citizen. We can set out these necessary conditions as follows:

The necessary conditions for being eligible to vote in federal elections in Canada are:
(1) being at least eighteen years of age,
(2) not being a judge, a person serving a prison sentence, or an insane person, and
(3) being a Canadian citizen.

These constitute all the necessary conditions for being eligible to vote in federal elections in Canada. But notice that these three necessary conditions are, *when taken together*, a sufficient condition. This is because any person who satisfies all three of these conditions is eligible to vote. Whenever we can list all the necessary conditions for something we will have listed the conditions that are **jointly sufficient** conditions.

In a similar way, we can sometimes find two or more different sufficient conditions for something. For example, according to the *Criminal Code of Canada* (section 222.(5)), a culpable homicide is committed when someone causes the death of a person:

(a) by means of an unlawful act,
(b) by criminal negligence,
(c) by causing that human being, by threats of fear of violence or by deception, to do anything that causes his death, or
(d) by wilfully frightening that human being, in the case of a child or sick person.

This section states four sufficient conditions for the crime of culpable homicide. If, in a particular case, any *one* of these conditions is met, the accused person will be found guilty of culpable homicide. If we take all four conditions together, that is, if we take section 222.(5) as a whole, we can say that it states the necessary condition for culpable homicide in the sense that at least one of these conditions must be met by every case of culpable homicide. This is because the absence of all four conditions means that an accused person would not be found guilty of culpable homicide.

So far, all our examples have dealt with criteria or entitlements. When dealing with causes, necessary and sufficient conditions work in the same way. When scientists search for a full account of the causes of some phenomenon, they are looking not only for the conditions that are individually sufficient, but also for the conditions that are individually necessary and jointly sufficient. However, if our sole interest is in controlling some phenomenon all we need is a partial account of the causes of that phenomenon. If we want to prevent something from happening we don't need a full account of its causal conditions, since if we can eliminate one necessary condition then we can prevent the event from occurring. For example, if we want to prevent a disease from spreading all we need to do is find and eliminate one of the necessary conditions for the spread of the disease. On the other hand, if we want to produce a certain effect, all we need to do is to find one (or one set) of its sufficient conditions that we can bring about. For example, if we want to lose twenty pounds we need to find only one way (for example, exercise) that works (i.e., is sufficient), and can ignore all the other ways (for example, dieting, diet pills).

3.9 Self-Test No. 7

State whether the italicized phrase in each of the following sentences states a necessary or a sufficient condition. (*Note:* Once you understand the two different meanings of each sentence, you will have to use your common-sense knowledge to decide which is the more likely meaning.)

1.   To bring down a fever, *apply a cloth dampened in cold water to the patient's face, arms, and legs.*

2.   *Any student who has not paid his or her tuition fee by the first day of the term, or who has not made arrangements with the bursar's office for delayed payment,* will be automatically required to withdraw from the university.

3.   To be admitted as a graduate student, *applicants must have a four year honours degree with a 75 per cent average on all courses taken in their last two years.*

4.   You cannot get an A average unless *you work hard throughout the whole term.*

5.   Essays will be returned to the student without being graded, if *they are submitted without a proper bibliography.*

6.   The Bruce Prize of five hundred dollars will be awarded to *the graduating student who has the highest cumulative average in all his or her philosophy courses.*

7.   No-one can become prime minister in our system of government unless *he or she is a Member of Parliament.*

8.   For the business community to regain confidence in the economy, *interest rates must come down.*

9.   *You have to have good physical co-ordination* to be a good skier.

10. No-one can become a university professor these days unless *they have a Ph.D. degree.*

3.10 Questions for Discussion

Comment on the following passages:

1.   We hold these truths to be self-evident, that all men are created equal, that they are endowed by their Creator with certain unalienable Rights, that among these are Life, Liberty, and the pursuit of Happiness. (from the *Declaration of Independence*)

2.   No rational person ever commits suicide.

3.   Adding Courses: All course additions to a student's program for a particular semester are to be completed by the end of the six-day add period. The addition of a course after the end of the add period will be consid-

ered only in exceptional circumstances and will require the approval of both the instructor for the course and the program counsellor of the program in which the student is registered. The program counsellor's signature should be sought first but does not presume the judgement of the instructor as to the appropriateness of the late addition for his or her particular course. (from *University of Guelph, Undergraduate Calendar, 1995-1996*, p. 66)

4. **Politician:** As far as we are concerned an impartial dispute-settling mechanism is an essential precondition for any free trade deal between Canada and the United States.
   Interviewer: So you are saying, then, that you would support a free trade deal as long as the Americans accept an impartial dispute-settling mechanism.

5. Suppose someone is drowning twenty feet from shore. We throw him ten feet of rope, and he drowns. It would be illogical to conclude: "Rope is useless in the prevention of drowning." But this is the logic of the speech given by the Premier last week to the Chamber of Commerce in which he asserted that most government-funded social assistance programs are "based on the assumption that any social problem can be solved simply by throwing enough tax dollars at it." No-one with any understanding of our social problems has ever made such a stupid and simplistic assumption, yet the Premier persists in spreading the myth that only such an assumption can justify social assistance programs.

6. For years, Canadian governments have persisted in lecturing other countries about their racist policies. Last week the Minister of External Affairs continued this tradition by lecturing the Indonesian government about its racist policies in East Timor. May I pose a question for the Minister and for all those who think the same way: Why should another country pay attention to the carping of foreigners whose own country still follows racist policies and practices? I refer, of course, to the large number of subtle ways in which our government discriminates against our native people. The overall effect of these policies is to bring about a slow cultural genocide.

7. Thou shalt not kill.

8.   The Association for the Mentally Retarded recently changed its name to The Association for Community Living. The Association felt that "retarded" was a derogatory term, and that dropping the term was an important step in their fight to change public attitudes towards a social group that has often suffered in the past from cruel and hostile treatment at the hands of the more unenlightened members of the community.

Chapter 4

Reconstructing Arguments

4.1 Reconstruction

Unfortunately, the arguments we encounter in real life do not come with their premises and conclusions neatly labelled. Even worse, they are usually embedded in extraneous material that, although it may aid in interpreting the argument, is not actually part of the argument itself. Before we can critically assess an argument, therefore, we have to determine what the actual argument is. What is its conclusion, what are its premises, and what is the precise relationship between them? The process of eliciting this information is called **reconstructing the argument**. The aim of reconstructing an argument is to produce a set of statements that represents the actual argument – the premises, the conclusion, the relationship between premises and conclusion – the author intended to present. The specific words used in the reconstruction need not be the actual words used by the author, for, as we have seen, it may be necessary to revise the words used in order to clarify the meaning or to remove ambiguities. What is important is to ensure that as far as possible the reconstruction does not violate the author's intent, and where this is unclear, does not violate the principle of charity.

Reconstructing an argument involves two phases. In the first, the premises and the conclusion of the argument must be identified. In the second phase the structure of the argument must be identified. When identifying the premises and conclusion of an argument that is presented in written form we will use the following conventions:

(1) The conclusion is underlined and represented by *C*.

(2) Premises are enclosed in brackets and represented by P1, P2, P3, etc.

(3) A missing premise or conclusion is represented by *MPx* or *MC*.

To see how this works in practice we will reconstruct the following argument:

> *The most important challenge facing educators today is to teach students how to write decent prose. By "decent prose" I do not mean elegant writing: I mean simple straightforward writing that conforms to the rules of English grammar and clearly conveys its meaning. The ability to write decent prose is important because those who lack it will be unable to understand the great achievements of our cultural heritage — whether of Homer or Hemingway — and, perhaps even more important, will be unable to communicate effectively in today's world.*

The first step is to identify the conclusion. What is the author's main point? What is the author trying to get the reader to accept? It seems quite clear that the conclusion is the first sentence: that the most important challenge facing educators today is to teach students how to write decent prose. We should always be careful here. It is extremely important that the conclusion be correctly identified, for if we misidentify the conclusion whatever we say about the argument will almost certainly miss the point and be a waste of everyone's time.

The second step is to identify the premises. What reasons does the author present to support the conclusion? There are two: (1) those who lack the ability to write decent prose will be unable to understand the great achievements of our cultural heritage, and (2) those who lack the ability to write decent prose will be unable to communicate effectively in today's world. The second sentence in the passage, it should be noted, is not a premise, since it cannot plausibly be regarded as providing a reason in support of the conclusion. Its function is to explain in more detail the meaning of the conclusion.

Following the suggested conventions, the passage should now look like this:

> <u>*The most important challenge facing educators today is to teach students how to write decent prose.*</u> *By "decent prose" I do not mean elegant writing: I mean simple straightforward writing that conforms to the rules of English grammar and clearly conveys its meaning. The ability to write decent prose is important because [those who lack it will be unable to understand the great achievements of our cultural heritage](P1) — whether of Homer or Hemingway — and, perhaps even more important, [will be unable to communicate effectively in today's world.](P2)*

Before moving to the second phase in reconstructing an argument, that is, identifying its structure, we need to consider how to deal with missing premises and conclusions.

4.2 Missing Premises and Conclusions

Many of the arguments we encounter in real life are incomplete, in the sense that if we consider only what the author says we will be forced to assume that the speaker has left something out. Consider:

> P. *Doug's birthday is tomorrow.*
> C. *Therefore, Bob should buy him a present.*

If this is the entire argument, it is quite weak. The mere fact that tomorrow is Doug's birthday is not by itself a good reason for Bob to buy him a present. Either the speaker is quite stupid, or something is missing, such as the fact that Bob and Doug are brothers or are close friends. The principle of charity requires us to assume that something is missing. If the author is present we need only ask; once we learn that Doug and Bob are brothers we have the missing premise that makes sense of the argument:

> P2. *Bob is Doug's brother.*

If the author is not present we have to use whatever knowledge we possess and whatever clues the context provides to supply a missing premise that makes the best sense of the argument. If, however, we lack the knowledge that would allow us to supply the missing premise, we should make only a tentative assessment of it. We should say that, unless there is some special relationship between Doug and Bob, the argument is a weak one.

Supplying missing premises is not always as simple as this. Consider the following argument:

> P1. *High crime rates are caused by the widespread use of probation and suspended sentences.*
> C. *Therefore, we should amend the criminal law to provide for mandatory minimum prison sentences for all crimes.*

A fair interpretation of this argument shows that there are two missing premises. The first is the relatively obvious one, that we are experiencing higher crime rates; clearly this is something the author believes. Thus we need to add the following:

MP2. Crime rates are increasing.

The second missing premise is a little less obvious. On reflection, however, it seems likely that the speaker is also assuming the following:

MP3. A policy of mandatory minimum prison sentences for all crimes will lead to a reduction in crime rates.

Supplying these two missing premises increases the strength of the argument. The strength of this reconstructed argument, it should be noted, is its logical strength: if its premises are true then its conclusion will also be true. (It is probably not a sound argument, however, since it is unlikely that P1 and MP3 are true.)

There is an important difference between the two missing premises. MP2 supplies some missing information that presumably the speaker knows or believes. MP3, on the other hand, is an assumption or **presupposition**; a principle which is needed to explain why the speaker believes that P1 and MP2 support the conclusion. Finding the presuppositions that underlie an argument can often be quite difficult and usually requires considerable care. Such presuppositions are important because frequently they are the real bone of contention between the two sides of an issue.

Let us return to the argument we started to reconstruct in section 4.1. We have already established the premises and conclusion:

P1. The ability to write decent prose is important because those who lack it will be unable to understand the great achievements of our cultural heritage.
P2. The ability to write decent prose is important because those who lack it will be unable to communicate effectively in today's world.
C. The most important challenge facing educators today is to teach students how to write decent prose.

Is there a missing premise in this argument? It is clear that the author is making the following assumption: that educators have a responsibility to give students an understanding of the great achievements of our cultural heritage, and to teach students how to communicate effectively. On the basis of what the author has said, it is almost certain that he or she is making this assumption. Otherwise it is difficult to imagine why the author thinks that the conclusion is supported by the given premises. So we must add the following premise:

MP3. Educators have a responsibility to give students an understanding of the great achievements of our cultural heritage, and to teach students how to communicate effectively.

How can we be sure that this is the actual presupposition of the author? If the author is available we can ask whether he or she accepts this assumption. If the author is not available there may be other of his or her writings we can consult. Otherwise we will have to follow the principle of charity, and attempt to work out the most plausible assumption and add it as a missing premise.

When eliciting assumptions of this sort there are two factors to be considered. We need to find a premise that if true actually provides support for the conclusion, and the premise should be as plausible as possible. Often these two factors pull in opposing directions: a premise that gives the argument logical strength may be less plausible than another premise that provides less logical strength to the argument. We might, for example, have tried another version of MP3:

MP4. Educators have the sole responsibility for giving students an understanding of the great achievements of our cultural heritage, and for teaching students how to communicate effectively.

This, however, is less plausible than MP3, since it denies that parents, for example, have any responsibility in these matters. But if we use it instead of MP3 in our reconstruction, the argument would have greater logical strength. The choice between MP3 and MP4 should be made on the basis of the principle of charity: which gives us a more reasonable version of the argument? In this case MP3 seems a much more reasonable presupposition than MP4.

Sometimes we encounter an argument with a missing conclusion. Usually it is easy to figure out what the conclusion should be. For example:

People who want to see the death penalty reintroduced in Canada should look at the United States. In the United States the death penalty is routinely applied for first degree murder, yet their murder rate is much higher than the murder rate in Canada.

The most likely interpretation of this passage is: it is an argument whose conclusion is that the death penalty should not be reintroduced in Canada. It is difficult to imagine a context in which the speaker would not intend his or her comment to be a reason for not reintroducing the death penalty. When reconstructing an argument with a missing conclusion, we should follow the guidelines suggested above for dealing with missing premises.

4.3 Self Test No. 8

Supply the missing premises or conclusions in the following arguments.

1. It is after midnight and the gas stations are all closed, so I won't be able to drive you home.

2. Whenever your car's engine is flooded, you should put the accelerator right to the floor and then try to start it. So floor it, and try again.

3. But you are still a Catholic, and Catholics are supposed to make a special effort to attend church at Easter.

4. Living in a large metropolis like Toronto is much more stressful than living in a small town. That must be why Jennifer is more uptight than her sister.

5. Well, it's no wonder he failed his mid-term. He skipped more classes than he attended.

6. I am not surprised. After all, children whose parents are extremely strict usually turn into teenage rebels, and Todd's father was tougher on him than any parent I know.

7. You broke my hearing aid, you clumsy oaf. Now I'll have to get a new one.

8. The highschool drop-out rate in our district is about 15 per cent higher than the provincial average. Clearly, the school board ought to introduce programs to persuade students not to drop out, as well as programs designed to make it easier for those who have already dropped out to resume their education.

9. I deserve a much higher grade on my essay than a D+. I worked really hard on it.

10. There ought to be a law prohibiting the use of animals in research. After all, we would not tolerate that kind of treatment of humans.

4.4 Near Arguments

Sometimes we encounter things which look very much like arguments but are not. We shall call these near arguments to remind us that their appearance is misleading. There are two types of near arguments. The first type consists of *reports* of arguments, and the second consists of *explanations*.

4.4.1 REPORTS OF ARGUMENTS

A report of an argument is a statement that says that so-and-so argued in a certain way. For example:

John refuses to vote in elections because he believes that all politicians are dishonest.

This statement tells us that John refuses to vote in elections, and that his reason for not voting is his belief that all politicians are dishonest. But the statement itself is not an argument: it simply tells us that John reasons in a certain way. A report of an argument is no more an argument than a photograph of an accident is itself an accident. Of course, since it is a statement, we can ask whether or not it is true, that is, if it correctly reports some facts about John. It may be false because John's refusal to vote may rest on his belief that despite their promises, all political parties behave the same if they win. Or it may be false because, although he believes all politicians are dishonest, he votes anyway. If the statement is true, however, that does not make it an argument, because its truth consists only in the fact that it reports correctly how John reasons. Here are two more examples of reports of arguments.

According to an editorial in The Chronicle, *standardized, nation-wide scholastic achievement testing will improve the quality of education because it will enable us to learn what works and what doesn't work in the classroom.*

In 1851 John Stuart Mill argued that we should never restrict freedom of expression because in the long run complete freedom of expression has beneficial social consequences, even if in some particular cases the consequences are harmful.

These are both reports of arguments put forward by someone other than the speaker. If we are asked whether we agree with these statements, we must be careful to distinguish between the speaker's actual statement and the argument that is being reported. We may agree that *The Chronicle* and John Stuart Mill did say what the speaker claims they said, but this does not mean that we agree with the arguments that are being reported.

Of course, the arguments that are reported can be considered as arguments in their own right. But to do this we must no longer regard them merely as reports of what others have said: we must view them as arguments that claim to give us good reasons for accepting their conclusions. Now we must ask ourselves whether standardized testing will improve the quality of education, and whether complete freedom of expression will in the long run have beneficial social consequences. What *The Chronicle* and John Stuart Mill believe is now irrelevant. What is relevant is only the argument itself.

It is sometimes difficult to know whether a report of an argument is intended by the speaker to be taken as an argument. Some people seem to prefer to take part in discussions by citing other people's arguments; they are inclined to agree with the arguments they report, but if they meet serious criticism they can easily back off by claiming that they don't fully agree with *The Chronicle* or John Stuart Mill. But often people who introduce another person's argument into a discussion clearly do mean to stand by it; they report the argument precisely because they think it is a sound argument. In these cases, we are entitled to interpret a report of an argument as itself an argument. There is no easy test to decide when we should treat a report of an argument as itself an argument. We can only rely upon the context and the principle of charity to help us decide.

4.4.2 EXPLANATIONS

The second type of near argument consists of explanations. An explanation is an attempt to show *why* or *how* something happens. For example:

My car won't start because it is out of gas.

The reason the Liberals lost the last election is that they were perceived by the voters as arrogant and uncaring.

Teachers, who in recent years have become increasingly sensitive to public criticism, are opposed to nation-wide scholastic achievement testing since they fear that the results could be used or misused in attempts to criticize them as poor teachers.

The Red Wings got a penalty because they had too many players on the ice.

There are several different types of explanations. Many explanations are causal: they explain an event by reference to its causes. But some explanations are non-causal. We explain how volleyball is played not by reference to the causes of volleyball, but to the rules of volleyball. We explain how to register as a university student by reference to the university's registration procedures. We explain people's behaviour by reference to their motives and goals. We explain what a hammer is by reference to its function.

Explanations are often confused with arguments because they share the same vocabulary. In the above examples, the words *because, reason,* and *since* are used to indicate that an explanation is being given, although these same words are often used in arguments as inference indicators. To avoid confusing arguments and explanations, we need to understand how their purposes differ. The purpose of an explanation is to show *why* or *how* some phenomenon occurred or some event happened; the purpose of an argument is to show *that* some view or statement is correct or true. Explanations are appropriate when the event in question is taken for granted, and we are seeking to understand why it occurred. Arguments are appropriate when we want to show that something is true, usually when there is some possibility of disagreement about its correctness.

Thus, when I say that my car won't start because it is out of gas, I am not trying to find a support for my belief that my car won't start. I know this already. What I want is an explanation for the fact that it won't start.

Is it because the engine is flooded, or because of an electrical fault, or because the car is out of gas? With arguments, on the other hand, what is at issue is whether the conclusion is true; the function of the premises is to supply reasons for believing that the conclusion is true or correct. Consider the following argument, which is superficially similar to an explanation:

Susan, you should visit your parents more often, because it gives them such pleasure when you do.

Here the speaker is trying to persuade Susan to do something she is reluctant to do by providing a reason for doing so. It would make little sense to interpret this passage as an explanation, that is, that the speaker and Susan both agree that she should visit her parents more often and are discussing *why* she should do so.

There are, however, cases where only the context can tell us whether we should treat something as an argument or as an explanation. For example:

Jim's health is good because he has a healthy diet and gets plenty of exercise.

We can imagine a context in which both the speaker and the audience know that Jim's health is good, and the speaker wants to explain why this is so. But we can also imagine a context in which they know that Jim has a healthy diet and gets plenty of exercise, and the speaker wants to argue that Jim is in good health. Usually, the context makes it clear whether something is an explanation or an argument.

Explanations are of course subject to debate, and there are many disagreements as to what is the correct explanation for some phenomenon or event. This means that sometimes explanations themselves become the subject of an argument. For example:

Women are economically disadvantaged in our society not because they have traditionally been socialized into accepting passive and supporting roles, but because they have been and still are excluded by men from economic power. The effects of the traditional socialization on women's attitudes are still very real in many cases, but it does not account for their economically disadvantaged position, since when women do seek careers in business, which is where the real wealth is to be made, they are systematically excluded by men from the corridors of real power and influence.

This is an argument about what is the correct, or best, explanation of the fact, which is not at issue, that women are economically disadvantaged in our society. The speaker is, however, not merely asserting an explanation, but attempting to argue that his or her explanation is correct. Arguments about explanations, like this one, can sometimes be difficult to distinguish from the explanations themselves. All we can do is rely upon the context to help us decide, bearing in mind, as always, the principle of charity.

4.5 Self-Test No. 9

Which of the following are not arguments? For those that are near arguments, indicate whether they are reports of an argument or explanations.

1. I find it extremely difficult to perform for an audience. When I was a child my parents used to brag all the time about what a prodigy I was, and they used to get so upset when I played badly that I was always terrified that they would stop loving me if I didn't play well. Consequently, I still imagine all sorts of things going wrong, like having a memory lapse, or dropping my flute.

2. David was so upset at what he had done that he ran all the way home to fetch the first aid kit and tried his best to bandage up the cut on Steven's foot. Then he helped Steven walk home, and explained to his mother what had happened. The fact that it was really Steven's fault – as even his mother realized – didn't make any difference to David at all; he felt responsible for his friend.

3. We'd better watch Gina closely for the next twenty-four hours. She has had a nasty knock on the head, and there could be a concussion. If we see any signs of grogginess or disorientation then we'll take her to the hospital.

4. There are several reasons why a child's school performance can suddenly deteriorate. Sometimes it is because a physical problem, which may be caused by a virus or a poor diet, affects the child's concentration. Sometimes it is because of a problem at school, such as an inexperienced teacher who has not learned how to recognize when children are only pretending they understand their lessons. Most commonly, it is because of a problem at home, such as the parents getting a divorce.

5. The reason your local taxes go up when you make improvements to your home and property is that the tax rate is based upon the value of your property. The more your property is worth, the higher your local tax. It may not be fair but that is how the system works.

6. According to a recent Canadian Supreme Court decision, the previous sexual conduct of a woman may be introduced by the defence in sexual assault cases. The court argued that the right of an accused to a fair trial was more important than the right of the victim to avoid possible embarrassment.

7. You should never turn off your computer without following the exit procedure for your software program. This is because you will lose the files you have been working on, unless you save them before you exit.

8. I have consulted my lawyer, and he advised me that unless you refund the entire purchase price I could take you to court and get my money back. And he says that if I complain to the Ministry of Commercial Relations, you could lose your licence.

9. Using juries in criminal trials is a stupid system. When there is only a judge trying the case, the prosecution has to persuade only one person that the accused is guilty. But when there is a jury, the prosecution has to persuade all twelve members of the jury that the accused is guilty. If only one juror has a grudge against the police, or has sympathy for the accused, or is just too dumb to understand the evidence, then a guilty person will go free. The jury system works to the advantage of criminals. We should abolish it.

10. Americans really don't understand the way our political parties operate, for they fail to realize the tremendous power that the leader of the party has over rank-and-file party members, and especially over the elected members of the legislature. In the U.S. the party leader's power is much more limited, even when the leader becomes president. This is because their constitution is based upon the separation of power between the legislative and administrative branches of government.

4.6 The Structure of Arguments

The structure of an argument is important because it can tell us how the premises are intended to support the conclusion and can give us some of the information we need in order to undertake a critical assessment of the argument. The easiest way to see the structure of an argument is to represent it graphically using what is called a tree diagram. A **tree diagram** is a schematic representation of the structure of an argument using letters (*P1*, *P2*, *MP3*, *C*, etc.) to represent the premises and conclusion, and an arrow to represent *therefore*. There are three basic argument structures.

4.6.1 SIMPLE ARGUMENTS

In section 1.1 we saw that every argument must have a conclusion and at least one premise, and that the premises and conclusion are connected by an implicit or explicit *therefore*. The simplest type of argument consists of a single premise and a single conclusion. Such arguments have a structure that we will call a **simple argument structure**. For example:

> P. *When Jim quit playing the trumpet he gave it to his younger brother.*
> C. *Hence, Jim won't be able to lend his trumpet to Andrew.*

The tree diagram for such simple argument structures is:

P

C

4.6.2 T ARGUMENTS

When we consider arguments with two premises, there are two possible structures the argument might have, and it is important to be aware of how they differ. Consider the following argument:

> P1. *Every medical doctor has had to tell someone that a loved one has died.*
> P2. *Beth is a medical doctor.*
> C. *Therefore, Beth has had to tell someone that a loved one has died.*

This argument has the following structure:

Notice that each premise, considered by itself, provides little or no support for the conclusion. By itself, the fact that every medical doctor has had to tell someone that a loved one has died provides no support for the conclusion. Similarly, the fact that Beth is a medical doctor does not by itself provide any support for the conclusion. If either premise were false, the remaining premise would provide little or no support for the conclusion. It is only when both are true that they provide support. An argument with this structure is called a **T argument**, because the lines joining the premises to the conclusion form a *T*.

T arguments may sometimes have three or more premises. Consider the following argument:

P1. Every physically handicapped person who has tried to find employment knows the anguish of rejection.
P2. Jody is physically handicapped.
P3. Jody has tried to find employment.
C. Therefore, Jody knows the anguish of rejection.

The tree diagram for this argument is:

4.6.3 V ARGUMENTS

The third basic structure can be seen in the following argument:

P1. Frances is very successful in her career.
P2. Frances has a secure and supportive marriage.
C. Therefore, Frances is a happy person.

This argument has the following structure:

Notice that two separate reasons are offered in support of the conclusion. Each operates independently of the other. If either premise is missing or false the remaining one still provides support for the conclusion. We shall call arguments with a structure of this sort **V arguments**, because the lines joining the premises to the conclusion form a *V*.

Like T arguments, V arguments can have three or more premises. For example, the argument above would be strengthened by adding another premise that functions in the same way as the first two:

P3. Frances had a stable and secure childhood.

Our argument now has the following structure:

Obviously, the diagram now looks more like a *W* than a *V*, but to keep things simple we will continue to call it a V argument.

The distinction between T and V arguments is important because they represent two different ways in which two or more premises can combine to support a conclusion. To distinguish the two types of argument structure it is necessary to ask whether the premises have to work together in order to provide support for the conclusion or whether they work independently of each other. The premises of a T argument work as a team, and both must be true to provide support for the conclusion; if either premise is false then the other by itself would provide no support for the conclusion. On the other hand, each of the premises of a V argument provides independent support for the conclusion: if either premise is false the other would still provide independent support for the conclusion. We shall see the importance of the distinction when we come to the assessment of arguments. If one of the premises of a T argument is false, then the argument is weak even if the other premise or premises are true. But if one of the premises of a V argument is false the argument may still be strong if the other premise or premises are true. It is important, therefore, to pay careful attention to the structure of arguments.

4.6.4 COMPLEX ARGUMENTS

The above are the three basic structures out of which more complex structures are constructed. Consider the following argument:

P1. *Max was born in Canada to Canadian parents.*
P2. *This means that Max is a Canadian citizen.*
C. *Therefore, Max can vote in federal elections.*

This argument has the following structure:

P1

P2

C

Note that the tree diagram contains two arrows. This is because the second premise is really a sub-conclusion that is supported by the first premise. In reality there are two arguments here; *P2* is the conclusion of the first argument and the premise of the second. The first argument is P1 therefore P2, and the second is P2 therefore C. The combined argument does not, however, present two separate reasons to support the conclusion, but only one. P2 presents a reason for C and P1 presents a reason for P2. We could delete either premise and the remaining one would still support the conclusion.

When reconstructing an argument that has two conclusions it is necessary to determine which is the main conclusion and which is the subordinate conclusion. Sometimes the argument makes this quite clear. When it does not we should ask which is best regarded as a premise for the other. Taking account of all the contextual clues and the principle of charity, which of the following makes better sense of the argument?

C1 therefore C2, or
C2 therefore C1.

Consider the following argument:

City Council should approve the proposed arts centre without delay, for several reasons. The need for a centre has been demonstrated many times; anyone who examines the evidence will agree that existing facilities are woefully inadequate. The financial benefit to the community is harder to pin down precisely, but no-one can deny that local merchants and the city's tax base will benefit. The only question is whether the city can afford to make a reasonable contribution to the annual operating costs. It is foolish to expect a consensus on this question: after all no-one likes higher taxes, no matter how worthy the cause. But the fact is that Guelph has a lower tax rate than most cities its size and is in excellent financial shape. And the proposed increase in taxes would amount to only two dollars per year. It is clear, therefore, that the city can afford the arts centre.

This passage has two conclusions. The opening sentence is a conclusion, which the passage goes on to give reasons for. But the final sentence gives another conclusion. We determine which is the main conclusion by asking which of the following makes the best sense of the whole passage:

(1) City Council should approve the proposal for an arts centre. Therefore, the city can afford an arts centre.
(2) The city can afford an arts centre. Therefore, City Council should approve the proposal for an arts centre.

It is obvious that (2) makes good sense while (1) does not. This means that we should regard the opening sentence of the passage as the main conclusion. The other is a sub-conclusion, or, the conclusion of a subsidiary argument that has been included to support one of the premises of the main argument.

Some arguments, however, are much more complex than these examples suggest. Here is another argument with a complex structure:

P1. When the Meech Lake agreement was negotiated it had the support of the Prime Minister and all provincial premiers, who represented all the major political parties.

P2. In several provinces the opposition parties voted to ratify the agreement.

P3. So politicians of all political parties all across Canada strongly supported the agreement.

P4. However, the vast majority of Canadians outside Quebec and a significant minority inside Quebec were strongly opposed to the agreement.

C. Therefore, the politicians were out of touch with the views of the people.

In this argument P1 to P3 constitutes a sub-argument: it is a V argument with P1 and P2 as premises and P3 as its conclusion. P3 is then used as a premise in a second argument: it is a T argument with P3 and P4 as premises and C as its conclusion. The tree diagram for this argument is thus a combination of a T and a V structure:

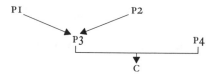

4.7 Self-Test No. 10

Label the premises and conclusion and draw a tree diagram for each of the following arguments. Where appropriate, supply missing premises or conclusions.

1. Anyone who has brains and ambition will go far in this world. Carla has certainly got plenty of both, so she will go far.

2. I have never had any problems with the last four Fords I've bought, so I don't think I'll have any problems this time.

3. The Blue Jays should win the American League pennant this year. They have solid depth in their pitching staff, their hitting has been consistently good this year, their coaching is excellent, and there is a good team spirit.

4. A recent public opinion poll showed that more than two-thirds of Canadians believe that most politicians are dishonest. Clearly, there is a crisis of confidence in Canadian politics.

5. In the last thirty years in Canada, there has been a tremendous increase in the university participation rate (i.e., the percentage of population in the eighteen- to twenty-two-year-old age group that attends university). In 1960, the participation rate in Canada was only 5 per cent. But by 1990 the participation rate was over 15 per cent.

6. Laura gets pretty good grades, she is the best gymnast in the school, she has a lot of friends, and she organized the campaign last year that forced the school to start a recycling program. I think she will probably win the election for president of the Students' Council.

7. If he tells his teacher he cheated he will be punished by the principal. But if he doesn't tell his teacher he cheated he will be punished by his parents. Either way he is going to be punished.

8. Since angle CAB is 60 degrees, and angle ACB is 40 degrees, then angle ABC must be 80 degrees.

9. Any reporter who says that good reporters never slant their stories but simply report the objective facts, must be either stupid or dishonest, since it is obvious that one cannot write anything without an element of interpretation creeping in....

10. ...and that reporter is obviously not stupid. He must be dishonest.

4.8 Another Warning

People talk about all sorts of things for all sorts of reasons. Sometimes we can be fooled into interpreting something as an argument when it really isn't. Sometimes people use language that makes it appear that they are presenting an argument when they are really just expressing a strongly held opinion and not attempting to defend it with reasons. For example:

> The press in this country seems quite uninterested in serious political discussion. Whenever an important political issue arises, such as aboriginal rights or free trade, the press seems interested only in personalities and whether the issue will hinder this

party's chances of re-election, or improve that leader's public image. I think the press should take a good hard look at itself and ask whether a truly responsible press would conduct political discussions at such a juvenile level.

Is this an argument? To answer this question we should ask whether we can, without doing violence to the author's apparent intentions, interpret it as presenting a conclusion accompanied by one or more supporting premises. Clearly, the author wants us to agree with his or her view that the press is irresponsible in its approach to serious political discussion. But it is probably unfair to the author to insist that any of the statements should be regarded as presenting a reason for this view. In fact, what is interesting about this passage is the absence of any real supporting evidence. All we are offered is the suggestion that the press ignores serious political discussion and deals only with peripheral matters, and if we regard this as a premise it is an extremely weak one. It is much better to interpret this passage as an expression of an opinion. The principle of charity supports this interpretation, since otherwise we would have to regard the argument as a very weak one.

However, since we are sometimes entitled to supply missing premises and missing conclusions, we may be tempted to turn a non-argument into an argument by reading a great deal more into a passage than is really there. When dealing with a doubtful passage we should therefore be careful not to assume that it must be an argument, or we may find ourselves reconstructing an argument that the author never intended. There is no simple way of determining when we are dealing with an argument and when we are not. We should remember that people do many things besides argue: they complain, express opinions, make observations, make accusations, tell stories, give illustrations, bestow praise, and so on. The principle of charity dictates caution. Common sense usually suggests the most plausible interpretation.

4.9 Questions for Discussion

Read carefully each of the following passages, and, if you decide it is an argument, work out the best reconstruction.

1. (Background: A father is talking to his sixteen-year-old son.)
    It wouldn't matter if everybody in the school was going to the rock concert. The point is that you know that you shouldn't go. You prom-

ised me that if we didn't give you a curfew any more you would ensure that every school assignment would be submitted on time. And there is no way you can finish your history essay if you go to that concert.

2.   (Background: A student who has missed a mid-term approaches the instructor to ask for a make-up test.)

I'm sorry I missed the test, but it really wasn't my fault. I went home on the weekend, and didn't get back until midnight. I studied until four in the morning and as a result I didn't hear my alarm and missed the test. It would be really unfair if I were to be punished for something that is not my fault.

3.   (Background: A letter to the editor commenting upon a recent U.S. court ruling that teaching scientific creationism in science courses in public schools is unconstitutional. Scientific creationism holds that the biblical account of creation is a legitimate scientific theory that should be taught in science courses along with the theory of evolution.)

Your recent report on scientific creationism was very interesting and I don't disagree with anything it said, but it failed to point out the true nature of these so-called "scientific" creationists. The fact is that they are a bunch of intellectual misfits and misguided crackpots who wouldn't recognize a truly scientific theory if you hit them over the head with it. They are either lamentably ignorant, or bigots, or both.

4.   (Background: Several students are discussing the U.S. war on Iraq. One, who supported the war, is responding to the objection that the U.S. has no right to act as a world policeman.)

But of course the U.S. has the right to police the world. The U.S. is one of the most powerful nations in the world; surely you don't deny that. Well, that's one of the things world powers can do. If a world power decides to act as a world cop, then it has that right.

5.   (Background: A lawyer is attempting to persuade a client not to sue his doctor for malpractice.)

I understand why you feel a sense of grievance, but I don't think it is a good idea. First, you have to prove that the doctor was negligent, i.e., that he failed to provide medical care that is up to the accepted standard. And given what you've told me, I don't think we would prove that at all. After all, he did explicitly warn you that there was only a 70 per cent chance of success. Secondly, a trial will be extremely stressful for your wife, since she will have to answer a lot of intimate personal questions which I'm sure she would prefer to avoid.

6.   (Background: From a talk on student stress given by an educational psychologist to a group of highschool teachers.)

Finally, we come to the type of stress that is induced by the learning process itself, for example, stress that results from getting low grades, from not understanding the material, from being late with assignments, or from asking dumb questions in class. Unlike other types of stress, this type is caused by you as teachers. If you want to reduce this type of stress the solution is in your hands: develop better methods of presenting material and motivating the students to master it, make sure students don't get into courses they cannot handle, be more reasonable about accepting late assignments, and be polite to students who ask dumb questions.

7.   (Background: A university student is talking to a friend about smoking marijuana.)

My mom and dad, and my older sister too, used to warn me about the evils of taking drugs. I remember the first time I went to a party where people were smoking pot; I mean, I thought I was in a den of iniquity and I left as soon as I could. But after a while you realize that there are all sorts of perfectly ordinary people walking around who smoke a bit of pot now and again. So I figure there can't be anything really wrong with it.

8.   (Background: From an article entitled "Technology: Boon or Doom?")

These astonishing achievements – achievements that earlier generations could only dream of – have produced in many a faith in the limitless capacity of technology to benefit mankind. During the past two decades, however, there has been increasing evidence that this faith is unreasonable. The space shuttle disaster, the Chernobyl and Three Mile Island nuclear accidents, acid rain, and a host of other technological misfortunes have each in their own way shown that there are significant limitations to what technology can do.

PART III

ASSESSING ARGUMENTS

Chapter 5

Strategies for Assessing Arguments

We now come to the assessment of arguments. Before we consider the details of how this should be done, we need to say something about the nature of the task. Every argument, as we saw in section 1.1, makes a double claim: (a) that its conclusion is true and (b) that its premises support its conclusion. Whenever we assess an argument we are really only asking whether these claims are true. An argument makes a kind of promise; assessing an argument is asking whether it can make good on its promise. A good argument is one that does what it claims to do, and a bad argument is one that fails to do what it claims to do. But how are we to tell whether an argument has made good on its promise?

Philosophers have developed two approaches for assessing arguments. The first and more traditional is the **fallacies** approach, in which we identify all the specific fallacies (or mistakes) that an argument can make, and then ask whether a given argument commits any of these fallacies. If it commits none of them it will be a good argument, and if it commits one or more of them it will be a bad argument. In recent years, however, philosophers have developed the **criterial** approach in which we appeal to the criteria, or standards, that a good argument must satisfy, and ask whether a given argument meets these criteria. If it meets them all it will be a good argument, and if it fails to meet one or more of them it will be a bad argument.

The criterial approach is the better of the two. It has several very important advantages over the fallacies approach, which will be noted below. Nevertheless, the fallacies approach is sometimes useful because it identifies certain common mistakes. In the following chapters we adopt the criterial approach but will introduce specific fallacies when they can help put us on our guard against certain mistakes. But first we need to discuss the two approaches in more detail.

5.1 The Fallacies Approach

The concept of a fallacy presents several theoretical difficulties for logicians that need not detain us here. For our purposes we can define a **fallacy** as any error or weakness that detracts from the soundness of an argument. For example, one traditional fallacy is the *appeal to pity*, as in:

Jane is a widow with three teenage children living in a two-bedroom basement apartment.
Therefore, her employer should promote her to supervisor.

Clearly, the fact that Jane is a widow with three teenage children living in a two-bedroom basement apartment is not a good reason for promoting her. Whether she should be promoted depends upon whether she has the qualifications and experience to be a good supervisor. The appeal to the pity we naturally feel for Jane is irrelevant to the question whether she should be promoted.

Logicians have long been fascinated by fallacies and have devoted much time and energy to identifying and explaining specific types of fallacies. Aristotle listed 13 types of fallacies, but modern logicians have identified approximately 150 different types. This proliferation of fallacies suggests a misleading picture of a logician as a kind of microbiologist of the intellect searching for new logical viruses. This picture is misleading because a fallacy is an error, and errors lack the kind of objective status that a virus has. One problem with the fallacies approach is that there is no limit to the number of ways in which an argument can be weak. We can never be sure that our list of types of fallacies is complete. Another problem is that as more and more types of fallacies are identified it has become increasingly difficulty to use them effectively as the basis for assessing arguments. Not only do we have to memorize a very long list of fallacies, but we often find arguments that clearly contain a weakness but where we have difficulty in deciding which particular fallacy has been committed.

The underlying problem with the fallacies approach is that it is negative in nature. This is an especially serious problem when we are trying to develop good arguments for ourselves, rather than merely criticizing other people's arguments. Rather than telling us what we want to see in a good argument, it only tells what we should try to avoid.

5.2 The Criterial Approach

The criterial approach, unlike the fallacies approach, is positive in nature. It begins by establishing the criteria that a good argument must satisfy, and then uses these criteria as the basis for assessing particular arguments. To develop these criteria we rely upon the concept of a sound argument. In section 1.1 we defined a logically strong argument as one whose premises, if true, support its conclusion, and a sound argument as a logically strong argument whose premises are true. It is now time to use these concepts to establish the criteria for a sound argument. They give rise to three criteria.

5.2.1 THE THREE CRITERIA OF A SOUND ARGUMENT

The requirement that a sound argument must have true premises is the basis for our first criterion for a sound argument: it should have true premises. Obviously, since premises are offered as support for a conclusion, if a premise is false then no matter how good the argument is in other respects the premise provides no support for the conclusion. But there is a problem here. Often we are not able to *prove* that our premises are true: most of us cannot actually prove, for example, that cigarette smoking is a health hazard. However, in most contexts there are reasons that justify the acceptance of such a claim even though we cannot prove it is true. The fact that our government requires all cigarette packages to include the claim as a warning, for example, makes it reasonable for us to accept it, even though such a reason is clearly not a proof. We must therefore expand our first criterion to take account of those contexts where all that we can reasonably demand is that there be good reasons for accepting the premises. Our first criterion, therefore, is that the premises must be **acceptable**. Of course, in some contexts, such as assessing mathematical proofs, the only good reason for accepting the premises will be that they can actually be proven.

Logical strength, the second requirement for a sound argument, gives rise to our second and third criteria. The second is that the premises must be relevant to the conclusion. We noticed in section 1.2 that an argument may have premises that are known to be true, but that nevertheless fail to provide any support for its conclusion. This is what happens when the premises are not relevant to the conclusion. Clearly, if the premises of an argument are to support its conclusion they must supply us with information that is relevant to the question whether or not the conclusion is true. Precisely what information is relevant to the truth of a particular conclusion may sometimes be difficult to determine, but it is clear that what we are looking for is *relevant* information. Our second criterion, therefore, is that the premises should be **relevant** to the conclusion.

The logical strength requirement also gives rise to our third criterion, namely, that the premises must be adequate to support the conclusion. A premise may be both true and relevant to the conclusion, but it may nevertheless not be adequate to support the conclusion. Adequacy is usually (but not always, as we shall see later) a matter of degree. In most cases a true, relevant premise can provide support that ranges from very little to a great deal. Consider the following:

> *My neighbour, my wife, and all the people I work with, all of whom voted Tory in the last election, have decided to vote Liberal in the next election. Therefore, the Liberals will probably win the next election.*

The premise of this argument is obviously relevant to the conclusion, and it does provide some, albeit minimal, support for the conclusion. It is, we might say, a straw in the wind. We would be foolish to bet on the outcome of the election on the basis of this evidence. By itself, therefore, this premise is not adequate. If, however, we keep asking friends and neighbours, or better yet undertake a proper public opinion survey, we may accumulate more information that shows that large numbers of voters are switching from Tory to Liberal. If this extra information is included as additional premises, then the support provided for the conclusion is much more adequate. The third criterion, therefore, is that the premises must provide **adequate** support for the conclusion.

Thus there are three different and independent criteria that a sound argument must meet:

(1) The premises must be acceptable.
(2) The premises must be relevant.
(3) The premises must be adequate.

We are not entitled to pass final judgement on any argument until we have assessed it against each of these criteria. If it meets all three criteria we should conclude that it is a sound argument. If it fails to meet any one criterion we should regard it as a weak or defective argument.

5.3 Seven Rules for Assessing Arguments

At this point it will be useful to present a set of rules that should be followed whenever an argument is being assessed. The brief comments included here are intended only to highlight points that are made elsewhere.

Rule 1. Identify The Main Conclusion

The way to identify the main conclusion should be familiar by now. (1) Look for the main point of the passage, by asking, *What is the author driving at?* (2) Look for inference indicators, such as *therefore, hence, so, consequently*, and so on. (3) Pay attention to the context and background for clues as to what the argument is all about. (4) Use the principle of charity when interpreting an ambiguous conclusion, or when supplying a missing conclusion. If the conclusion is difficult to elicit it may be because we are not dealing with an argument at all. We have already come across several passages that look like arguments but should not be regarded as genuine arguments. Near arguments (see section 4.4) and forceful assertions can be especially troublesome. Remember that every argument presents a claim *and* a reason to support that claim.

Rule 2. Identify the Premises

The next step is to identify the premises. If the conclusion has been correctly identified the rest of the argument will include the premises. But it may also include some irrelevant material, such as illustrations and examples. It may also include alternative versions of what is really a single premise. The question we should ask here is, *What information or reasons does the author provide to support the conclusion?* As always, it is important to pay attention to the context and the principle of charity when identifying the premises and when supplying missing premises.

Rule 3. Identify the Structure of the Argument

Once the conclusion and the premises have been identified the structure of the argument must be identified. If the argument has a simple structure (see section 4.3.1) we can pass straight on to the critical assessment. In all other cases care should be taken to ensure that the structure of the argument has been correctly identified, if necessary by drawing a tree diagram.

Rule 4. Check the Acceptability of the Premises

In Chapter 6 we will consider how truth-claims should be approached. Two warnings should be mentioned here. First, if the argument is intended to be a counterfactual argument (see section 1.3) it is irrelevant to ask whether the premises are true, since the author is not claiming that they are true. Second, we need to note that a false premise does not always deprive the conclusion of all support. If an argument has two independent premises, as in a V argument, the fact that one of them is false has no bearing on whether the other premise is true, and if the other premise is true then the conclusion may still have some support.

Rule 5. Check the Relevance of the Premises

In Chapter 7 we will examine some common ways in which premises can seem relevant when in fact they are not. It should be stressed that the premises must be considered in context, for a premise that is irrelevant when considered by itself may have its relevance established by other premises in the argument.

Rule 6. Check the Adequacy of the Premises

In Chapter 8 we will examine the common ways in which premises can fail to provide adequate support for the conclusion. When assessing adequacy it is important to notice the degree of support which the argument claims is provided by the premises.

Rule 7. Look for Counter-arguments

Finally, we should look for counter-arguments. Are there any reasons we can think of that would support a conclusion that is inconsistent with the conclusion of the argument being assessed? Strictly speaking, this goes beyond the assessment of a given argument, but if there is a sound counter-argument we know that the given argument must be deficient. Otherwise, we would have two sound arguments with inconsistent conclusions, which is, or should be, impossible. We will discuss the role of counter-arguments in Chapter 12.

Chapter 6

Assessing Truth-Claims

6.1 Theories of Truth

Pontius Pilate, before sentencing Christ to death, asked, *what is truth?* but, being a practical man, did not stay around to debate the question. In its most general sense, the question is deeply troubling, for no-one has yet been able to provide an entirely satisfactory answer. Philosophers have made numerous attempts to develop theories of truth, but all are open to plausible objections. However, our interest in truth, like Pilate's, is more practical than theoretical, so we need not delay too long over purely theoretical issues. Nevertheless, we should note the three main theories of truth, for they provide a useful background to our discussion of how truth-claims are to be assessed.

6.1.1 THE CORRESPONDENCE THEORY

What makes a statement or belief true? (We can speak interchangeably here of beliefs or statements.) The most obvious answer is that a statement or belief is true when it corresponds to the facts. The statement *My birthday is October 22* is true if, and only if, it is a fact that I was born on October 22. The fact that I was born on October 22 is a necessary and sufficient condition for the truth of the statement *My birthday is October 22*. Anyone who is not sure whether this statement is true need only check my birth certificate. It seems reasonable, therefore, to hold that truth consists of a correspondence between a statement and a fact; that when the correspondence holds, the statement is true; and when it does not hold, the statement is false. This is the **correspondence theory of truth**.

There are a number of objections to this account of truth. The most obvious is that there are many statements that we believe to be true for which there seem to be no corresponding facts. But according to the correspondence theory, if there are no corresponding facts then we would have to conclude that these statements are false. Consider the following statements: what facts would we check to determine whether they are true?

There is no greatest prime number.
You should keep your promises.
God created the universe.
Bach was the greatest composer of the eighteenth century.
If Hitler had died in 1918, World War II would not have occurred.

Supporters of the correspondence theory have developed some ingenious strategies to overcome this objection. Some have held that there really are facts that correspond to these statements. They claim that there are mathematical facts, moral facts, etc. But these are not ordinary facts since they are not accessible to us in the way that facts about my birthday are, so the introduction of these queer facts solves nothing. Others have argued that some or all of these statements are not really true or false at all. They hold that when we say that you ought to keep your promises we are expressing an attitude, and that it is a mistake to regard our statement as making a truth-claim.

Despite this difficulty, the correspondence theory is an adequate account of one kind of truth. Sometimes the truth of a statement or belief does consist of a correspondence between the statement and certain facts. Whenever a statement makes a factual assertion, then, as long as there are facts that could be checked to determine whether they are as the statement claims they are, we can use the correspondence between the statement and the facts as our criterion of truth. But when a statement makes a non-factual assertion, or asserts a fact that is non-checkable, we cannot use correspondence as a criterion of truth.

The notion of checkable facts is important and needs some elucidation. We can only check facts, either directly or indirectly, by making observations. This is another way of saying that the fact must be empirical. An **empirical fact** is a fact that is observable in principle, that is, it could be observed if we could get ourselves into the right place at the right time. The notion of an empirical fact allows us to define an empirical statement as a statement that asserts an empirical fact (or set of empirical facts). The correspondence theory of truth, therefore, provides an appropriate criterion of truth for all empirical statements. And since the world around us consists, by and large, of empirical facts, the correspondence theory is an appropriate criterion for our knowledge of the external, observable world.

6.1.2 THE COHERENCE THEORY

But the critics have a second objection to the correspondence theory. Besides claiming that it is inadequate as a criterion for non-empirical statements, they also object that it is inadequate even for empirical statements. They point out that the theory presents us with two distinct and separate worlds, the world of facts and the world of statements and beliefs. Its claim that truth consists of a correspondence between empirical facts and statements or beliefs requires that the world of facts must be *brute* facts, or facts that are independent of our beliefs about them. Otherwise, we could not compare the facts with our beliefs about them in order to see whether they correspond. But, the critics ask, how can we know anything at all about the world of facts, since as soon as we turn to the facts the only thing we can obtain is yet another belief about the facts? We can never, it seems, have any knowledge of such brute facts, for we can never get beyond our *beliefs* about them. Brute facts presumably exist but we can never know them directly. The very act of recognizing or knowing that something is a fact necessarily involves an element of selection and interpretation. Facts, as many philosophers of science claim, are never brute but are always theory-laden. The empirical facts upon which correspondence theorists rely, therefore, presuppose that some theory or interpretation is already true, which means that the correspondence theory not only fails to provide a criterion of truth but presupposes some other criterion of truth.

This objection has led the critics to propose the coherence theory of truth, according to which truth is defined by reference to the reasons we have for believing something to be true. When we consider whether any particular belief is true we appeal to reasons, but these reasons are themselves beliefs. The only things available to us as justifications for believing something to be true are other beliefs. A particular belief, therefore, may be regarded as true when it is part of a coherent set of mutually supported beliefs. To show that any belief is true we appeal to our other beliefs: if it can be supported by some of them and is not inconsistent with the rest we are entitled to regard it as true. But if it is inconsistent with one or more of our other beliefs then one of the inconsistent beliefs has to be rejected, since we cannot simultaneously hold two inconsistent beliefs. In short, according to the **coherence theory of truth**, a belief or statement is true if, and only if, it coheres with a system of beliefs or statements.

Where do the beliefs that make up this system come from? They come from our experience. Some beliefs impress themselves upon us very strongly (for example, that you are now reading a book) while others seem less secure (for example, that you spent New Year's Eve, 1991, with your cousin). But the question whether any of these beliefs is true is not to be answered by looking at their source; this is the error made by correspondence theorists. Rather it is to be answered by appeal to other beliefs. Ultimately, the only test of truth lies in the appeal to the coherence of our beliefs.

The issue between correspondence and coherence theorists is quite theoretical and abstract, and we will not attempt to resolve it here. Since our interest is essentially practical, however, we should note that the coherence theory is strongest precisely where the correspondence theory is weakest – when dealing with non-empirical statements. Consider again the examples of non-empirical statements given in section 6.1.1. It is obvious that we can only deal with the question of their truth or falsity in the way the coherence theory suggests. The coherence theory, therefore, is an appropriate criterion of truth for non-empirical statements.

6.1.3 THE PRAGMATIC THEORY

Some philosophers reject both these theories on the ground that they ignore the problem-solving function of human beliefs. They argue that all human activity, including thinking and using language, arises from our need to solve problems. This is true at the level of the human species: humans would never have learned to notice colours if, for example, colours were not helpful in deciding when fruit is ripe enough to eat. It is also true at the individual level: we learn the multiplication table because it is useful in figuring out how much wallpaper to buy to paper a room. Since thought and language are essentially problem-solving tools, they argue, truth should be thought of as a property of beliefs or statements that can actually solve problems. A true statement or belief is one that is useful in solving a problem.

Not all the problems we face are practical problems, but the pragmatic theory is not limited to practical problems. Any real problem can give rise to a true solution. To understand what a real problem is, we have to ask the following sorts of questions. Why do we want to know whether World War II would not have occurred had Hitler died in 1918? What difference would it make if this claim were true rather than false? What would we do differently if we knew it were true? Such questions force us to reflect upon what the solution is needed for. For pragmatic theorists a problem is only a real problem if we have to solve it in order to go on to do something else. Otherwise it is only a pseudo-problem, one that makes no difference to anything. Thus, for the **pragmatic theory of truth** a statement or belief is true if, and only if, it leads to the successful solution of a real problem.

One basic objection raised against the pragmatic theory is that many beliefs that we are quite certain of cannot be regarded as solutions to problems. Mathematicians are quite certain that there is no greatest prime number because they are certain that they have a valid proof, although they would be hard pressed to say what the real problem is to which their belief is a solution. We can be reasonably sure that Caesar crossed the Rubicon in 44 B.C., even though this is unlikely to help in the solution of any real problem. At a more mundane level, it can be proven that when people hiccough, air travels through their windpipes at speeds of up to 140 kilometres per hour, but for what conceivable problem could this be a solution?

A rather different objection arises when we look at other types of problems. What problem is the belief in God's existence intended to solve? Suppose we say that the problem is how to find solace in a vast universe that seems to have no purpose? If, as is usually the case, belief in God does provide this kind of comfort, then we would have to conclude that a belief in God is true. But this puts the cart before the horse. Doesn't the belief in God have to exist *before* it can provide solace? Would the argument that belief in God provides spiritual solace to believers prove to an atheist that God actually exists? Surely not.

Critics of the pragmatic theory argue that while there is a connection between truth and problem solving, it cannot be as close as the pragmatic theory claims. It is true that when we act on the basis of true beliefs our actions are much more likely to be successful than when we act on the basis of false beliefs. But it is a mistake to conclude that every belief that leads to a successful action must therefore be true. Consider the following situation:

I believe (a) that there is only enough gas in my car to drive 300 kilometres, and (b) that it is 250 kilometres from Guelph to Parry Sound. On this basis I conclude that I can drive to Parry Sound without refuelling.

Clearly if both (a) and (b) are true, I will be able to drive to Parry Sound without refuelling. But (a) or (b), or both, may be false and yet I may still get to Parry Sound without refuelling. Suppose that (a) is false because there is really enough gas in my car to drive 400 kilometres; in this case if (b) is true I will still be able to drive to Parry Sound without refuelling. Or suppose that (b) is false because it is really 285 kilometres to Parry Sound; in this case if (a) is true I will still get to Parry Sound without refuelling. Or suppose both (a) and (b) are false, because I really have only enough gas to drive 250 kilometres, and because it is really only 225 kilometres to Parry Sound; in this case I will still get to Parry Sound without refuelling. So false beliefs do not necessarily lead to unsuccessful actions.

It is also a mistake to hold that every belief that leads to unsuccessful actions must therefore be false. Many medical researchers have dedicated years to searching for the causes of cancer, although as yet none has been entirely successful. They all believe that cancer does have causes, that is, that it is not a purely spontaneous or uncaused phenomenon. This belief is one of the factors that has led them to conduct their unsuccessful research. Does this mean that their belief is false? Surely not.

These objections suggest that the pragmatic theory is not really a theory of truth at all, but rather a theory of meaning. When I say that there is only enough gas in my car to drive 300 kilometres, what I mean is that since it is only 250 kilometres to Parry Sound I have enough gas to get to Parry Sound without refuelling. If it then turns out that there is enough gas to drive 350 kilometres it is a mistake to conclude that (a) is false. In this context, (a) is still true because its real meaning is different from what it appears to be. Many statements are intended to solve problems, even though this intention may not be immediately apparent, and recognizing the problem solving function of statements obviously tells us something important about their meaning. This feature of meaning is one of the strengths of the meaning-as-use theory discussed in section 2.2.3.

The weakness of the pragmatic theory can also be seen when we consider what we have to do in order to tell whether a problem has actually been solved. To know whether we have solved a problem, we have to appeal either to empirical facts (as the correspondence theory tells us to do) or to reasons (as the coherence theory tells us to do). The empirical facts tell me whether or not I drove to Parry Sound without refuelling, and reasons tell me whether I have really solved a mathematical equation. So, far from being a theory of truth, the pragmatic theory actually presupposes the two other theories of truth.

Our brief examination of these three theories of truth has led us to the following conclusions. (1) The correspondence theory provides a criterion for the truth of empirical statements. (2) The coherence theory provides a criterion of truth for non-empirical statements. (3) The pragmatic theory does not really provide a criterion of truth at all, but warns us not to overlook the fact that when we interpret the meaning of statements we should take into account their problem-solving function. Let us now consider how the two criteria should be applied in practice.

6.2 Types of Truth-Claims

Every statement can be regarded as making a claim to be true, or, in other words, as making a truth-claim. The process of determining whether or not a truth-claim is true is called verification. If we can show that a truth-claim is true, it has been **verified**. If we can show that it is false, it has been **falsified**. (Sometimes, of course, we can do neither, so the truth of the claim remains undetermined.) The method of verification we use depends upon the type of truth-claim being made. There are two main types of truth-claims, the empirical and the non-empirical. The first step in verifying any truth-claim should always be to decide which of these two types of claim we are dealing with. Since a non-empirical truth-claim is simply a truth-claim that does *not* make an empirical claim, it is best to begin by asking simply, *Is this an empirical claim?* If it is not, we will know that it is non-empirical.

6.2.1 EMPIRICAL TRUTH-CLAIMS

In section 6.1.1 we defined an empirical fact as a fact that could be checked, i.e., a fact that is observable in principle. Thus, when we want to verify an empirical truth-claim, we must be prepared to do the appropriate checking. Consider the following:

My car won't start.

Jim has shaved off his moustache.

The library owns a first edition of Fielding's Tom Jones.

These are empirical statements because we can attempt to verify them by checking the relevant facts. If you doubt my claim that my car won't start, you can check it by trying to start the car yourself; if you cannot start it then you will agree with my claim, and if you can then you will have proven that my claim was false. If you doubt the claim that Jim has shaved off his moustache all you need to do is look at him and you will know whether it is true or false. And you can check whether the library owns a first edition of Fielding's *Tom Jones* by looking in the catalogue.

However, not all empirical claims can be verified as easily as these: some are more difficult to deal with. Statements about the past or about the future rest only indirectly on the empirical facts that support them. For example:

Caesar crossed the Rubicon in 44 B.C.

Sebastian first ran a four-minute mile five years ago when he was still in high school.

Beth will win the gold medal in physics next year.

It will rain tomorrow.

It is obvious that the empirical facts that would directly verify or falsify these statements are not available to us. For statements about the past we have to rely on records and memories. For statements about the future we have to use empirical evidence about the past and present that makes the predicted event likely to occur. Of course, we could wait and see whether the predicted event actually occurs, in which case we would have direct empirical support.

Our examples so far have been of **particular empirical statements**, that is, statements about particular empirical facts. Sometimes, however, we have to deal with statements about *classes* of objects or events. These are called **general empirical statements**, and have to be approached somewhat differently because they usually make a claim that goes beyond the available empirical evidence. There are two types of general empirical statements. The first are **statistical empirical statements**, which make claims about some, or a certain proportion of, a class of objects or events. For example:

A majority of Canadians support the use of capital punishment.
90 per cent of snapping turtles do not survive the first three months of life.

These claims would be impossible to check if we had to do a su /ey of the entire population of Canada and every snapping turtle in th₍ world. However, there is a procedure – called inductive generalizatic n – that can provide us with an empirical basis for statistical statements. It allows us to use a representative sample of a class as an empirical basis for making statements about the entire class. Public opinion polls, for example, work on this basis. We will examine this procedure in detail in section 10.2.

The second type of general empirical statement consists of **universal empirical statements**, or statements about *every* member of some class. These are even more difficult to check. Consider the following:

All swans are white.

This is a statement about all swans, and, like statistical empirical statements, it too makes a claim that goes far beyond any available empirical evidence. But there is an important difference between statistical and universal empirical statements that allows us to approach universal statements differently: universal empirical statements can be refuted by a single exception. If we can find one swan that is not white the universal statement must be false. In other words, even though we cannot verify the statement we can *falsify* it on the basis of empirical evidence. This suggests a procedure for dealing with universal empirical statements that gives them a secure empirical basis. If we make a systematic attempt to find exceptions to some universal empirical statement and nevertheless fail to find any, we are entitled to assert that it is true. But since this procedure does not rest upon direct empirical evidence, we must always regard universal empirical statements as tentative. They are tentative because we will never be in a position to rule out the possibility of finding an exception. In principle, they can never be verified, but can only be falsified.

When gathering empirical evidence we must be careful not to misinterpret it. Since empirical evidence rests upon observation it can sometimes be misinterpreted in ways we are unaware of. Under artificial light an object that looks blue in natural light may look green. Railway tracks really do look as if they come together in the distance. Sometimes we misinterpret our observations because we have not observed carefully enough. We think the bowl contains sugar because it looks like sugar, but had we tasted it we would have realized it is salt. We will later look at certain ways in which empirical facts can be misinterpreted, but in general there are no rules that will prevent us from misinterpreting empirical evidence except for the injunction to be careful.

All the various types of empirical statements rest, one way or another, on empirical facts. To decide whether a statement is an empirical statement, we must ask whether there could be empirical evidence that would verify or falsify it. If there could be such empirical evidence then it is an empirical statement, and all that remains is for us to do our best to obtain this empirical evidence. On the other hand, a statement that could never be verified or falsified by empirical evidence must be non-empirical.

6.2.2 NON-EMPIRICAL TRUTH-CLAIMS

We now turn to non-empirical statements. Non-empirical statements are identified by the fact that empirical evidence would not be sufficient to verify or falsify them. Consider:

The government should provide free day-care programs.

What empirical facts could possibly show that this statement is true or false? It is an empirical fact that many people believe that the government should provide free day-care programs, but this clearly doesn't show that the statement is true. Nor does the fact that many people believe that the government should not provide free day-care programs show that the statement is false. It might be an empirical fact that the government promised it would provide free day-care programs, but by itself this doesn't show that the statement is true; to do so it would have to be assumed that governments should keep their promises, and *this* is not an empirical fact. It is impossible to specify any empirical evidence that would be sufficient to show the statement to be true or false, so we must conclude that it is a non-empirical statement.

How then are we to determine whether non-empirical statements are true or false? According to the coherence theory of truth we have to look not to the empirical facts but to other beliefs we have that are secure enough to serve as justifying reasons. What these justifying reasons will be depends upon the nature of the non-empirical statement we want to verify. If we want to verify the mathematical statement that the square of the hypotenuse of a right-angle triangle is equal to the sum of the squares of the other two sides, we have to work out the mathematical proof. It is not sufficient to draw several right-angled triangles and then measure their sides: mathematics teachers won't let us get away with this manoeuvre since it uses empirical evidence where a proof is required. If we wish to verify a moral statement like the one in the preceding paragraph we must appeal to some general moral principle that is secure enough to justify it. We might, for example, appeal to the principle that governments ought to respond to the wishes of the majority of the voters, and this, along with the empirical claim that a majority of voters wants free day-care programs, would be sufficient to justify the moral claim. In short, non-empirical statements are verified or falsified by appealing to other non-empirical statements that can serve as justifying reasons.

There are several different types of non-empirical statements. Analytic and contradictory statements (see section 3.4) are clearly non-empirical: once we know what they mean we can determine their truth or falsity without reference to any empirical facts. Most ethical statements, like the example above, are non-empirical. So too are most aesthetic statements. For example:

J.S. Bach is the greatest composer of the eighteenth century.

Any empirical evidence about Bach's music and the music of his contemporaries is not going to be sufficient to show whether this claim is true or false. Most religious statements are non-empirical as well. For example:

God is eternal and unchanging.

It is clear that there could not be any empirical evidence that we can appeal to that would be sufficient to determine whether this claim is true or false. It is, most theologians believe, something that must be accepted on faith, although some would regard it as analytic. For all such statements, determining whether they are true or false depends not on empirical evidence but on the strength of the justifying reasons we can provide.

Not all ethical, aesthetic, and religious statements are non-empirical, for sometimes they make claims that can be supported by empirical evidence. For example:

People who are treated unjustly feel entitled to compensation or retaliation.
Of all Dickens's novels, Pickwick Papers *relies most extensively on the use of caricatures.*
Jesus Christ was crucified by Roman soldiers.

Each of these statements is empirical, because empirical facts are sufficient to determine their truth or falsity. Sometimes, however, it is difficult to tell whether statements are empirical or non-empirical. For example:

In democratic countries, citizens have a duty to vote.
All music must have a recognizable rhythm.
God created the world.

These are difficult statements to deal with precisely because it is difficult to know how to determine whether they are true or false. If we regard them as empirical we would need to look for the appropriate empirical evidence, and if we regard them as non-empirical we need to look for non-empirical justifying reasons. Each of these statements can plausibly be interpreted in both ways, so whether we should regard them as empirical or non-empirical will depend upon what we think is the most reasonable interpretation of them. Ultimately, it is up to anyone who makes such claims to interpret them in one way or the other. It is, after all, the speaker who should be the final arbiter of what he or she means.

Finally, we should mention an important class of non-empirical statements consisting of what might be called foundational principles. These are principles that lie at the basis of all knowledge claims, including empirical claims. Consider what is sometimes called the Law of Causality:

Every event must have a cause.

It would be quite irrational to suggest that this is false. There is a great deal of empirical evidence that supports it: think of all the events whose causes we know. Nevertheless, it is not an empirical statement. If it were we would have to reject it, for there are some events (for example, the occurrence of cancer) whose causes we do not know. We would only be able to claim that most events have a cause. Unlike most scientific laws, the Law of Causality is not an empirical law. It is a presupposition that underlies all of science, and all common sense as well. How we are to show that the Law of Causality is true is a difficult philosophical question about which there are different and conflicting theories.

Many foundational principles are not as secure as the Law of Causality. We saw in section 6.1 that there are at least three plausible theories of truth. These theories express alternative foundational principles about the nature of truth, all of which are non-empirical in nature. Most foundational principles are like this: there is agreement that some foundational principle is needed, but disagreement on precisely what it is. Some foundational principles are subject to even deeper disagreement. The statement that God exists is a foundational principle for those who believe in God, but is a principle that atheists reject altogether. Foundational principles also underlie moral reasoning, and we will examine some of these in Chapter 11.

6.3 Acceptability

In section 5.2 we noted that it is not always appropriate to demand that truth-claims be *proven*. Conclusive proofs are often hard to come by, and if we were not entitled to make assertions unless we could prove them we would have a great deal less to say. Fortunately, we do not need to insist on a proof for every truth-claim we make. The first question we need to ask about a truth-claim is not *Can it be proven?* but *Are we justified in accepting it?* Sometimes, indeed, we do need a proof in order to be justified in accepting a truth-claim, but usually proofs are not needed. In fact, there are varying standards of acceptability, depending upon the nature of the statement and the context in which it is made.

The most stringent standard of acceptability is that of a strict proof. There are in fact two types of strict proofs, depending upon whether the statement is empirical or non-empirical. In section 6.2 we saw how empirical statements rest on empirical evidence in various ways. An empirical proof is one in which the empirical evidence is subjected to scrutiny designed to eliminate as far as possible any error. The evidence is, as it were, cross-examined. Is the evidence available to any normal observer? Does it avoid questionable interpretations? Have alternative explanations been refuted? Only when these questions have been answered satisfactorily are we entitled to regard empirical evidence as constituting a proof.

Non-empirical statements, we saw, rest on justifying reasons rather than on empirical evidence. A non-empirical proof, therefore, is an argument in which the premises are shown to be true and whose conclusion follows necessarily from them. Of course, showing that the premises of the proof are true requires another proof of the same sort, which in turn requires yet another proof. If we are to avoid an infinite regress we must ultimately reach premises that we are entitled to assert in the absence of proof. In other words, the premises from which a non-empirical proof is derived must ultimately be statements whose truth we can be quite certain of without proof. There are profound philosophical difficulties about the notion of statements whose truth is certain but not provable, which need not detain us here. It is sufficient for our purposes that there are premises that seem certain to us even though we cannot prove them. The best examples of non-empirical proofs are found in mathematics, for in mathematics we typically begin from premises that are known to be true and deduce conclusions that follow necessarily from them.

Strict proofs, of either the empirical or non-empirical sort, are only rarely called for. In most contexts it is irrelevant and a waste of time to demand, or to attempt to provide, a strict proof for every truth-claim. In other words, it is often reasonable to demand or provide less stringent support for our claims. When is it appropriate to look for strict proofs, and when is it not? The answer depends upon the context in which the claim is made. Suppose someone claims that a low-cholesterol diet reduces the chances of a heart attack. What can we demand of the speaker in order to show that the claim is acceptable? If it is made in the context of a discussion among people who are only interested in a healthy diet for themselves and their families, it would be sufficient to defend the claim by referring to what doctors and nutritionists commonly say or are reported as saying in magazine articles. But if the claim is made by a professor who is giving a university course on nutrition, we should demand better evidence. If the professor defends the claim by saying,

> *Well, a lot of nutritionists say that a low-cholesterol diet reduces the chance of heart attack, and besides there was an article in a recent issue of* Reader's Digest *that says so,*

we would suspect the competence of the professor. The claim ought to be defended by citing research that has been generally accepted by qualified nutritionists. Finally, if the claim is made by the researcher who conducted the research, we should not allow that researcher simply to refer to his or her own published articles on the subject, but should expect a defence of the research itself.

Deciding what kind of support is required by the context is largely a matter of common sense. Unfortunately, most of us have a tendency to accept or reject claims too readily because we fail to pay attention to the context. We should use our common sense to answer the question, *What is the appropriate defence for this claim in this context?* but should be cautious about using our common sense to answer the question *Is this claim true?* In the latter case we have a tendency to make one of two errors. If we want to believe something, we tend to ignore the context if it requires a stronger defence than we can easily provide. On the other hand, if we want to reject something we tend to ignore the context and demand a strict proof where such a demand is not warranted.

In some contexts there are statements that are a matter of common knowledge and for which it is quite unnecessary to require a defence. Consider the following:

Canada has ten provinces.
Christmas day is December 25.
Snow melts when the temperature is above freezing.
Shakespeare wrote Hamlet.

In most contexts such statements will be common knowledge among all those involved in a discussion, and any demand that they be defended will be inappropriate. When used as premises in arguments they will be acceptable, even though we might find it difficult to defend them. If we are challenged to defend them we should first attempt to discover the reason for the challenge, for this will tell us what kind of defence is needed. It may be sufficient merely to check an encyclopedia, if, for example, the challenger is obviously ignorant of the common view. But it is possible that the challenger may require a more thorough defence. There are people who believe that many of the plays usually attributed to Shakespeare were in fact written by Francis Bacon; if this is the reason for the challenge we should be prepared to admit that we may be wrong and that a great deal of careful analysis and argument would be needed to settle the issue. The idea of *common knowledge* is a relative term that depends upon the shared assumptions of a community or group. If some item of our common knowledge is challenged we should be prepared either to defend it or to concede that there is a possibility that we are mistaken.

Let us consider some examples of statements where the kind of defence required depends upon the context and purpose of the argument:

> *Christ died on the cross for our sins.*

If said by a preacher in a sermon or by a theology student in a course on New Testament theology, this statement would be acceptable because it has a biblical source. But if said in an ethics or philosophy course, it could not adequately be defended by appeal to the Bible.

> *The Liberal party lost the 1911 general election because it ran on a platform of free trade with the United States.*

If said by a student in a history essay, this claim would be acceptable if it could be supported by the textbook for the course. If said by a historian, it should be supported by historical documents and analysis of the evidence.

> *Smith is guilty of first-degree murder.*

If said by a member of the jury while attempting to reach a verdict, this should be supported by a very careful assessment of the evidence presented in court. If said by someone after the trial, it should be supported by newspaper accounts of the verdict.

To decide whether or not a statement is acceptable, then, we should proceed as follows:

(1) If the statement is common knowledge, we should regard it as acceptable, unless the context requires a higher standard of proof.

(2) If the statement is not common knowledge, we should ask for, or be prepared to offer, the evidence upon which it is based, and accept it only if the evidence meets the appropriate standard, for example, personal experience, appeal to a recognized authority, or strict proof.

It is important to remember, however, that whenever we rely upon anything less than a strict proof, there is a possibility that a truth-claim may turn out to be false. All the weaker standards of acceptability presuppose that a strict proof could be found if we were to take the trouble to look for it or to work one out for ourselves, and this is a presupposition that may turn out to be false. History is littered with discarded "truths" that were once believed to be true in the absence of a strict proof. We should not forget this lesson.

6.4 Self-Test No. 11

Which of the following are empirical claims?

1. The Conservatives lost the last New Brunswick election.

2. My children are hoping for a white Christmas this year.

3. St. Paul's Cathedral in London is one of the great architectural achievements of Western civilization.

4. Human beings will not survive the destruction of the ozone layer.

5. The sum of the interior angles of a triangle is 180 degrees.

6. If the Toronto Maple Leafs win the Stanley Cup this year, I'll eat my hat.

7. If the Canadian government ever succeeds in eliminating the federal deficit there will be a substantial reduction in taxes.

8. Paula won the prize last year for the best student in the school.

9. It is a sad reflection upon our society that suicide rates are highest around Christmas.

10. The illegal killing of elephants in Africa has been significantly reduced by the international ban on the sale of ivory.

6.5 Questions for Discussion

The following statements require some analysis and interpretation in order to determine whether they are empirical claims. Several contain both empirical and non-empirical claims that must be carefully distinguished.

1. Christians believe that the Bible is the word of God.

2. The human race was not created by God, but evolved from lower forms of life.

3. Everyone has a conscience, even those who deny it.

4. You should apologize to Miss Rothwell as soon as possible.

5. Every society has the values that are most appropriate for that society.

6. I know that President Gorbachev was very unpopular in the former Soviet Union, but you really have to admire him for bringing about the end of communism in what was one of the largest countries in the world.

7. I absolutely adore Robertson Davies' novels.

8. Science explains why things happen.

9. People who believe in God generally lead happier lives than atheists.

10. The fact that suicide rates are highest around Christmas is a sad reflection upon the failure of our society to deal with the breakdown of the family structure.

6.6 Assessing The Acceptability of Premises

Clearly, an argument with one or more unacceptable premises suffers from a major defect. Since the function of premises in an argument is to provide support for the conclusion, if the premises are unacceptable then the argument provides no support for its conclusion. Such an argument fails to meet the first of our three criteria for a sound argument. Whenever we have reason to think that a premise lacks appropriate support, we can charge the argument with failing to meet the first criterion. To back up the charge, however, we must be able to state our reasons for claiming that it lacks the appropriate support.

In section 6.3 we examined what we need to do to determine whether a statement is acceptable. When a statement functions as a premise in an argument we should approach the question of its acceptability in the same manner. Sometimes we know that a premise is false and can easily refute it. But often we are sceptical of the truth of an opponent's premise without being able to refute it. For example:

P1. *Potential murderers would be less likely to commit murder if they knew they would be executed if they were caught.*
P2. *We should do whatever will reduce the number of murders in Canada.*
C. *Therefore, we should reinstate the death penalty.*

In this example, P1 cannot be defended on the ground that it is common knowledge. Anyone who has followed the debate on capital punishment will be aware that many people who have examined the statistical evidence believe that it shows that P1 is false. Even if we are not familiar with this evidence ourselves, we should at least ask the speaker to produce the evidence he or she believes supports P1. In this case the evidence will be empirical, and will consist of facts about the frequency of murders in countries where murderers are normally executed, as compared to the frequency of murders in countries where murderers are not executed. If the evidence produced does not seem to be solid and accurate we should charge the argument with violating our first criterion. Any good reason for thinking that a premise is unacceptable entitles us to raise this objection.

So the application of the first criterion for a sound argument is simply a matter of asking whether each of the premises is acceptable, and we do this using the approach outlined in section 6.3. We should always begin by deciding which of the various standards of acceptability we should use, and this, as we saw, should be decided on the basis of the context. In fact, the argument itself provides important information about the context that is usually helpful in deciding which standard of acceptability we should use.

6.7 Some Particular Fallacies

We now turn to four particular fallacies that describe special kinds of unacceptable premises. The first two – *begging the question* and *inconsistency* – are important because they identify arguments where it is unnecessary even to ask whether its premises are acceptable. The other two – *equivocation* and *false dichotomy* – are easy to commit and often difficult to spot if we are not on our guard, and deserve special mention for this reason.

6.7.1 BEGGING THE QUESTION

An argument **begs the question** when its premises presuppose, directly or indirectly, the truth of its conclusion. An argument of this sort obviously fails to support its conclusion, since any reason we might have for doubting the conclusion will obviously also lead us to doubt any premises that presuppose it. The function of the premises of an argument is to support its conclusion, and if we have to accept the truth of the conclusion in order to accept the premises then obviously the premises have failed to do their job. The argument actually presupposes what it is supposed to prove. Begging the question is sometimes referred to by its Latin name: *petitio principii*.

Begging the question typically arises when we want to defend some strongly held conviction, yet have difficulty in finding reasons that will persuade others of its truth. For example:

> *The Bible frequently says that it is the word of God and the word of God must obviously be true. Therefore whatever the Bible says is true.*

The conclusion of this argument may be true, but the premises offered do not support it because they presuppose it. Only someone who already accepts the conclusion would be able to accept the premises.

We are even more likely to beg the question when we are challenged by a sceptical opponent to defend an important claim. For example:

> North: *I believe I was justified in lying to Congress because I was doing so in order to protect the national interest.*
> South: *How can you defend such a position?*

North: *Because a good citizen should always protect the national interest even if they have to tell lies to do so.*

Notice that North's second statement (the premise) is roughly equivalent to the first statement (the conclusion). Anyone who is unwilling to accept North's conclusion will obviously be equally unwilling to accept North's premise. Perhaps telling lies to protect the national interest is justified, but the argument fails to show this because it begs the question.

A somewhat more complex way of begging the question is when we use premises that are clearly different from the conclusion, and thus do not beg the question directly, but that are themselves defended by other premises that presuppose the truth of the original conclusion. For example:

East: *I deserve a larger salary than you because as sales manager my job is more important to the company.*
West: *I dispute that. As production supervisor my job is just as important as yours.*
East: *No it isn't. My job is more important because I get paid more than you.*

East is arguing in a circle: *A therefore B, and B therefore A*. Notice that neither of East's two arguments begs the question when considered in isolation from the other. It is only when they are taken together that they beg the question.

6.7.2 INCONSISTENCY

The fallacy of **inconsistency** arises when an argument contains, implicitly or explicitly, a contradiction, usually between two premises. In section 3.3 we defined a contradictory statement as one that is false by definition. The kind of contradiction we are now referring to is that where two statements, neither of which is contradictory on its own, create a contradiction when they are asserted together. For example, consider the following statements:

Mary is older than Tom.
Tom is older than Mary.

Neither statement by itself is a contradiction, but asserting them together amounts to saying,

Mary is older than Tom and Tom is older than Mary.

Since this is a contradiction we know that it must be false, without having to check the facts. We may not know which of the contradiction's components is false, but we know that one of them must be. Clearly, any argument that includes a contradiction must fail to provide support for its conclusion.

Arguing from a blatant inconsistency is not common, doubtless because even the most irrational person can see that an argument with contradictory premises is not going to succeed. But when under pressure we sometimes get carried away and contradict ourselves. Most parents will recognize the following:

> Father: *I'm sorry, son, but you know you are not supposed to eat any cookies without permission, so you are going to have to go to bed early to-night.*
> Son: *I shouldn't have to go to bed early, Dad, because I didn't take any cookies, honest I didn't.*
> Father: *How come you have cookie crumbs all over your face?*
> Son: *But I only took one cookie. I could have taken a whole bunch, but I only took one. Really I shouldn't have to go to bed early to-night.*

The son argues that he shouldn't have to go to bed early because (a) he didn't take any cookies, and (b) he only took one cookie. Since (a) and (b) are inconsistent, his argument is fallacious.

In practice, however, the fallacy of inconsistency usually arises when the contradiction is implicit rather than explicit. In these cases we need to make the contradiction explicit by showing how it arises. For example:

> There are three reasons why the free trade agreement with the U.S. is bad for Canada. First, open competition has created a significant increase in unemployment and will eventually produce a drastic reduction in the GNP as more and more branch plants are closed by their American owners and Canadian industries are driven into bankruptcy. Second, we are under continual pressure to dismantle social programs such as medicare and family allowances, which the Americans regard as "unfair" subsidies to industry. Third, all the new wealth that is being created in Canada is concentrated in the hands of a prosperous middle class while the workers become poorer.

Now, it certainly seems that the first and third reasons are inconsistent with each other. The first predicts a *drastic reduction in the GNP* while the third admits that *new wealth is being created*. Are these two claims really inconsistent? The principle of charity would require us to give the speaker a chance to explain, or explain away, the apparent inconsistency, but in the absence of a convincing explanation we can charge the argument with committing the fallacy of inconsistency because it relies on inconsistent premises.

A more common type of inconsistency in argument is between what someone says in the course of an argument and other relevant things they have said on other occasions. For example:

> Jock: *The city cannot afford a performing arts centre. Taxes are already too high, and cause hardship for many ordinary people.*
> Art: *Wait a minute. Last year you made a presentation to City Council in support of a proposal to build another hockey arena, and that would have cost even more than a performing arts centre. Fortunately, the Council turned down that proposal.*

Art's charge is that Jock has presented two arguments dealing with the same subject (i.e., city taxes) that contain inconsistent premises. In the above argument Jock has used the premise that taxes are too high, while in his earlier argument he used the premise (or perhaps presupposed as a missing premise) that taxes are not too high. But this by itself does not entitle Art to charge Jock with the fallacy of inconsistency. Because the inconsistency arises between two arguments presented at different times, Art must allow for the possibility that Jock has changed his mind. Jock might respond to the charge by saying that since last year he has reconsidered his position, and now thinks that his earlier argument was unsound because it used a premise he now believes is false. If Jock takes this line then Art's charge of inconsistency will fail. Of course, Jock may be only pretending to have changed his mind in order to avoid having to respond to Art's charge. In this case Jock will have avoided the charge of inconsistency at the price of being a hypocrite.

There is another type of hypocrisy, however, that can give rise to the charge of inconsistency. This is where the inconsistency is between what someone says and what he or she does, that is, between words and actions. For example:

Mary: *I'm just appalled at my sister-in-law. She had an affair and then when my brother found out she expected him to forgive her. That sort of thing is unforgivable and I think he should leave her. It would be good riddance to bad rubbish.*
Francine: *Cool it, Mary. I know about the little extramarital fling you had a couple of years ago, and when your husband found out you were grateful when he forgave you.*

Francine's accusation of hypocrisy is probably justified, assuming she has her facts right. Mary's premise is that an extramarital affair should not be forgiven by a spouse. But, as Francine points out, Mary not only had an affair herself but wanted her husband to forgive her. Clearly, Mary's premise is inconsistent with her earlier actions, and her conclusion – that her brother should not forgive, and should leave, her sister-in-law – lacks real support. Francine should, however, give Mary a chance to explain her apparent hypocrisy. Perhaps her affair took place during a period when her husband was also having an affair and this might allow her to argue that the two situations are not parallel. But in the absence of some such explanation, Francine is justified in refusing to accept Mary's premise and charging her with the fallacy of inconsistency.

6.7.3 EQUIVOCATION

In Chapter 3 we examined various ways in which language can be ambiguous, and we indicated the importance of ensuring that the meaning of what we say is clear and unambiguous. We now consider some ways in which ambiguities can destroy or weaken an argument. The fallacy of **equivocation** arises when a premise has two interpretations, one acceptable and one unacceptable, and when it is the unacceptable interpretation that is required by the conclusion.

Here is a silly example that clearly illustrates the nature of this mistake:

Noisy children are a real headache.
An aspirin will make a headache go away.
Therefore, an aspirin will make noisy children go away.

There is a sense in which noisy children are a headache, but it is only a metaphorical sense. When taken literally, the claim is false. The conclusion of this argument, however, follows only if the first premise is literally true. The argument, therefore, commits the fallacy of equivocation.

Usually, the equivocation arises in more subtle ways. For example:

> *There's a lot of talk these days about how we shouldn't discriminate. Well, I don't agree at all. Everybody discriminates all the time. It is unavoidable. We discriminate when selecting a wine or buying a car or choosing new wallpaper. We discriminate when deciding which friends to invite to a party or which candidate to vote for. We discriminate when we hire someone, or admit someone to a college. We always make such decisions on the basis of the qualities we admire: i.e., we discriminate. So there is nothing wrong with discrimination.*

The equivocation here is with the term *discrimination*. In the premises the speaker uses the term to mean *making decisions on the basis of relevant qualities*. This is an accepted sense of the term, which is reflected in sentences like *He is very discriminating in his choice of clothes*. But the conclusion uses the term to mean *making decisions on the basis of irrelevant qualities such as race, religion, or gender*. This is the sense of the term that is obviously used by those who believe we should not discriminate. The sense in which the premises are true is not the sense required by the conclusion, so the argument commits the fallacy of equivocation.

Any of the types of ambiguity we discussed in Chapter 3 can give rise to the fallacy of equivocation. Sometimes it may rest on a failure to recognize linguistic ambiguities, for example, the ambiguity between the collective and distributive use of a term. Or it may arise through the failure to distinguish between the analytic and synthetic interpretations of a statement, between the descriptive and evaluative meanings of a term, or between necessary and sufficient conditions.

Here are two more examples of arguments that commit the fallacy of equivocation:

> *Professor Jones says that no-one will get an A in his course unless they attend every seminar. Well, I've attended every seminar so I'm expecting an A.*

> *According to Judge Wapner's ruling the Country Club cannot build an indoor swimming pool unless the membership agrees. Well, I am a member and I most certainly do not agree. Therefore, the Club cannot build its new pool.*

We often have to deal with alternatives. Sometimes there are only two alternatives: either we are pregnant or we are not. But frequently, when we are offered two alternatives, there are really more than two: we may be neither rich nor poor, neither young nor old, neither hairy nor bald. In addition, some alternatives do not exclude each other. When we are offered a choice of cake or pie for dessert, we may, if we are lucky, be able to choose both. With any range of alternatives we can ask whether they are exhaustive and whether they are exclusive. Alternatives are **exhaustive** when they cover all the possibilities. *Being pregnant* and *not being pregnant* are exhaustive alternatives, for there is no other possibility. *Being young* and *being old* are not exhaustive alternatives, for there is a third possibility: *being middle-aged*. Alternatives are **exclusive** when the choice of one rules out the other(s). For example, the designations *a.m.* and *p.m.* are exclusive, at least when applied to time on earth. *Being a faculty member* and *being a student* are not exclusive, since some faculty are also students.

Thus, every set of alternatives will be either exhaustive or non-exhaustive, *and* either exclusive or non-exclusive. The famous choice between liberty or death (*Give me liberty or give me death*) is exclusive but not exhaustive. It is exclusive because one cannot choose both liberty and death, but it is not exhaustive because one could choose neither liberty nor death, but slavery. The American bumper sticker *America: Love It Or Leave It* presents a choice that is neither exhaustive nor exclusive. It is not exhaustive because it is possible to neither love it nor leave it: for example, to be indifferent to it but stay. It is not exclusive because it is possible to love it and to leave it.

The fallacy of **false dichotomy** arises when the premise of an argument presents us with a choice between two alternatives and assumes that they are exhaustive or exclusive or both when in fact they are not. Most commonly it arises when the alternatives are presented as if they were exhaustive when in fact they are not. For example:

> David: *Let me get this straight, Paul. You mean that you have been going out with your girlfriend for almost a year, and she never told you she has a three-year-old daughter by a previous marriage?*
> Paul: *That's right. And I only found out by accident last week.*
> David: *Well, whatever you do, Paul, don't marry her. She is a liar.*

David is assuming that telling the truth and telling lies are exhaustive alternatives, when in fact not telling the truth is not the same as telling a lie. We can fail to tell the truth by not saying anything, which is what Paul's girlfriend did, and this is quite different from telling a lie. Here are three more examples of the fallacy of false dichotomy:

> I'm against giving aid to countries in which people are starving. We will never be able to eradicate starvation completely, so it is a waste of time even trying.

> Good students will study and learn if there are no examinations, and bad students won't study and will learn nothing even when there are examinations. So exams are useless.

> These days students have to choose whether they want to get good grades or whether they want to have fun. Well, Alex has decided he wants to have fun at college, so I guess he's not going to get good grades.

6.8 Self-Test No. 12

Identify the weaknesses in the following arguments, after making sure you have correctly identified the conclusion.

1. If we want economic prosperity for Canada, we should be looking for wars to get involved in. Every nation that has fought a major war in this century emerged from the war economically stronger than it was before. It seems to be the one sure path to economic prosperity.

2. In our democratic system, government is supposed to be based on the consent of the governed. Well, I am one of the governed, and I certainly do not consent to the GST. So the government has no right to force me and others who think the way I do to pay this iniquitous tax.

3. The outboard motor I bought last year turned out to be a real lemon. As soon as the warranty expired everything started going wrong; it has cost me over six hundred dollars in repairs so far this year. The trouble is there's nothing I can do about it. I thought about suing the manufacturer, but the lawyer's fee would cost more than I could ever hope to win.

4. History shows that only in democracies does the human spirit flourish. And the reason is clear: undemocratic societies deny to most of their

members any opportunity to take part in the political life of the community, and without such participation the human spirit withers and dies.

5. Members of the jury, there are two compelling reasons why you should find my client not guilty. First, the prosecution has failed to prove beyond a reasonable doubt that he was anywhere near the warehouse on the night the theft occurred. And second, even if he was there I have presented evidence to show that he was acting under threats from his companions. In either case he should be found not guilty.

6. Most people are much more interested in local issues – such as property taxes, garbage collection, their children's education, and zoning by-laws – than they are in provincial and national political issues. This is shown by the fact that a much higher percentage of the electorate votes in municipal elections than in provincial or federal elections.

7. It never ceases to amaze me that so many scientists deny that the miracles reported in the Bible actually took place. After all, science itself has presented us with many miracles, such as lasers, antibiotics, computers, and space flight. Since scientists accept that these modern miracles actually exist, they should accept that biblical miracles also actually occurred.

8. The choice confronting us is clear. Do we want a defence policy that relies upon the threat of nuclear annihilation to deter aggression, or do we want a non-aligned foreign policy that is aimed at reducing international tensions? It is obvious that we should reject the first alternative since it embodies a dangerous and outmoded cold war mentality, and that we should therefore adopt a non-aligned foreign policy.

9. Last year I took a great course in history of science that was developed and team taught by Professors Smith, Jones, and Brown. They were excellent teachers; in fact they received an award for teaching excellence for the course. So I am going to register next term for a new course being offered by Professor Smith. I am sure it will be a great course, too.

10. There are thirteen chapters in this book, and I am now almost finished Chapter 6. Therefore, I am almost halfway through the book.

6.9 Questions for Discussion

Each of the following arguments involves a weakness, although it may take careful analysis to identify the precise nature of the weakness.

1. There is no such thing as an unselfish act. If you examine any so-called unselfish act, such as donating money to charity, you will always find that there is a selfish motive. There has to be, for nobody can do anything unless they think it will give them some kind of satisfaction. Seeking self-satisfaction is the only reason why anybody does anything. So every act is selfish.

2. Individuals are born, struggle through childhood, grow to maturity, and after a few years decline and finally die. So we should expect all societies, which are mere aggregations of individuals, to do the same.

3. I have attended several operas, and I always come away with the same reaction, which is that opera is a vastly over-rated art form. The plots could never be described as great literature, and some are as bad as any TV melodrama. Even when performed superbly, the music itself is always a mixture of good and mediocre, usually more mediocre than good. The costumes and the staging are often well done, but the whole experience is always destroyed for me by the atrocious acting. Why can singers never learn to act? The fact that opera lovers always seem to be unaware of these drawbacks is a great mystery to me.

4. The great experiment in communism that began in Russia in 1917 with such high hopes finally came to an inglorious end in 1991, and all that is left is to diagnose the fatal flaw that destroyed the noble dream. The view one hears most frequently is that it was the failure of the communist system to provide its citizens with material goods that brought it down. But this view ignores the role of the denial of freedom that has characterized the Soviet Union since its inception. If the history of the Soviet Union proves anything, it is that the human spirit needs freedom not merely to flourish but to survive. People will tolerate the denial of their freedom for a time in order to achieve security, but eventually the demand for freedom will burst forth, destroying everything that stands in its way. The death of communism can only be explained by its denial of freedom, not by its admitted failure to give its citizens material prosperity.

5.   In his book *Utilitarianism*, John Stuart Mill defends the view that the ultimate test of right and wrong is the greatest-happiness principle. The principle states that we should always seek to promote the general happiness, which he defines as the greatest happiness of the greatest number of people. To show that the principle is true, Mill argues as follows: Each person's happiness is a good to that person. Therefore the general happiness is a good to the aggregate of all persons.

Chapter 7

Assessing Relevance

7.1 The Criterion of Relevance

Our second criterion for a sound argument is that the premises must be relevant to the conclusion. An argument whose premises are irrelevant to its conclusion obviously suffers from a major weakness. But what precisely is relevance? What are we looking for in an argument when we ask whether its premises are relevant? What we need from our premises, if they are to be relevant to the truth of the conclusion, is that they should make it more likely that the conclusion will be true. We cannot expect that the truth of a premise will always guarantee the truth of the conclusion, but we can demand that it make the conclusion more likely to be true than it would be if the premise were false. In brief, a premise is relevant when it helps to make it reasonable to accept the conclusion.

The idea of relevance is easier to grasp if we compare some examples of arguments with relevant premises and arguments with irrelevant premises:

> *You should vote for Johnson because she is honest and is well informed about the issues.*
> *You should vote for Johnson because her mother used to be my kindergarten teacher.*

The first of these arguments supplies two reasons for voting for Johnson, both of which are clearly relevant. Anyone who thinks they are irrelevant would have to hold that it is a matter of indifference whether a politician is honest or well informed about the issues, and would see no reason to vote against a politician who was dishonest or poorly informed about the issues. Such a view is unacceptable to most of us because we are convinced that being honest and well informed are desirable qualities in a politician. If pressed we could defend this view by pointing to the disastrous social and political consequences of having dishonest or poorly informed politicians. The second of the above arguments supplies an irrelevant reason for voting for Johnson. It is difficult to imagine why anyone would seriously think that the fact that the candidate's mother was a kindergarten teacher is a good reason to vote for that candidate. If pressed to justify our view that this is an irrelevant premise, we could argue that there is no evidence that the children of kindergarten teachers make better politicians than anyone else.

Thus, for any premise we can always ask whether it has any relevance to the acceptability of the conclusion. Usually it is quite clear whether a premise is relevant, but where it is not clear we can address the question directly by trying to find an argument that will determine the question one way or the other. This is not always a straightforward matter. Consider the following:

> You should vote for Johnson because she is the only female candidate.

Is the fact that Johnson is a woman a relevant reason to vote for her? This is a debatable question. Many people believe that there should be more women elected to public office, and they defend this view by arguing that women bring a different and better perspective to politics, that women are more likely than men to address women's issues seriously, that women are still handicapped in politics by their gender, and so on. On the other hand, many people reject this view on the ground that we should vote only for candidates whose policies we agree with, and that not all women candidates support the policies we may agree with. It is not obvious whether a candidate's gender is relevant: to decide whether it is we have to grapple with the issue on its own terms.

There is one complicating feature of questions of relevance we must note. Sometimes the question whether a premise is relevant depends upon the standard of acceptability that is appropriate in the context. In section 6.2 we discussed the different standards of acceptability that we can use when determining whether statements are acceptable. These varying standards also have a bearing on whether premises are relevant. If we want to show that a high-cholesterol diet increases the chances of a heart attack, the context will determine which premises are relevant and which are not. Appealing to an article in *Reader's Digest* will be relevant in a casual conversation with friends about diet, but irrelevant in a discussion by nutritionists about recent research. Again, measuring the interior angles of a triangle with a protractor to show that they add up to

180 degrees may be relevant in some contexts, but irrelevant when a mathematical proof is called for. Generally, when the standard of acceptability is very demanding, premises that may be relevant with a lower standard of acceptability will become irrelevant. Whenever we raise the question of relevance about a premise we should always take account of the standard of acceptability that is appropriate in the context.

7.2 Recognizing Irrelevant Premises

The traditional term used to describe arguments with irrelevant premises is *non sequitur*, which means, literally, *it does not follow*. It is an unfortunate human tendency to believe that much more follows from premises than really does. We are too willing to appeal to premises that may be irrelevant on the off chance that they might convince others, or even ourselves. Fortunately, it is usually easy to decide whether a premise is relevant if we can remember to ask ourselves whether it is really relevant. Simply raising the question often suggests a plausible argument that shows whether the premise is relevant. The kind of argument we need is not usually a lengthy one, but it should be clear and specific. For example:

> *Tom Thompson is a better artist than Jack Shadbolt, because Thompson's paintings usually sell for a higher price than Shadbolt's.*

We can show the irrelevance of the premise of this argument by noting that there is no reason to believe that the price of an artist's painting always or even usually reflects the quality of the artist. The price of paintings is determined by a variety of market considerations of which the quality of the artist is only one factor.

Here are two more arguments with irrelevant premises:

> *I am opposed to the proposed anti-smoking by-law, and will vote against it at the Council meeting. Such a by-law is inappropriate in a city in which the Imperial Tobacco Company is one of the largest employers.*

> *The movie of Anna Karenina was pretty boring; it is really nothing more than a soap opera set in Imperial Russia. I'd always thought it was supposed to be a great novel. I guess I was wrong.*

The irrelevance of the premise of the first argument can be shown by arguing that the fact that the Imperial Tobacco Company is one of the city's largest employers has no bearing on whether the citizens want or are entitled to an anti-smoking by-law. Would anyone argue that Windsor should get rid of its No Parking zones merely because Ford is one of its largest employers? In the second case, a comparison of even a few great novels with films that have been based on them is sufficient to show that the quality of the film usually has very little to do with the quality of the novel.

There is no limit to the kinds of irrelevant premises people can appeal to except for the limits of their imagination. Certain types of irrelevant appeals, however, occur so frequently that they have been given particular labels. These labels are useful because they remind us of the common kinds of irrelevancies we should be on the lookout for, and because they help us to explain why the premises are irrelevant. The *appeal to pity* that we mentioned in section 5.1 is one such. Here is another example of an appeal to pity:

> *The judge was very unfair. He shouldn't have found Evelyn guilty. She is a single parent with three small children and an ex-husband who refuses to make his support payments, and I'm sure she would not have started shoplifting if she weren't really hard-pressed for money.*

Evelyn certainly deserves our pity (or sympathy), but this has no bearing on whether or not she is guilty of shop-lifting. If there is strong evidence that she shoplifted, then the judge has no option but to find her guilty. There are situations, however, where the appeal to pity is relevant. If the conclusion of the above argument were

> *The judge shouldn't have given Evelyn a jail sentence*

then the appeal to pity would be relevant, since we could argue that single parents with small children should not be jailed for non-violent criminal offences.

Another type of irrelevant appeal is the *appeal to force*. It arises when the premise of an argument threatens the use of force (either physical force or other kinds of pressure, such as economic pressure or emotional blackmail) as a reason for accepting the conclusion. Obviously, an appeal to force normally provides no reason for accepting the truth of a claim, although it might well provide a good reason for pretending to accept it. For example:

Listen, I'm telling you that my son did not cheat on his exam: if you don't agree, we'll step outside and settle the matter man to man.

Clearly, the son's innocence cannot be established by beating up his teacher, although the son might nevertheless be innocent. And even if the teacher agrees with the father out of fear, the son has obviously not been shown to be innocent.

Occasionally, however, the appeal to force is relevant. When the conclusion of the argument is a claim about the use of force, the threat might be considered relevant. Consider the following argument:

My father can beat up your father, and if you don't agree I'll get my father to come over and beat up your father.

Here the threat is logically relevant to the truth of the conclusion, so we cannot claim that the premise is irrelevant. And an appeal to force may be relevant when it is used in an attempt to get someone to *do* something, rather than to accept a truth-claim. However, in order to decide whether we are justified in using threats of force to get people to do something, we must establish a moral or political principle to serve as an additional premise. The criminal law, for example, works on the basis of the principle that society is entitled to use the threat of punishment to secure obedience to the law. If we accept this principle, then it is relevant to argue that people should not commit murder because otherwise they will be punished.

Another type of irrelevant appeal worth mentioning is the *appeal to popularity*. It arises when an argument uses the popularity of a belief as a reason for holding that the belief is true, when its popularity is irrelevant to its truth or falsity. Obviously, the mere fact that a belief is popular is usually no guarantee that it is true. History provides many examples of discarded beliefs that were once widely held to be true. Typically, the popularity of a belief is not a good reason for accepting it. For example:

Well, obviously capitalism is the most efficient economic system ever devised by humankind. Everybody knows that.

Phrenology is unscientific nonsense. Nobody believes it any longer.

Clearly, the popularity of capitalism does nothing to show that it is the most efficient economic system, nor does the unpopularity of phrenology do anything to show that it is false. It is also easy to recognize the cases where the appeal to popularity is relevant, that is, cases where the conclusion makes a claim that depends upon the popularity (rather than the truth) of some belief. If we are trying to predict who will win an election, or the future sales of a product, or the size of an audience for a concert, we will obviously need to use the appeal to popularity.

There are, however, harder cases where the relevance of the appeal to popularity is unclear. For example:

> *According to public opinion polls more than 60 per cent of Canadians are in favour of the death penalty for first-degree murder. This is supposed to be a democratic country, so the government ought to reinstate capital punishment.*

Is this a sound argument? It does not attempt to show that capital punishment is justified in itself, but only claims that it ought to be reinstated because the majority support it. It thus relies upon a missing premise: the political principle that government policy ought to reflect the will of the majority. It is on the acceptability of this principle that the strength of the argument depends. If it is acceptable then the argument is strong. If it is not acceptable then the argument is weak, for it appeals to an irrelevant premise.

For the remainder of this chapter we will examine four issues that often arise when questions of relevance are being discussed.

7.3 Appeals to Authority (1)

Often in discussion we make numerous claims that we do not attempt to defend. When we are challenged to do so, a common response is to cite an authority, in other words, we present an argument of the form:

> *So-and-so says X.*
> *Therefore, X is true (or probably true).*

The authorities we appeal to in order to defend a claim are many and varied: the prime minister, the family doctor, Uncle Fred, the weatherman, mom, the encyclopedia, a physics professor, the media, Wayne Gretzky. In each case the argument is in effect claiming that the mere fact that so-and-so says something is a good reason for us to accept it as true.

It is obvious that sometimes such appeals are quite irrelevant and give rise to very weak arguments. When Uncle Fred tells me that the Tiger-Cats are the best team in the CFL, it is unreasonable for me to agree with his view merely because he holds it. He is an enthusiastic fan, but he knows very little about football. What he says is irrelevant to the issue whether or not the Tiger-Cats are the best team in the CFL. But not all appeals to authority are as obviously weak as the appeal to Uncle Fred. Consider the following examples:

Albert Einstein, even after all his research into the nature of the universe, still believed in God. He once wrote, "I do not believe that the universe was the result of blind chance." If belief in God made sense to Einstein then it makes sense to me.

I've decided not to take any more philosophy electives. Some philosophy is kind of interesting, but the problem is that it consists merely of opinions and not knowledge. At least that's what my psychology professor says.

These arguments may seem plausible, but they appeal to irrelevant authorities. It is (or should be) evident that the fact that a famous physicist believed in God is not a good reason for believing in God. And the fact that a psychology professor thinks that philosophy consists merely of opinion and not knowledge is not a good reason for accepting his or her claim.

However, not all appeals to authority are irrelevant. In fact, our lives would be intolerable if we were never to rely upon authorities. The reason we consult lawyers, doctors, architects, and engineers, is that we have to rely upon their advice on matters about which we lack knowledge. In general, an appeal to authority is relevant whenever the following two conditions are met: (1) we lack information or experience that is needed to make a reasonable decision, and it is difficult or impossible on the matter in question to obtain it directly for ourselves, and (2) the authority appealed to is entitled to authoritative status. The first condition recognizes that if we could get the needed information and experience directly and without appealing to some authority, we ought to do so. For example, we should not rely upon someone else's view that a book is offensive if we could easily read it and decide for ourselves. Similarly, we shouldn't accept the view that euthanasia is right merely because someone we admire holds that it is. The appeal to authority, even when it is legitimate, should always be regarded as second best; if we are in a position to learn about the matter and decide for ourselves, we should do so. Only in situations where we lack the expertise needed to make some decision or judgment are we entitled to turn to an authority, such as a doctor, lawyer or engineer. But when we do so, we must bear in mind the second condition and make sure we are relying upon the judgment of someone who really is entitled to be treated as authoritative on the matter in question. There should be good reasons to believe that what the authority says really is likely to be true. How much reliance we should place on authorities will be discussed in section 8.2.

7.4 Some Particular Fallacies

The particular fallacies described in this section all involve an irrelevant appeal of some sort. They deserve a more extended discussion because they are so common, and because recognizing them requires sensitivity to their complexities. They figure prominently in arguments about virtually every controversial issue, and account for much of the frustration we typically experience when we are drawn into such debates. Understanding them will not only help us to avoid them but also show us how to respond when our opponents use them against us.

7.4.1 AD HOMINEM

The **ad hominem fallacy** is committed when the premise of an argument provides information about the author of some statement in an attempt to show that this statement is false, when this information is irrelevant to the truth or falsity of the statement. Loosely speaking, the ad hominem fallacy involves a personal attack upon someone in an attempt to discredit what that person says, when such an attack is irrelevant to the issue. The traditional name for this fallacy is *argumentum ad hominem*, which literally means *argument against the man*. Some contemporary logicians call this fallacy *abusing the person*, or *attack on the person*, but the Latin name is still widely used in ordinary speech, and we shall follow this usage here.

Let us look at some examples of arguments that commit the ad hominem fallacy:

According to the supporters of capital punishment, the death penalty is an effective deterrent against murder. This is nonsense. These people are not interested in deterrence at all. They want vengeance pure and simple. They suffer from a kind of bloodlust; they are the people who flock to see Dirty Harry movies. They get turned on by the thought of shooting up the bad guys.

What makes this an ad hominem is that the facts (or alleged facts) cited about the personal qualities of supporters of capital punishment are completely irrelevant to the question whether or not the death penalty is an effective deterrent against murder. Here is another example:

The Ontario Medical Association claims that the government's ban on extra-billing will produce a second-class system of medical care. It is difficult to accept their claim, however, since it is so obviously self-serving. Let us not forget that the OMA is essentially nothing more than a trade union, and that it is trying to negotiate a contract that gets the best deal for its members.

Once again, the evidence provided to show that the OMA's claim should not be accepted is quite irrelevant. It is true that the OMA is a kind of trade union and that it is presumably trying to negotiate a good deal for its members. But these facts do not show that its claim about the effects of a ban on extra-billing is false.

The ad hominem is usually easy to detect as long as we can remember to separate our views about the personal qualities of people whose opinions we do not share from our views about their opinions. We may not like to admit it, but nasty people sometimes say what is true and sometimes argue impeccably. The ease with which so many people commit the ad hominem fallacy doubtless derives from the fact that it is psychologically satisfying to attack nasty people. This also explains why an ad hominem can be so successful in public debates and discussion: audiences enjoy seeing nasty people under attack and often feel that such attacks actually refute their opinions and arguments. It is important, therefore, not to allow ourselves to be taken in by such attacks when they constitute an ad hominem, especially in situations where we feel very strongly that someone's opinion is not only false but deeply immoral as well. These are the types situations where we may commit an ad hominem without realizing it. We should strive to develop the intellectual self-discipline to separate our views about our opponents from our views about the truth or falsity of what they say.

Not every attack upon a person's personal qualities, however, constitutes a fallacy. It is only when such attacks are irrelevant to the point at issue that the fallacy arises. Sometimes the personal qualities of someone are precisely what is at issue. When we are looking for a baby-sitter, or considering asking someone out on a date, our decisions should be based upon a judgement about personal qualities. In such cases the personal qualities of the person are not used as a basis for rejecting what the person says, and for this reason no ad hominem fallacy is committed.

There are two types of arguments that seem to, but do not actually, commit the ad hominem fallacy. First, in some situations it is appropriate to argue that a person's opinions should not be relied upon because he or she is untrustworthy. When we are trying to assess the reliability of someone's testimony about an event, it is relevant to point to facts about the person's character. If you tell me that you have no idea how my bicycle came to be in your garage, the fact that you were convicted for bicycle theft last year is relevant to the question of whether I should accept your claim of innocence. This does not, of course, prove that you stole my bicycle, but it is relevant to the question of whether or not it is reasonable to believe you. Or, if I tell you that you will get better grades in school if you buy a particular encyclopedia, the fact that I get a 10 per cent commission is relevant to the question of whether you should accept my claim.

Second, sometimes it is appropriate to argue that a person's opinions should not be taken into account because of a conflict of interest. When a body such as a city council or school board makes decisions that might affect the financial interests of its members, it is an accepted principle that any member whose financial interests might be affected should not participate in such decisions. Here we do not dispute what a person says, but rather whether that person's views ought to be taken into account in the decision-making process. An argument that someone ought to abstain from voting on an issue because of a conflict of interest does not commit the ad hominem fallacy.

The **tu quoque fallacy** is a special case of the ad hominem. Like the ad hominem, it typically arises in an argumentative context when someone attempts to refute or rebut something said by another person. The tu quoque fallacy is committed when the conclusion of an argument claims that an accusation is unwarranted and supports it by claiming that the accuser is also open to a similar accusation. This fallacy is sometimes called the *Two Wrongs* fallacy, but we shall use the traditional Latin name (pronounced tew-kwoh-kway), which means *you too*.

It is clear that a tu quoque response to an accusation can never refute the accusation. Consider the following:

Wilma: *You cheated on your income tax. Don't you realize that's wrong?*
Walter: *Hey, wait a minute. You cheated on your income tax last year. Or have you forgotten about that?*

Walter may be correct in his counter-accusation, but that does not show that Wilma's accusation is false. Wilma's guilt can in no way reduce or eliminate Walter's guilt.

It is easy to understand why tu quoque arguments are so popular. After all, what better way to avoid an accusation than to hurl the same accusation back at our accusers. Many important public issues suffer from an abundance of tu quoques. For example:

I don't see why our company should be singled out by the city just because of some leakage problems at our chemical storage facility. The city should pay more attention to the more serious pollution that is occurring at its landfill site.

The opposition is in no position to attack the government for increasing the deficit. When they formed the government a few years ago they created a massive deficit that we are still coping with.

Tu quoque arguments are probably popular because they are deceptively similar to a type of argument that is sound. For example, when the issue is not whether an accusation is true, but whether someone has the right to make that accusation, it may be legitimate to use a tu quoque response. Recall our example from section 6.7.2:

Mary: *I'm just appalled at my sister-in-law. She had an affair and then when my brother found out she expected him to forgive her. That sort of thing is unforgivable and I think he should leave her. It would be good riddance to bad rubbish.*
Francine: *Cool it, Mary. I know about the little extra-marital fling you had a couple of years ago, and when your husband found out you were grateful when he forgave you.*

Here the issue is not whether Mary's sister-in-law has had an extramarital affair, but whether she should be forgiven for it. Since Francine is really charging Mary with hypocrisy, Francine herself does not commit a fallacy. In such cases an underlying moral principle is being invoked. We shall discuss how these arguments work in more detail in section 11.3.

7.4.3 STRAW MAN

This too is a very common fallacy. It usually arises in debates over controversial issues when one side is attempting to avoid or deflect criticisms presented by the other side. The **straw man fallacy** is committed when someone attacks a position that appears similar to, but is actually different from an opponent's position, and concludes that the opponent's real position has thereby been refuted. The opponent being attacked, however, is not the real opponent but an unreal opponent, a *straw man* who has been constructed by the attacker solely for the purpose of destruction. To recognize this fallacy we must, of course, know what the opponent's real position is, in order to see that it is different from the position being attacked. The question we need to ask when a position is under attack is, *Is the position being attacked really held by those under attack, or is it a false interpretation of their position?*

Examples of the straw man fallacy abound. When the issue is controversial, the straw man fallacy is often committed by both sides. Consider the following arguments:

What I object to most about those people who oppose capital punishment is that they believe that the lives of convicted murderers are more important than the lives of the policemen and prison guards who protect us.

Those who want the death penalty restored have not really thought their position through. They hold that every murderer would have been deterred from committing

murder had the death penalty been in force, and this is absurd. Otherwise, countries
with the death penalty would have no murders, which is obviously false.

With regard to the first argument, there is no evidence that anyone who is against the death penalty has ever believed that the lives of murderers are more important than anyone else's lives. With regard to the second argument, there is no evidence that anyone who supports the death penalty has ever seriously argued that the death penalty would deter all potential murderers. In both cases the accusers have attacked an unreal position, and have thus committed the straw man fallacy.

Clearly, the principle of charity is being ignored in these cases. We have no difficulty recognizing when our opponents have committed a straw man fallacy by attacking a travesty of our position. We know that they have violated the principle of charity. It is more difficult for us, however, to avoid stooping to the same level as our opponents. We need to remind ourselves that committing the straw man fallacy accomplishes nothing other than perhaps making us feel better for the moment. Our opponents are certainly not persuaded by such arguments; neither should anyone else be persuaded, since the position our opponents really hold has not been attacked at all and survives unscathed. Even worse, people who are not yet committed to either side of the issue may well conclude that our position must be very weak indeed if our straw man attack is the best that can be said against the other side.

Here are some other examples of straw man arguments:

If the New Democratic Party ever forms the government in Canada they would nationalize the whole economy. After all, they have repeatedly made it clear that they are opposed to business and to the profit motive.

The government's new immigration laws are designed to make it virtually impossible for refugees to enter Canada. This is an indefensible policy. What we want are laws that will make it easy for legitimate refugees to enter Canada, while at the same time requiring all non-refugees to apply to immigrate like anyone else.

The demands made by the aboriginal peoples are totally unacceptable. They claim that the whole country was stolen from them without their consent, and are demanding compensation for their loss. This is crazy. There isn't enough money in the world, let alone in Canada, to pay compensation for the whole country.

7.5 Self-Test No. 13

Explain the weaknesses, if any, in the following arguments.

1. I wouldn't take his word for anything, if I were you. His father has been convicted for fraud, and you know what they say: Like father, like son.

2. Seinfeld is the best show on television. It must be the best because it gets higher ratings than any other show.

3. Many mathematicians used to believe that formal logic could provide a foundation for the whole of mathematics. But they were wrong. Their view was decisively refuted by Kurt Gödel in his famous paper published in 1931.

4. How can anyone seriously believe in evolution? I certainly don't. How can you take seriously a theory that claims that humans are just monkeys with less hair and that our ancestors were apes?

5. I'm fed up with the feminist movement. I used to think they had some valid concerns, but they are just another special-interest group who are upset because they aren't getting all the good jobs. They talk a lot about justice but it all comes down to selfishness.

6. Throughout recorded history, the family unit has always had a single head, usually the father, but sometimes the mother or a grandparent. But in recent years this tradition has been challenged by those who think that the mother and father can be equal partners. Do these people really think that their limited perspective is better than the wisdom of history? The idea is preposterous.

7. I hate flying, and I don't see why everyone thinks I'm just being silly. Look at Janine. She hates flying as much as I do.

8. My son wants to be an opera singer, but he'll have to do it without any support from me. I've tried to persuade him to go into something useful, like business or law, but he insists on being a singer. He seems to think that everybody should be free to do whatever they want in life. Well, where would we be if everybody did whatever they wanted? That's what

I said to him when he told me he wanted to study music at university. And his only response was to walk out of the room.

9. For years francophone Quebeckers had to put up with an economy that was dominated by anglophones. Often they could not even get a job, and usually could never get a promotion, unless they spoke good English. The shoe is now on the other foot. Now, because of the measures adopted by the Quebec government, anglophones are finding that they are barred from many jobs unless they can speak good French. In my view, this is entirely justified. Let the anglophones suffer for a change.

10. (Background: A schoolteacher resigned his position, charging that the principal persistently treated him in an unfair and arbitrary manner. A school board official gave the following response.)

We conducted a thorough investigation to determine whether or not there is any validity to the charge, and we have concluded that there is not. The teacher in question seems to have embarked upon a campaign to undermine the authority of the principal. It is not clear whether his reasons for doing so were ideological or personal, but in either case he seems to have been a troublemaker.

7.6 Questions for Discussion

Each of the following arguments relies upon a premise that might be regarded as irrelevant. Identify the offending premise and suggest an argument that shows it is irrelevant.

1. There are no absolute values, i.e., no values that are valid for all times and all places. To see this you only have to look at the wide variety of values that have been held by other societies and at earlier times in our history. Pick any value you like: there will be some society somewhere that has rejected it. You simply cannot find a value that has been valid at all times and all places.

2. Although there are no strict proofs that God exists, it is still rational to believe that He does exist. Suppose God does exist: in this case heaven and hell exist and God will send unbelievers to hell for eternity, while believers stand a good chance of going to heaven. Obviously it is rational to do whatever is necessary to avoid hell and to get to heaven, so it is rational to believe in God if He actually exists. On the other hand, suppose God

doesn't exist: in this case there is no heaven or hell, so even if we believe He exists we run no risk of being punished for having a false belief. It is rational, therefore, to believe in God even if He does not exist. So it is rational to believe God exists, whether He exists or not.

3. The Israeli government should accept the right of Palestinians to a national homeland, because otherwise the Palestinians will continue their campaign of terrorism indefinitely. Israel will never have peace until it recognizes this right.

4. Recently, a number of manufacturers have begun marketing so-called green products, i.e., products that are supposed to be environmentally friendly. The supermarket shelves are now full of them, everything from detergent to peanut butter. These companies seem to think that these products will show their concern for the environment. This is absurd. They have developed these products not because they care about the environment but because they think they can make more money. Sadly, they probably will make more money because the public wants to help preserve the environment and thinks that buying green products will make a difference. But don't be fooled into thinking that these manufacturers care about the environment. It is profit, pure and simple, that motivates them.

5. There are a few people who believe that prostitution is morally acceptable, but in fact it is immoral behaviour. It is contrary to the accepted standards of our community as reflected in public opinion and in the legal system. The vast majority of Canadians strongly believe that prostitution is immoral and therefore quite properly reject any proposal to legalize prostitution.

6   Why does the public get so upset when people refuse to render assistance to someone in need? That incident last month where a woman was beaten in a park by her boyfriend while several hundred people looked on and did nothing produced a great outpouring of righteous indignation. But I can't for the life of me see why everyone gets so upset at the bystanders. According to the law, these people did nothing illegal, since the law imposes no duty on ordinary citizens to go to the aid of someone who is in distress. That's what the law says so I don't see that the bystanders did anything wrong at all.

Chapter 8

Assessing Adequacy

8.1 The Criterion of Adequacy

Our third criterion of a sound argument is that its premises should be adequate to support its conclusion. We need this criterion because even if an argument satisfies the first two criteria (i.e., its premises are true and are relevant to its conclusion), the premises may nevertheless be inadequate to support the conclusion. Clearly, an argument with premises that are inadequate to support its conclusion suffers from a major weakness. Relying on premises that are inadequate to support a conclusion is sometimes called *jumping to conclusions*, or reaching a *hasty conclusion*.

We saw in section 5.2.1 that adequacy is a matter of degree. In this respect the criterion of adequacy differs from the first two criteria. If the premises of an argument are *unacceptable* then they give us no reason to think that its conclusion is true. If the premises are *irrelevant* then they give us no reason to think that the conclusion is true. But if the premises are inadequate they may still provide some support for the conclusion, although this support may be too weak or inadequate to make the conclusion acceptable. The fact that premises may be partly but not entirely adequate to support a conclusion is often reflected in the tentative way we assert the conclusion. For example:

> Look at those dark clouds on the horizon. We might be in for some rain, so maybe we should head back to the car.

Notice the tentative nature of the inference. By using the words *might* and *maybe*, the speaker is acknowledging that the evidence is not conclusive. Suppose, however, the argument had been:

> Look at those dark clouds on the horizon. It's going to rain, and if we don't head back to the car right away we're going to get soaked.

Here, the inference is not tentative at all. The speaker is arguing that the dark clouds mean that it *will* rain, and since, as we all know, the presence of dark clouds on the horizon does not always mean that it will rain, the argument violates the criterion of adequacy.

When assessing the adequacy of the premises of any argument, therefore, we always need to look for the degree of strength that the argument claims to have. If it claims to *establish* or *prove* its conclusion, it is more likely that it may violate the criterion of adequacy. If its conclusion is presented tentatively, it is less likely to violate the criterion. It is important to interpret an argument with this question in mind before asking whether it violates the criterion of adequacy. Frequently, it is unclear what degree of strength a speaker is claiming for an argument, and we have to rely upon the contextual clues and the principle of charity when interpreting the argument.

However, we also need to make a judgement regarding the degree of support the premises actually provide for the conclusion, as opposed to the degree of support that is claimed by the speaker. This degree of support can range from none to a great deal and may fall anywhere in between. When an argument violates the criterion of adequacy it may be because the premises provide no support for the conclusion, but it may be because the premises provide some, although not enough, support to justify accepting the conclusion. Thus, many arguments that violate the criterion of adequacy can easily be amended to meet the criterion by changing the wording of the conclusion to reflect the degree of support actually provided by the premises. This is what we did in the above example. To determine the degree of support provided by a set of premises, we need to examine the full context and use whatever relevant background knowledge we possess in order to make the best judgement we can.

Once we have decided, however, that an argument violates the criterion of adequacy, we must be prepared to say why the premises are inadequate to support the conclusion. The reasons we offer will depend upon the content of the argument. In the above example, we pointed out that a few dark clouds on the horizon do not always mean that it is going to rain. In other cases we will explain the inadequacy of the premises by pointing out other relevant factors. For example:

> Steve always got A's in high school, so we expect him to get high marks in university.

All Margot's classmates think that Mr. Braithwaite is a great teacher, so I'm sure she does too.

The fact that Steve always got A's in high school provides some support for concluding that he will get high marks in university, but, as many of us know to our sorrow, it is no guarantee. And that Margot's classmates think Mr. Braithwaite is a great teacher is no guarantee that she agrees with them. We would have to know more about both Margot and Mr. Braithwaite to know how much support this argument provides for its conclusion.

When assessing the adequacy of an argument, it is sometimes important to take account of what the consequences would be if the conclusion turns out to be false or unacceptable. If we are considering major surgery the consequences could be very serious if the operation fails; and in a matter as important as this we should normally demand a very high standard of adequacy, and it would therefore be reasonable to seek a second medical opinion. But when an automechanic recommends that we use higher octane gasoline the relative unimportance of the consequences, if it turns out to be bad advice, means that it would normally be inappropriate to demand a second opinion.

Jumping to conclusions, and thus violating the criterion of adequacy, is the product of a very widespread human tendency. We have a small amount of relevant evidence, and cannot resist claiming that we have a good argument, or even a proof. We all know of cases like the following:

Classical music is terrible; I sang in the school choir for a year and we had to do some really boring classical music.

Sure, I believe in astrology. The day I broke my leg my horoscope said I should avoid risky situations, but I went skiing anyway. After that, I started taking it seriously.

Indeed there seems to be no limit to the different ways in which we can violate the criterion of adequacy. For this reason, it is difficult to classify into types most of the arguments we meet in real life that violate the criterion of adequacy. There are, however, a few types of arguments where determining the adequacy of the premises raises special difficulties.

8.2 Appeals to Authority (2)

In section 7.3 we saw that appeals to authority are relevant in circumstances where we lack information or experience that is needed for some decision and which we are unable to obtain for ourselves directly. But not all appeals to authority are equally strong. The adequacy of any appeal to authority depends upon a number of factors, all of which must be taken into account. There are five criteria we should use when determining the adequacy of any appeal to authority.

1. **The authority must be identified**. The reason for insisting that an authority must be identified is obvious: if we don't know who the authority is we cannot determine whether he or she is reliable. An anonymous authority is like a cheque: we won't know whether it is any good or not until we try to cash it. Beware of unnamed authorities.

2. **The authority must be generally recognized by the experts in the field**. The characteristics someone must have to be an authority depend upon the particular field in question. In some fields there are licensing requirements that are intended to ensure an appropriate level of expertise, as in medicine, dentistry, and many other professions. In fields where there are no licensing requirements, there are often generally accepted standards of expertise, such as a Ph.D. or a diploma in automechanics. Meeting licensing requirements or accepted standards, however, does not by itself guarantee that what an expert says is true. There are "qualified" crackpots in every field. The best general test is whether the expert is generally recognized as an expert by other experts in the field. Beware of authorities who lack the support of their fellow-experts.

3. **The particular matter in support of which an authority is cited must lie within his or her field of expertise**. No-one is an expert on everything, and the authority that experts can legitimately claim is limited to their field of expertise. Bank presidents are presumably experts on banking, but when they make pronouncements on what is a fair tax system they probably lack the relevant kind of expertise. Beware of authorities who make claims beyond their area of expertise.

4. The field must be one in which there is genuine knowledge. In certain fields individuals may have a great deal of experience, but this experience does not produce genuine knowledge. By *genuine knowledge* we mean a systematically ordered body of facts and principles that are objective in nature. In this sense, an experienced novelist may not have any knowledge of how to write a good novel and may be an abysmal teacher. In some fields there is no expertise: experience may produce familiarity but no genuine knowledge and hence no expertise. Experience is sometimes not merely the best but the only teacher. Beware of authorities who pretend to have expertise in a field in which there is no genuine knowledge.

5. There should be a consensus among the experts in the field regarding the particular matter in support of which the authority is cited. In virtually every field of knowledge there are some controversial issues. This is true in mathematics, law, medicine, economics, accountancy, and molecular biology, as well as in plumbing, wine-making, and coaching athletes. Such controversies mean that on that particular issue there is no knowledge, even though the field in general may have a secure knowledge base. Always be cautious when authorities disagree among themselves.

When deciding whether an appeal to an authority is adequate, we should always apply these criteria as best we can. In practice, it is sometimes difficult to gather the information that would show they have all been satisfied, but at the very least we should always look for evidence that one or more criteria is not met. To the extent that the criteria are not satisfied by some authority we should reduce our reliance upon that authority, especially when there is something important at stake. We can be forgiven if we accept the authority of our grandmother that chewing a garlic bud will stave off a cold, but it would be foolish in the extreme to accept our horoscope as an authority on whether to undergo surgery.

8.3 Analogical Reasoning

Reasoning by analogy is probably the most creative form of reasoning. Whenever we encounter something we do not understand, it is a natural reaction to try to understand it by reference to something that is familiar to us. When we see a man behaving erratically in a way that reminds us of Aunt Ethel, we conclude that he too is suffering from Alzheimer's disease. When an election gives the winning party a minority of seats, political commentators immediately look at past minority governments in order to understand the possibilities of the new situation. When scientists seek an explanation for a new phenomenon, they always begin by attempting to subsume it under laws or principles they are familiar with. In all such cases the reasoning presupposes an analogy between two things (objects, classes of objects, situations, relationships) one of which is familiar and one unfamiliar.

Some analogies are better than others, and some are downright misleading. The quality of an analogy depends upon the purpose of drawing it. If the purpose is merely to clarify a difficult concept, any analogy will be a good one if it succeeds in clarifying the concept. For example:

According to quantum mechanics particles move in accordance with wave-like principles. They are not physical waves, however, but probability waves. They are not like the waves on a lake, but are more like a crime wave.

The crime-wave analogy is helpful in grasping the concept of a probability wave, and for this purpose is a good analogy. In general, any analogy that helps us to understand something is a good one.

Another purpose of analogical reasoning is to suggest possible explanations. Charles Darwin got the idea for the principle of natural selection, which is central to the theory of evolution, by reading a book on economics by Thomas Malthus. Some scientists have used the digital computer as a source of possible explanations for how the human mind works. In these cases, the analogy is used not to prove anything but merely to suggest a hypothesis that would have to be defended independently of the analogy.

Our concern, however, is with analogies that are used in arguments, that is, where the analogy is being used to provide support for a conclusion. Here we need to be careful in choosing our analogies, for a weak analogy will fail to provide the support our conclusion needs. Analogies by themselves are never sufficient to prove anything, and if an argument claims to prove its conclusion any premise that introduces an analogy would be irrelevant. However, a strong analogy can provide an adequate reason for conclusions which are claimed to be only probably true. For example:

Last year I put some fertilizer on my strawberries in the fall and got about 20% more strawberries. You should do the same with your stawberries, since you've got the same kind of soil. You'll probably get more strawberries too.

Clearly, this is not a compelling argument, but the analogy between your soil and mine is strong enough to make it reasonable to accept the conclusion, at least tentatively. A weak analogy, on the other hand, is one that is used as a premise in an argument but fails to provide adequate support for the conclusion. For example:

Driving a car is basically just like riding a bicycle: it's all a matter of physical co-ordi-nation and keeping an eye on where you are going. Well, I taught myself how to ride a bicycle, so I reckon I can teach myself how to drive a car.

Clearly there are some similarities between riding a bicycle and driving a car, but the analogy is not strong enough to provide much support for the conclusion of this argument.

To determine the strength of an analogy we examine the similarities and dissimilarities between the two things being compared. A strong analogy is one in which there is a large number of relevant similarities and a small number of relevant dissimilarities between the two things being compared. A weak analogy is one in which there is a small number of relevant similarities and a large number of relevant dissimilarities between the two things being compared. It is important that the similarities and dissimilarities are relevant. The fact that riding a bicycle and driving a car are done in a sitting position is not a relevant similarity. The fact that I learned to ride a bicycle in June whereas I am proposing to teach myself to drive a car in September is not a relevant dissimilarity. On the other hand, the fact that both require good physical coordination is a relevant similarity. And the fact that cars are faster and more powerful than bicycles is a relevant dissimilarity. The relevance of a similarity or dissimilarity depends upon the subject matter of the analogy and the conclusion being inferred. For each of the above similarities and dissimilarities we would have to be prepared to say why we think it is or is not relevant, and to do this we would have to rely upon what we know about riding bicycles and driving cars, as well as what we know about learning to drive a car. Determining the strength of an analogy in-volves weighing the relevant similarities against the relevant dissimilari-ties. We have to make a judgement, in the light of the similarities and dissimilarities, as to whether the analogy is strong enough to support the conclusion. There are no hard and fast rules here: all we can do is to look for relevant similarities and dissimilarities and make our judgement on that basis.

Here are two arguments that rest upon analogies. In both cases the strength of the analogies would have to be carefully assessed in order to determine the strength of the arguments.

> *Giving fathers a period of paid leave when their wives give birth would not be prohibitively expensive. In Sweden, where such a policy has been in effect for more than a decade, only 12 per cent of Swedish men take the leave.*

> *Many people support gun control legislation because they think it will reduce the number of murders. They are making a serious mistake, however. Have they forgotten the failure of prohibition to reduce the amount of drunkenness?*

8.4 Appeals to Ignorance

Sometimes people defend a claim by appealing to the fact that there is no evidence that it is false. By itself this is a completely inadequate reason, for it assumes that in some mysterious way the absence of evidence that something is false supports the claim that it is true. For example:

> *I believe in astrology, and always read my horoscope in the paper every day. I can't actually prove that it is true, but nobody can disprove it.*

In fact, the absence of evidence against something is by itself never a good reason for believing it. Otherwise, we would have a good reason to believe all sorts of silly things. For example:

> *The world will come to an end at exactly 12:00 noon EST on a Saturday.*

> *There are seven invisible leprechauns living in my garden.*

> *Ronald Reagan was never the president of the United States. The real Ronald Reagan died in his sleep in 1979, but his body was taken over by creatures from outer space.*

None of these statements can be disproved, even though there is no evidence that they are true.

In certain contexts, however, the absence of contrary evidence can be a good supporting reason for a conclusion. If we have some evidence that supports a claim, then the absence of contrary evidence does add some additional support. This additional support is even stronger if we have actually looked for contrary evidence and failed to find any. This is what medical doctors sometimes do when faced with a condition that is difficult to diagnose. The symptoms suggest the patient has a certain disease; a test is performed that could prove that the patient does not have that disease, but the test result is negative. The absence of this piece of contrary evidence is then used as additional support for the initial diagnosis. The legitimacy of the appeal to the absence of contrary evidence in such cases, however, clearly requires that there be some direct supporting evidence. And even then, the additional support it provides can never be more than secondary in importance. Thus, the tree diagram for an argument with an appeal to the absence of contrary evidence as a premise would have to be a T-argument structure, since it only provides support when joined to other premises. Even in cases where such an appeal is relevant, however, its adequacy as a supporting premise should be assessed by appeal to the criterion of adequacy in the usual way.

8.5 The Slippery Slope Fallacy

We often want to assess a proposal to take some action or adopt a new policy. One important and legitimate way of doing so is to examine the consequences that would result if the action were taken or the policy adopted. If the action or policy is likely to lead to undesirable consequences then we have a good reason to reject it, and if it is likely to lead to desirable consequences then we have a good reason to support it. This method of assessment involves making predictions about the future, and it is important to realize that such predictions are always somewhat tentative. Even when there is a wealth of empirical support for predictions we know how easily they can be wrong: think of weather forecasts and stock market predictions. There is one important aspect of predictions that needs to be noted. When we chain predictions together in the following way:

A will probably lead to B; B will probably lead to C; C will probably lead to D; D will probably lead to E, and E will probably lead to F;

we are not entitled to conclude that A will probably lead to F. This is because when we multiply probabilities the resulting probability is always reduced. There may be a 50 per cent chance that the next person to walk around the corner will be a woman, and a 50 per cent chance that the woman will be married, but that means that there is only a 25 per cent chance that the next person to walk around the corner will be a married woman. So if each of the probabilities between A and F is 80 per cent, the probability that A will lead to F is only 33 per cent. Clearly, to conclude that A will probably lead to F would be a mistake. Such arguments commit the *slippery slope fallacy*. The premises of a slippery slope argument present a chain of predictions each of which may be very strong, but the chain as a whole is weak. The conclusion of such an argument is not adequately supported.

Usually, when we make a chain of predictions we cannot, or do not bother to, assign numerical probabilities to each step in the chain. But it is clear that even a chain of "pretty likely" predictions will become weaker as it becomes longer. And if, as often happens, one step in the chain violates the criterion of acceptability, then the prediction of the final outcome will be very weak indeed. For example:

If abortion on demand were to become legal there would be a great increase in abortions. And once abortion became commonplace there would be a weakening of respect for human life in general. Once the respect for human life was weakened we would see an increase in euthanasia of all kinds: the elderly, the mentally handicapped, and the physically disabled. Before long we would be getting rid of anyone who is unproductive. In short, it would threaten our civilization. Therefore, we should oppose any move to broaden the grounds for legal abortions.

This is a clear example of a slippery slope fallacy. Which step is the weakest in the chain is debatable, for none of them is very strong. But the second step — that if abortions become commonplace there would be a weakening of respect for human life in general — seems especially weak. It might be true that there would be a weakening of respect for human life in general, but there is very little evidence to support this claim.

This example shows another common characteristic of slippery slope arguments: they often omit some of the steps in the chain. It is possible that if society began to get rid of anyone who is unproductive our civilization would be threatened, but clearly there must be a number of intermediate steps, which the argument omits. There are missing premises that would have to be supplied in order to undertake a complete assessment of the argument.

Sometimes slippery slope arguments omit all the intermediate steps in the chain. For example:

> *You should never drink during the day. Once you start doing that you will end up as a skid-row bum.*

The only charitable interpretation of this argument is to regard it as having a series of missing premises that would provide the intermediate steps in the chain. Of course, it is difficult to assess a series of missing premises of this sort. All we can do is use our own knowledge to decide whether the chain would be a strong one if it were spelled out in detail.

Slippery slope arguments are superficially similar to another kind of argument that is not open to the same kind of objection. Sometimes we explore the consequences of a policy by predicting the different consequences that would arise if we were to adopt the policy. Here our reasoning is as follows:

> *A (the policy) will probably lead to B; A will probably lead to C; A will probably lead to D; A will probably lead to E, and A will probably lead to F.*

If these consequences are bad we will reject the policy, and if they are good we will accept the policy. But we need to note that each of these predicted consequences is independent of the others, and thus they do not constitute a *chain* of predictions. Chained predictions can be diagrammed as follows:

A ⟶ B ⟶ C ⟶ D ⟶ E ⟶ F

We are now considering a series of independent predictions that are diagrammed as follows:

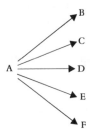

It is important to understand the crucial difference between the two types of reasoning. In slippery slope arguments our interest is in the last item in the chain, and it, as we have seen, is vulnerable to the weakness that results from the cumulative effect of each step being only probable. But when we work out a series of independent predictions our interest is in all the predictions taken together. Any weaknesses in our predictions are therefore not cumulative. In slippery slope arguments a single false prediction breaks the chain, whereas a single false prediction in a series of independent predictions leaves the others intact. An argument whose conclusion rests on a series of independent predictions thus is not a slippery slope argument.

Here are two more slippery slope arguments. Note that the first is part of a reductio ad absurdum argument:

Revenue Canada's recent decision that many of the perks employers give their employees are taxable benefits is a silly and dangerous precedent. It is one thing to tax food and lodging when it is routinely provided by employers. But now they are going after things like free parking. Next will be the pencils and paper clips we all take home from work. Then it will be office Christmas parties: there will be auditors hovering, clipboards in hand, keeping track of how many free drinks and peanuts we have consumed. And when they realize that for many of us the greatest perk is being able to daydream on the job, they will even begin to tax our dreams.

Everyone accepts the general principle that lying is immoral. Many people also believe that some exceptions to the rule are permitted. This, of course, raises the question of what these exceptions should be. People always start with the easy ones: we should be prepared to lie, they say, if it is the only way of preventing the death of an innocent person, and they point to examples such as lying to the Gestapo to protect Jews. But then, they argue, since lying in these cases is justified, surely it is justified to tell lies to protect your country in wartime; for example, when captured by the enemy. And then, of course, lying would be justified to protect your country in peacetime, and so also must lying to protect your government. It is then but a very short step to lying to protect your reputation if you happen to be a government official. Once you allow that any lie is capable of being justified, you are inexorably led to telling lies whenever you feel like it.

8.6 Causal Fallacies

We now come to a group of fallacies that often arise when reasoning about causes. But first we need to say something about the concept of causality. The idea of a cause is an extremely elusive concept, and a great deal of philosophical and scientific energy has been devoted to giving an adequate account of it. Scientists usually avoid the term altogether and refer instead to correlations between variables. It is clear, however, that these correlations are intended to reveal causal factors. These causal factors can best be expressed as statements of necessary and sufficient causal conditions in the way described in section 3.8.

It is misleading to speak of an event as having a single cause, for there are always a large number of causal conditions involved in any event. When we ask, *What caused the explosion at the mill?* we are not usually looking for a complete causal explanation of the explosion. We don't want to know about the various necessary conditions (the presence of oxygen, the presence of a combustible gas, etc.). We are usually looking for the one condition that, along with these necessary conditions, is sufficient to cause the explosion. In explaining the causal fallacies, we shall simplify the causal picture by assuming that events have only a single cause. It is possible to explain these fallacies without this simplifying assumption, but the explanations would be extremely cumbersome. The nature of the fallacies is the same in either case.

8.6.1 POST HOC

If A causes B then A must occur before B occurs, since the cause must always precede the effect. If boiling water causes it to evaporate, then we have to boil the water before we can expect it to evaporate. But the fact that a cause must always precede its effect does not mean that everything that precedes some event must be its cause. It is a necessary, but not a sufficient, condition of a cause that it must precede its effect. If we forget this distinction we can be led to commit the fallacy of **post hoc**. The name comes from the Latin phrase *post hoc ergo propter hoc*, which means *after this therefore because of this*. The fallacy of post hoc is committed when it is argued that something that occurs before some event must be its cause. For example:

> The stove in your apartment was working perfectly until you moved in, but the next day the oven stopped working. It must be something you're doing that has caused the problem.

This inference is obviously fallacious. It is possible that the landlord's conclusion is correct, but the argument provides very little support for it.

Here are some more examples of post hoc fallacies:

> In the 1960s the trend towards married women working outside the home began to emerge. Within a few years we began to see a significant increase in the divorce rate, which has now reached alarming proportions. Obviously, if we value the family as an institution we should try to prevent married women from working outside the home.

> I tried some Russian caviar at Mattie's cocktail party last Saturday and was so sick when I got home that I got almost no sleep that night. There must have been something wrong with the caviar or else I'm allergic to the stuff.

> In Aesop's fable, the rooster reasoned as follows: Every morning without fail, the sun rises just a few minutes after I start crowing. I must be the greatest creature in the world since I cause the sun to rise every day.

8.6.2 CONFUSING CAUSE AND EFFECT

If A causes B, then whenever A is present we will always find B as well. If inflation causes unemployment then wherever we find inflation we should also find unemployment. This fact can sometimes make it difficult to know which is the cause and which is the effect. The fallacy of

confusing cause and effect is committed when an effect is identified as a cause and the cause is identified as the effect. For example:

> According to a recent Statscan report, married couples with no children have approximately 20 per cent more disposable income than married couples with children. This shows that it is affluence which causes declining birth rates.

The conclusion of this argument clearly is not supported by the premise. The argument gets the causal connection backwards: it is the fact that people have children that leads to their having less disposable income.

Here are some more examples of arguments that commit (or seem to commit) the fallacy of confusing cause and effect:

> Almost all military experts hold that we must have standing armies because of the continuing threat of war. The reality is quite different: the continuing threat of war is caused by the existence of standing armies.

> Did you notice at the party last night that as soon as Kevin and Paula arrived she told him not to drink too much, and then Kevin proceeded to get really drunk? That always seems to happen when they are at a party together: she always complains about his drinking and he always gets drunk. If only she would shut up about it he probably wouldn't get drunk at all.

> Most people are afraid of hospitals. They have friends and relatives who have gone into hospital for routine surgery or for some tests, and then either die or come down with some chronic debilitating illness. In fact, when you come to think of it, almost everyone who dies seems to die in a hospital. Hospitals really are dangerous places.

8.6.3 COMMON CAUSE

One reason why A and B may always occur together is that one of them causes the other (either A causes B or B causes A). But there may be another explanation: it may be that A and B are each caused by some third event, C. In these cases, if we ignore C we can easily misinterpret the causal relationship. The fallacy of **common cause** is committed when it is claimed that there is a causal relation between A and B when in fact both A and B are caused by a third factor, C. For example:

During the trial of a seventeen-year-old Toronto youth accused of raping and then murdering a twenty-six-year-old suburban housewife, the prosecution presented evidence that the youth had a large collection of pornography hidden in the attic of his home. He had over five hundred magazines of what is normally classified as hardcore pornography, and thirty-seven pornographic video-cassettes. Before passing sentence, the judge made the following observation: "If anyone still needs persuading that pornography causes violence against women, this case provides conclusive proof."

The relationship between pornography and violence is a complex one, and we cannot say that the judge's conclusion is false. But the judge's evidence is quite weak. The evidence cited is probably better interpreted as showing that the youth's fascination with pornography and his crime were both caused by some underlying psychological factor.

Here are some more arguments that commit (or seem to commit) the fallacy of common cause:

Recent studies have shown that people who are commonly regarded as being successful have much larger vocabularies than average. This is no accident. Having an extensive vocabulary is an important factor in producing success.

The solution to the problem of poverty in Canada is obvious. People who live below the poverty line normally have very little education: more than half have less than a grade eight education. Therefore, the way to overcome poverty is to provide incentives and encouragement for poor people to go back to school to complete their education.

The best way to clear up the sinus congestion that usually accompanies a sore throat is to get rid of the sore throat by taking some of those medicated throat lozenges you can get at the drug store. After all, it's the sore throat that causes the congestion: haven't you noticed that you always get a sore throat just before your head gets stuffed up?

8.7 Self-Test No. 14

Explain any weaknesses in the following arguments:

1. They say there is no proof that living near nuclear power plants causes birth defects. Well, my sister-in-law, who lives only two kilometres from the Pickering nuclear power plant, had a miscarriage last year, and they can't prove that it wasn't caused by the power plant.

2. The Indonesian government is following a policy of genocide in West Papua and East Timor. Accurate information is hard to get, but many thousands of people have been killed by government troops. This shows that Indonesia has the worst record of human-rights violations of any government in the world.

3. A recent study showed that students who cram immediately before examinations usually get lower grades than those who do not. Well, I certainly won't make that mistake this term. I'm not even going to open a book during the exam period.

4. Our major objection to the free trade deal with the United States is not with the short- and medium-term consequences, since it is likely that, on balance, Canada will benefit economically. Our concern is with the long term. Gradually, our governments will lose the ability to interfere in the market place in ways designed to benefit the people of Canada, unless the U.S. government approves. Each time the government capitulates to U.S. pressure it will be another nail in the coffin of Canadian independence, and the final outcome will be the complete loss of Canadian sovereignty.

5. I was in good health until they started that darn fluoridation program. Within a few weeks I started getting an upset stomach every day or two, and within three months I was having really bad stomach cramps. I went to the doctor, who discovered that I had a duodenal ulcer. The doctor treated me, of course, but I knew what I needed to do − start drinking bottled water, which I do now. That was two years ago and I've been fine ever since. But it just goes to show how dangerous fluoridation is.

6. The high-school drop-out rate in Ontario has declined by more than 50 per cent since 1950. During the same period, there has been an increase of about 40 per cent in the rate of juvenile delinquency. I can't believe this is a mere coincidence. Clearly, we should have higher academic standards in school to force the weaker students out and into the real world where they will develop a sense of responsibility.

7. The proposal to give clean needles to prison inmates to stop the spread of the AIDS virus from the use of dirty needles is ridiculous. It is like giving bank robbers normal bullets to stop them from using dum-dum bullets, which are much more damaging to the victim.

8. (Comments by a city politician on a proposal that the city should fund a drop-in centre for unemployed workers.)

    I would be prepared to support the proposal if I thought there was a need for it. But I really don't see that there is a need. I get phone calls from taxpayers about all sorts of things, but I cannot recall ever getting a phone call from anyone suggesting we need such a centre.

9. All the public opinion polls for the last year have shown that the government has a lower approval rating than either of the two opposition parties. So the Premier obviously knows the government is not going to be re-elected, and will postpone calling the election until the last possible moment.

10. Last weekend there was a large demonstration in front of the U.S. Consulate by people protesting against U.S. involvement in Central America. There were so many people that they spilled out all over the northbound lanes of University Avenue, so the police had to re-route traffic. Like many other innocent people, I was seriously inconvenienced by the inconsiderate behaviour of the demonstrators. The incident has convinced me that the time has come to ban all demonstrations on public property.

8.8 Questions for Discussion

Comment on the strengths and weaknesses of the following arguments:

1. Perhaps we cannot know for certain that many animals feel pain, but there are three reasons for holding that they do. First, they exhibit behaviour that in humans is invariably associated with feeling pain. Second, they have a central nervous system that is similar to humans'. And third, the ability to feel pain would have the same kind of evolutionary advantage for many animals that it does for humans.

2. There has been a great deal of criticism recently of the quality of high-school education in Ontario. People seem to think the quality is declining. But the statistics don't bear this out; in fact they show that quality is increasing. The average grades of high-school graduates have increased by at least 10% since 1967.

3. Almost everyone would throw a life preserver to a drowning person; indeed, someone who could easily do so but refused would be regarded by

everyone as a sick or immoral person. The same thing applies to nations when a famine occurs in a Third World country. We should be prepared to throw them a life preserver in the form of emergency aid. Yet we continually hear complaints from those who are opposed to such aid. Surely we are entitled to regard them as sick or immoral people.

4. People who believe they have a duty to help those who are less fortunate than themselves almost always get pleasure from their unselfish actions. This just proves that it is the expectation of pleasure which causes people to act morally or to adopt their moral beliefs.

5. Athletes who earn multi-million-dollar salaries deserve them. Those who are so critical of these "astronomical" salaries conveniently overlook two reasons that make such salaries entirely justified. First, these athletes are supremely talented. They are able to perform better than almost everyone else, including most other athletes. Second, they have only a few short years to make their fortune, since in most cases they will have retired from professional sport by their mid-thirties. To compare their salaries with what most people earn you would have to spread athletes' million-dollar salaries out over forty years to make the comparison fair.

6 Ken is the leading scorer on the university hockey team this year. He is averaging one goal per game this year whereas last year he scored only three goals in the entire season. He claims that what made the difference is that he found God last summer; before each game he prays to God to give him the strength and concentration to score at least one goal. Well, maybe he's right, and we should try to get the rest of the team to get religion. If it works for Ken who is to say it won't work for the other players.

Chapter 9

Deductive Reasoning

In this and the next three chapters we consider three types of reasoning, each of which has distinctive features and that therefore requires special treatment. All three types still rely upon the three criteria of a sound argument for assessment, but the application of the criteria requires a detailed understanding of how these arguments work.

9.1 The Nature of Deductive Reasoning

In section 1.2, we defined logical strength as the property of an argument whose premises, if true, support its conclusion. We also pointed out that logical strength is a matter of degree, and we distinguished deductive and inductive arguments on that basis: deductive arguments are those whose premises guarantee the truth of the conclusion, and inductive arguments are those whose premises make it reasonable to accept the conclusion but do not absolutely guarantee its truth. To understand the nature of deductive reasoning it is essential to understand the fundamental difference between the two types of reasoning.

Most of the logically strong arguments we have considered so far in this book have been inductive arguments, i.e., arguments that do not provide absolute guarantees. This is not necessarily a weakness, for in many cases the most we can expect of an argument is a degree of strength that falls somewhat short of constituting an absolute guarantee. Consider the following inductive argument:

> *The Gordon Street bridge is regularly inspected by qualified engineers.*
> *Vehicles have been driving over it for years.*
> *Therefore, it will be safe to drive over it tomorrow.*

This is a logically strong argument, but it does not provide an absolute guarantee that it will be safe to drive over the bridge tomorrow. There is a remote possibility that it will collapse at the very moment I cross it. If the premises are true then the conclusion will very likely, or probably, or almost certainly, be true; but the truth of the premises cannot absolutely rule out the possibility that the conclusion will be false. In other words, the conclusion might turn out to be false even though the premises are true.

But deductive arguments are not like this. The conclusion of a logically strong deductive argument cannot possibly be false if its premises are true. Consider the following argument:

> *If you are under the age of eighteen then you are legally a minor.*
> *If you are legally a minor then you cannot be sued.*
> *Therefore, if you are under the age of eighteen then you cannot be sued.*

Unlike the argument about the Gordon Street bridge, it is impossible for the conclusion of this argument to be false unless at least one of the premises is also false. If its premises are true the truth of the conclusion is guaranteed.

Logically strong deductive arguments are able to guarantee, or conclusively establish, their conclusions because the logical strength of deductive arguments does not depend upon their specific content, but on their form or structure. Consider another example of a deductive argument:

> *If Ellen lost her purse then she lost her student ID card.*
> *If she lost her student ID card then she won't be allowed to write her exams.*
> *Therefore, if Ellen lost her purse then she won't be allowed to write her exams.*

This argument has the same logical form or structure as the previous example. This form can be expressed as follows:

> If p then q.
> If q then r.
> Therefore, if p then r.

What is significant about these arguments is not merely that they have the same form, but that their logical strength is derived from their form. If we ask why the premises provide strong support for the conclusion, we can ignore the particular content of the arguments because the facts about being under eighteen or losing ID cards have no bearing on the logical strength of the argument. It is the form of the argument (i.e., the form or structure of the premises and conclusion, and the formal relationships among them) that makes these arguments strong. They are strong arguments *because* of their form. This means that *every* argument with this form will be a logically strong argument. It is their form that determines their strength.

9.2 Truth-Functional Statements

Deductive reasoning relies upon what are called truth-functional statements: every deductive argument includes at least one truth-functional statement. In order to understand deductive reasoning, therefore, it is necessary to understand what a truth-functional statement is. All statements can be divided into two classes: simple and complex. A simple statement is one that does not contain any other statement as a part, and a complex statement is one that contains another statement as a component part. Here are some simple statements:

Virginia got a job with the Bank of Montreal in 1973.

I lost the keys.

Mark has had a great deal of experience dealing with emotionally disturbed children.

Shirley loves him.

Here are some complex statements with the component statements underlined:

Virginia got a job with the Bank of Montreal in 1973, and she became a vice-president after twenty-two years.

Either I lost the keys, or they have been stolen.

It is false that Mark has had a great deal of experience dealing with emotionally disturbed children.

Tom believes that Shirley loves him.

Truth-functional statements are a sub-class of complex statements, that are distinguished by the way their truth is determined. Ordinarily, when we want to determine whether a statement is true, we look directly for facts or reasons to tell us whether what the statement says is true. With truth-functional statements, however, the procedure is a little different. We have to proceed indirectly, for the truth of truth-functional statements is determined not by directly seeing whether what *it* says is true, but by seeing whether *its components* are true. The truth of truth-functional statements is thus a function of the truth values of its component statements.

Consider the first example given above. It is a truth-function because in order to determine whether it is true, we must separately determine the truth or falsity of its two component statements. If they are both true then the complex statement will also be true. But if either component is false – either because Virginia did not get a job with the Bank of Montreal in 1973, or because she did not become a vice-president after twenty-two years – then the statement as a whole will be false. The second example is also a truth-function. Unlike the first example, however, it asserts an *either/or* relationship between its two components. In order for the statement as a whole to be true only one of the component statements needs to be true. The third example is also a truth function. It is true only when its component statement is false.

The fourth example, however, is not a truth-function even though it is a complex statement, because its truth is not a function of the truth value of its component statement. Tom might believe that Shirley loves him even when she does not, in which case the statement *Tom believes that Shirley loves him* will be true even though the statement *Shirley loves him* is false. Or, Tom might not believe that Shirley loves him even when she does, in which case the statement as a whole will be false even though the component statement is true.

Each of these truth-functional statements includes what is called a **logical operator**: *and, either/or,* and *it is false that.* The presence of the logical operator is crucial, since it tells us precisely how the truth of the statement as a whole is determined by the truth values of its component statements. The logical operators define the different kinds of truth-functional statements. There are four kinds of truth-functions that are important for understanding deductive reasoning. We shall follow the standard convention in logic and use the letters *p, q, r,* and so forth, to stand for the component statements, which may be either simple or complex statements.

1. **Negation**   The statement *p is false* is a negation. (Sometimes, negations are written as *not-p*.) A negation is true when its component statement is false, and false when its component statement is true. Thus, the statement *p is false* is true when *p* is false, and false when *p* is true. For example:

> *It is false that falcons mate while flying.*

This statement is true if the statement *falcons mate while flying* is false. If falcons do mate while flying, then the statement is false.

2. **Conjunction**   The statement *p and q* is a conjunction. It is true only when *p* is true and *q* is true; it is false when *p* is false, or when *q* is false, or when both *p* and *q* are false. For example:

> *Ted and Alice have been married for six years and they have no children.*

This statement is true only if both its component statements, or conjuncts, are true. If either conjunct is false then the conjunction as a whole is false. If Ted and Alice have been married for only five years then the statement is false even though it may be true that they have no children. If they have a child then the statement is false, even though it may be true that they have been married for six years.

3. **Disjunction**   The statement *p or q* is a disjunction. It is true when *p* is true, or when *q* is true, or when *p* and *q* are both true; it is false when both *p* and *q* are false. For example:

> *Either Mac did it or Bud did it.*

This statement is true if either or both of its component statements, or disjuncts, is true. If both disjuncts are false then the disjunction as a whole is false. If Mac did it then the statement is true. If Bud did it then the statement is true. If they both did it then the statement is true. If neither of them did it, however, the statement is false.

It is important to note that in a disjunctive truth-function the two disjuncts are exhaustive but not exclusive. (Recall the discussion of false dichotomy in section 6.7.4.) This means that the disjuncts cannot both be false, since they are exhaustive, but both may be true, because they are not exclusive.

4. **Implication**   The statement *if p then q* is an implication. The two component sentences in an implication have different names since, unlike conjuncts and disjuncts, each plays a different role: the first is called the antecedent, and the second is called the consequent. An implication such as *if p then q* is false only when *p* is true and *q* is false; in all other cases (i.e., when *p* is false, or when *q* is true), it is true. For example:

If Moe studies hard then he will get an A average.

This statement is true if both the antecedent and the consequent are true, that is, if Moe studies hard and also gets an A average. And it is clearly false if the antecedent is true while the consequent is false: if Moe studies hard and does not get an A average. But what about the other two possibilities? If both the antecedent and consequent are false – if Moe doesn't study hard and fails to get an A average – logicians regard the original implication as still being true. And if the antecedent is false while the consequent is true – if Moe doesn't study hard and yet does get an A average – logicians also regard the original implication as true. These last two cases are somewhat counter-intuitive. What we want to say is that the original implication *could* still be true in these cases, but not that it *is* true. Logicians admit the oddity but defend it by pointing out that it results from treating implication as a truth-function, and that the power of deductive reasoning is greatly enhanced when implication is given a truth-functional interpretation.

Truth-functional statements are expressed in a variety of ways in English, but it is usually easy to recognize that they are truth-functions. Here are some alternative ways of expressing negations:

It is not true that organized crime is controlled exclusively by the Mafia.

John did not win the Alexander Prize for Physics.

His claim that he was at a concert when the break-in occurred isn't true.

It is easy to see how these statements can be rewritten in the standard *p is false* form.

Here are some truth-functional conjunctions that do not use the word *and* but rely on an equivalent word or phrase:

Sarah always worries about getting poor grades, even though she has never had a grade of less than B+.

The rent on my apartment has increased by 40 per cent in the last ten years but my income has only increased by 35 per cent during the same period.

Our conference lost more money this year despite the fact that twice as many people attended as last year.

All these statements express truth-functional conjunctions, since each asserts that both its component statements are true.

Here are some disjunctions that are expressed in variant terms:

You should either fix his lawnmower or buy him a new one.

He must have been extremely upset to have trashed his bicycle like that; or maybe he was just drunk.

There are just two possibilities: raising taxes or reducing expenditures.

Each of these statements is clearly equivalent to a disjunction expressed in the standard *p or q* form.

Implications may be expressed in wide variety of different sentences. For example:

Since your lease has expired the landlord is free to raise the rent up to the limit set by the Rent Review Board.

Being a teenager these days means that you have to face a tremendous amount of peer pressure.

Anyone who takes horoscopes seriously must be very gullible.

The theory of evolution implies that God did not create human beings in the way described in the Bible.

Whenever the pressure reaches 300 psi the release valve automatically opens and reduces the pressure to a safe level.

Being wealthy entails having obligations to those who are less fortunate.

If we rewrite these statements in the appropriate *if p then q* form, we can see that their meaning remains the same:

If your lease has expired then the landlord is free to raise the rent up to the limit set by the Rent Review Board.

If you are a teenager these days then you have to face a tremendous amount of peer pressure.

If someone takes horoscopes seriously then that person must be very gullible.

If the theory of evolution is true then God did not create human beings in the way described in the Bible.

If the pressure reaches 300 psi then the release valve automatically opens and reduces the pressure to a safe level.

If you are wealthy then you have obligations to those who are less fortunate.

9.3 Formal Validity and Soundness

The concept of logical strength is central in our approach to the assessment of arguments, since, as we saw in section 5.2.1, it provides the basis for the second and third criteria of a sound argument. When applied to deductive arguments, however, the concept of logical strength has a narrower meaning than it does when applied to non-deductive arguments. Logical strength is the property of an argument whose premises, if true, provide support for its conclusion. But the support claimed by a deductive argument amounts to a guarantee of the truth of its conclusion. The term formal validity is used to describe this special kind of logical strength; a formally valid argument is defined as an argument such that if its premises are true then its conclusion must also be true. The phrase _must be_ in this definition is to be interpreted strictly. Since it expresses the idea of a guarantee, it does not mean is _very probably_, but is _necessarily_.

The concept of formal validity has a corollary that it is useful to note. It follows from the definition of formal validity that a valid argument cannot have true premises and a false conclusion, and this means that if we know that the conclusion of a valid argument is false, then we know that at least one of the premises must be false. Otherwise, the argument would violate the definition of a valid argument.

Notice that the definition of validity does not claim that the premises of a valid argument _are_ true, but only that _if_ the premises are true then the conclusion must also be true. Saying that an argument is valid thus does not mean that it satisfies the first criterion of a sound argument. On the other hand, all valid arguments satisfy the second and third criteria. This is the great strength of deductive reasoning: once we know that a deductive argument is valid, we know that it completely satisfies both the second and third criteria, and we know this simply because the form or structure of the argument constitutes a valid argument form. A valid argument form thus guarantees both that the premises of the argument are relevant to the conclusion, and that they are adequate to prove the truth of the conclusion. Let us now identify some of these valid argument forms.

9.4 Valid Argument Forms

A valid argument form is any set of truth-functional statements such that every argument with that form is a valid argument. In other words, if an argument has a valid argument form, then if its premises are true its conclusion must also be true. To show that an argument is valid, therefore, we need only to show that it has a valid argument form. There are a great many valid argument forms, but we shall consider only four basic ones. They are basic in the sense that they frequently occur in everyday use, and that all other valid argument forms can be derived from these four forms.

1. Affirming the Antecedent

If p then q
p
Therefore, q

2. Denying the Consequent

If p then q
Not-q
Therefore, not-p

3. Chain Argument

If p then q
If q then r
Therefore, if p then r

4. Disjunctive Syllogism

Either p or q
Not-p
Therefore, q

Whenever we find an argument whose form is identical to one of these valid argument forms we know that it must be a valid argument. We identify the form of a deductive argument by reconstructing it. But when reconstructing deductive arguments we proceed a little differently from the way described in Chapter 4. Consider the following argument:

> *If the police knew that Jones had a motive for the crime then he would be a suspect. But he is not a suspect, so they obviously don't know that he hated the victim.*

To reconstruct this argument we first need to identify the truth-functional statements and their logical operators. This would give us:

> **If** *the police knew that Jones had a motive for the crime* **then** *Jones would be a suspect.*
> *Jones is not a suspect.*
> **Therefore**, *the police do not know that Jones had a motive.*

But now, instead of numbering the premises and drawing a standard tree diagram, we symbolize the statements to bring out their truth-functional relationships:

If p then q.
Not-q.
Therefore, not-p.

Now, we simply compare this form with the valid argument forms. If it matches one of them then it is a valid deductive argument. Our example has the form of denying the consequent, so we know that it is a valid argument. Note that the tree diagram for each of these valid argument forms is always a T-argument structure, since clearly it is only if both premises are true that they provide support for the conclusion.

When reconstructing deductive arguments, there are two things we need to watch for. First, we must be careful to ensure that the meaning of the component statements is the same each time it appears in the argument. If a statement is used ambiguously in an argument, the argument will not be valid. In the above example, for example, we have changed the wording of the conclusion from *They obviously don't know that he hated the victim* to *The police do not know that Jones had a motive.* In the context of the argument it is clear that these two statements have the same meaning, since hating the victim means that Jones had a motive.

Second, we must be consistent in symbolizing negative statements. A statement such as:

Jones is not a suspect

can be symbolized either as *not-p* or as *p*. If the argument has the form of affirming the antecedent or of a chain argument it is better to symbolize a negative statement simply as *p*. But in arguments whose form is denying the consequent or disjunctive syllogism the negative statements play a special role, and if a negative statement appears in the first premise it should always be symbolized simply as *p*. For example:

If he has an alibi then he is not a suspect.
But he is a suspect.
Therefore he does not have an alibi.

The first premise should be symbolized as *if p then q*. And this means we must symbolize the second premise as *not-q* since it is the negation of the consequent of the first premise. Since the conclusion must be symbolized as *not-p* it is now easy to see that the argument has the form of denying the consequent.

As long as we have correctly identified the form of an argument as valid, then, to repeat the point made earlier, we will know that if its premises are true its conclusion must also be true. Of course, when a valid argument has false premises the guarantee is voided: the conclusion may be true or it may be false, for we have lost our guarantee.

These valid argument forms underlie many arguments we encounter in a variety of contexts. Often they are combined together in the same argument, and sometimes produce quite complex logical structures. Consider the following argument:

> *If we want a healthy economy then we must have a balanced budget, and if we are to have a balanced budget then government funding for social programs will have to be cut back drastically. But if government funding for social programs is cut then the private sector will have to do more to support education, health care and private welfare organizations. So, if we are to have a healthy economy then the private sector must provide much more support for social programs. The question is whether the private sector is willing to provide this support. There is little doubt that the private sector wants, indeed demands, that a healthy economy should be our top priority. Therefore, I am confident that the private sector is willing to do much more to support social programs.*

When we reconstruct this argument we have the following:

> *(1) If we want a healthy economy then we must have a balanced budget.* (if p then q)
> *(2) If we are to have a balanced budget then government funding for social programs will have to be cut back drastically.* (if q then r)
> *(3) If government funding for social programs is cut then the private sector will have to do more to support education, health care and private welfare organizations.* (if r then s)
> *(4) Therefore, if we are to have a healthy economy then the private sector must provide much more support for social programs.* (if p then s)
> *(5) There is little doubt that the private sector wants, indeed demands, that a healthy economy should be our top priority.* (p)

(6) Therefore, I am confident that the private sector is willing to do much more to support social programs. (s)

Is this a valid argument? If the premises are true, must the conclusion be true as well? Even though some of the premises may be false or unacceptable (for example, 2 and 5), this is a valid argument. To show that it is valid, however, requires us to show that it uses only valid argument forms. To do this we first write down the forms of the statements that constitute the argument:

(1) If p then q
(2) If q then r
(3) If r then s
(4) If p then s
(5) p
(6) s

To show the validity of this argument we reason as follows:

(a) 1 and 2 are the premises of a chain argument whose conclusion is *if p then r.*

(b) This conclusion (i.e., *if p then r*) and 3 are the premises of another chain argument whose conclusion is 4. (This means that 4 is validly derived from 1, 2, and 3.)

(c) 4 and 5 are the premises of an argument affirming the antecedent whose conclusion is 6.

(d) Therefore 6 has been validly derived from the given premises.

In other words, if 1, 2, 3, and 5 are true (these are the premises whose truth we are being asked to accept) then we can derive 4 and 6. Therefore the argument is a valid one. If we believe that the premises are true then we must accept the conclusion. On the other hand, if we believe that the conclusion is false, we will have to reject one of the premises.

9.5 Formal Invalidity

Just as there are certain arguments whose strength depends solely upon their form, there are certain arguments whose weakness depends solely upon their form. Such arguments are called formally invalid. A formally invalid argument is one that lacks formal validity; if its premises are true its conclusion may nevertheless turn out to be false. Formal invalidity is not always a crushing verdict on an argument, for many strong arguments (including most strong inductive arguments) lack formal validity. Arguments can be strong even when they are formally invalid, but their strength cannot be the strength of formal validity. The strength of such arguments depends upon their particular content; the premises do provide support for the conclusion but the support does not derive from the logical form of the argument.

However, there are two types of fallacies involving formal invalidity that are worth considering. Both occur frequently in real life, and sometimes it is difficult to recognize them because of their similarity to the valid argument forms of affirming the antecedent and denying the consequent.

1. Fallacy of Denying the Antecedent

If p then q
Not-p
Therefore, not-q

For example:

If the police knew that Jones had a motive for the crime then he would be a suspect. But the police do not know that Jones had a motive. Therefore, he is not a suspect.

The form of this argument shows that it commits the fallacy of denying the antecedent. We can see why this is a fallacious argument by noting that there are other reasons for regarding someone as a suspect besides knowing that the person had a motive. For example, those who had the opportunity to commit a crime are usually treated as suspects. So the fact that the police do not know that Jones had a motive does not rule out the possibility that he may still be a suspect. Thus, the truth of the premises of this argument would be consistent with the falsity of the conclusion, which of course means that the argument must be invalid.

2. Fallacy of Affirming the Consequent

If p then q
q
Therefore, p

For example:

If the police knew that Jones had a motive for the crime then he would be a suspect. And he is a suspect. Therefore, the police must know that he has a motive for the crime.

The form of this argument shows that it commits the fallacy of affirming the consequent. We can see why this is a fallacious argument by noting that there are other reasons the police might have for regarding Jones as a suspect. They may, for example, have an eyewitness who claims to have seen Jones at the scene of the crime. In this case, the fact that Jones is a suspect might not rest on the police claim that he has a motive but on the testimony of the eyewitness. Thus, the truth of the premises of this argument would be consistent with the falsity of the conclusion, which means that the argument must be invalid.

9.6 Self-Test No. 15

Reconstruct the following deductive arguments and determine whether they are formally valid, and, if they are not, whether they are formally invalid.

1. Look, if you buy a new coat you won't be able to buy your text books for next term. And if you don't have the textbooks your grades will suffer. So if you get a new coat your grades are going to suffer.

2. I'm sure it wasn't Ellen who violated the confidentiality of the committee by revealing what took place at the meeting. If she had done that, then she would have harmed herself more than anyone else. And you know what Ellen is like: she would never do anything that was not in her self-interest.

3. I have an appointment to see my doctor this afternoon. He called yesterday to tell me that after consulting several specialists he has decided that surgery would be useless, but he wants to see me today. In general, as I understand it, there are only two treatments for my condition that are likely to do any good: either surgery or a long program of physiotherapy. So I suppose he wants to see me to set up a physiotherapy program.

4. The coach is worried that the football team will lose if it rains during the game next Saturday: he thinks the team doesn't play very well when the field is muddy. But the weather forecast is for sunny weather for the whole weekend. That's good news; it means we will win the game on Saturday.

5. If the Conservatives had won more than 50 per cent of the votes in the 1989 election then they certainly would have gained a mandate from the voters to implement the free trade agreement with the United States. But although the Conservatives won more seats than either of the other parties, they received less than 40 per cent of the popular vote. So they certainly did not have a mandate to implement the free trade agreement.

6. Chris has decided to run for president of the students' council. That's a pity because he is bound to lose. If Chris is going to win the election he will have to be known to a lot of students. But hardly anyone knows Chris.

7. I told you Chris would lose the election. If he had been known to a lot of students then he would have won. But hardly anyone knew who he was.

8. Left-wing radicals talk a great deal about their right to freedom of speech when they are under attack, but are strangely silent when it is the freedom of speech of conservatives that is under attack. If they were really committed to freedom of speech then they would defend freedom of speech whenever and wherever it comes under attack. Their silence when conservative intellectuals like Philippe Rushton are under attack shows that they are not really committed to freedom of speech at all.

9. If this is really question 5 then I must be losing my mind. But this is not question 5, so (thank heavens) I'm not losing my mind.

10. If I have not lost my mind then this must be question 8. This is question 8. Therefore, I have not lost my mind.

9.7 Questions for Discussion

The following deductive arguments may combine two or more argument forms, and may have missing premises.

1. Ken says that he does not have a logical mind: he complains that whenever he hears the word *validity* he goes into a state of intellectual shock. Well, he is just being perverse. Anyone who can pass university-level courses must be able to think rationally, and anyone who can think rationally must have the capacity to reason logically. And Ken is obviously successful in passing his courses. So he must have the capacity to reason logically.

2. *Jay:* There is a rumour going around that Fred is going to resign. This creates a really interesting situation. You see, if Fred resigns then Grace will be promoted to Fred's position. And if Grace gets promoted then Howard is going to be so upset that he will certainly quit. So, if Fred resigns then Howard will quit.
   Alf: But I happen to know that Fred is definitely not going to resign. Therefore, Howard will not quit.

3. If he tells his teacher he cheated he will be punished by the principal. But if he doesn't tell his teacher he cheated he will be punished by his parents. Either way he is going to be punished.

4. Despite the fact that the social sciences must, if they are to sustain their status as sciences, claim to be able to make accurate predictions of human behaviour, it is not surprising that the social sciences have such an abysmal record when it comes to making actual predictions. To predict anything, including human behaviour, one must rely upon a deterministic theory about the causes of whatever behaviour one is trying to predict, whether it is the movements of the planets, a rise in the inflation rate, or an increase in violent crime rates. Therefore, since the social sciences are committed to the claim that they can predict human behaviour, they must rely upon a deterministic theory of human behaviour. But these deterministic theories are false, as can be seen by the following argument. If some human behaviour is genuinely free then it is false that all human behaviour is subject to deterministic laws. But we all know from our personal experience that some of our behaviour is free: every time we deliberate about something, we are directly conscious that what we decide is not determined by anything, but is a decision freely arrived at. Otherwise, we would not waste our time thinking about the matter, and would just let deterministic fate decide for us. So, since we know that some human behaviour is free, we know that deterministic theories must be false. This, of

course, means that the social sciences cannot really predict human behaviour, and their failure to do so should no longer surprise us.

5. In Dostoevsky's novel, *The Brothers Karamazov*, Alyosha tries to persuade his brothers that if God did not exist then everything would be permitted. He means by this that if there is no God then anything we do would be morally acceptable. Alyosha's brother Dmitri happily accepts Alyosha's claim, apparently because he reasons that since there is no God then everything really is permitted. The other brother, Ivan, is deeply troubled by Alyosha's claim. He believes that not everything is permitted, since he is convinced that the slaughter of innocent children is inherently wrong. But he is unwilling to accept Alyosha's claim because then he would have to accept that God exists. He refuses to believe in God because he believes that if God exists, He would not tolerate the slaughter of innocent children.

Chapter 10

Inductive Reasoning

10.1 The Nature of Inductive Reasoning

Inductive arguments are distinguished from deductive arguments by the fact that they lack the ability to guarantee their conclusions. (The ability to guarantee their conclusions, as we saw in Chapter 9, is a defining characteristic of valid deductive arguments.) It will help us to understand the nature of inductive reasoning if we explain this difference in more detail. The ability of valid deductive arguments to guarantee their conclusions derives from the fact that deductive reasoning merely draws out, or makes explicit, information that is already contained in the premises. Consider any formally valid argument and it can be seen that the premises always implicitly contain the information that is stated in the conclusion. Often this is quite obvious, but sometimes it is not. When it is not obvious, however, seeing that the argument is formally valid is the same thing as seeing that the conclusion is implicit in the premises. But if the conclusion is implicitly contained in the premises, then to assert the premises *is* to assert the conclusion. Clearly, then, if the premises are true then the conclusion must also be true. Stating that the conclusion is true is only making explicit what has already been stated in asserting that the premises are true.

But this characteristic reveals the major weakness in deductive reasoning, namely, that its usefulness is limited to exploring the implications of what we already know or assume to be true. Wherever there is an organized body of knowledge or truth-claims – as in science, law, theology, history, mathematics, indeed in any academic discipline – deductive reasoning can generate new knowledge, but this knowledge is always implicit in our current knowledge. Genuinely new knowledge, however, cannot be derived from deductive reasoning alone. When we want to generate genuinely new knowledge we must rely upon inductive reasoning. Almost every increase in scientific knowledge and most new common-sense knowledge is genuinely new and was not implicit in our previous knowledge. The knowledge of the causes of cancer or of how the stock market will behave in the next three months cannot be discovered merely by drawing out the logical implications of our current knowledge. Our current knowledge is indeed necessary as a basis for such discoveries, but it is not sufficient. Genuinely new knowledge can only arise through the use of inductive forms of reasoning. Inductive reasoning is thus much more powerful than deductive reasoning. It can overcome ignorance in a way that deductive reasoning cannot.

But the power of inductive reasoning comes at a price. The absolute guarantee that valid deductive reasoning can provide for its conclusions is beyond the capacity of inductive reasoning: the conclusion of an inductive argument can never be more than probably true. The probability that a conclusion reached through inductive reasoning is true may be very high, and may even approach certainty. But certainty can never, in principle, be achieved. There is only one way of achieving certainty through reasoning, and that is by using a deductive argument. If we want to reach new knowledge that goes beyond what is implicit in our premises, we have to settle for something less than certainty.

The strength of inductive arguments depends not on their form but on their content. Only deductive arguments derive their logical strength from their form alone. This means that we cannot produce a catalogue of logically strong inductive argument forms as we could for valid deductive arguments. There are certain important inductive argument forms, but these forms by themselves tell us nothing about the logical strength of the arguments. To determine the strength of an inductive argument we must always examine its content. For example, as we saw in section 8.2, in order to determine whether appeals to authority are legitimate we have to examine the particular authority being appealed to and the particular claim involved. Indeed, most of the weaknesses described in Chapters 6, 7, and 8 rest upon an analysis of content.

There are, however, three types of inductive arguments that are widely used and that are strong arguments when certain conditions are met. It is useful to examine briefly these inductive argument forms, in order to learn what these conditions are and what weaknesses to look for. If any of these weaknesses is present then the probability that the conclusion will be true is reduced. Each inductive argument form is prone to its own type of weaknesses, so it is important to be able to recognize the form of an inductive argument before assessing it. The three inductive argument forms we will examine all play a significant role in both the natural and social sciences, but they are also frequently and legitimately used outside the domain of science.

10.2 Inductive Generalization

All inductive generalizations have the following form:

> Z per cent of observed F's are G.
> It is probable, therefore, that Z per cent of all F's are G.

For example, suppose we want to know what percentage of students at a particular university believe in God. Clearly, it would be extremely difficult to ask every student at the university whether they believe in God. It is much easier to select a sample of students and determine their religious beliefs, and then to generalize the results to the whole student body. Whenever we use a sample of some population as the evidence from which we draw a conclusion about the whole population, our reasoning will be in the form of an inductive generalization. Thus, our example would be written out as follows:

> *Sixty per cent of students at the University of X who were questioned believe in God. It is probable, therefore, that sixty per cent of all students at the University of X believe in God.*

There are two possible weaknesses in inductive generalizations, both of which pertain to the nature of the sample. The first and most important is that the sample may not be representative of the population it is drawn from. If it is an *unrepresentative* or *biased* sample, the argument is significantly weakened. So when assessing any inductive generalization we should always ask:

(1) Is the sample representative?

In other words, is the sample of observed F's referred to in the premise representative of the entire class of F's referred to in the conclusion? Suppose we had questioned only science students. Would this weaken the argument? Unless we are sure that studying science (rather than economics or philosophy) has no bearing upon one's religious beliefs, we would have to conclude that the argument is weak, since the sample is unrepresentative or biased in a way that might affect the conclusion. In a similar way the sample would be biased if our sample included only graduate students, or only first-year students, or only students who were in the pub on Friday night. Ideally, the sample should reflect the same percentage distribution as the entire student body at the University of X as regards degree program, major, year, grade average, age, sex, place of birth, type of religious upbringing, drinking habits, and marital status, to name a few variables. The more closely the sample is representative of the entire student body, the stronger the argument.

The second weakness that can arise with inductive generalizations is that the sample may be too small, and thus there is a second question we should ask:

(2) Is the sample large enough?

Even if a sample is adequately representative, it may nevertheless be so small that an inductive generalization from it is weak. We might, for example, be fortunate and discover a sample of 20 students who are more or less representative of students at the University of X in general, but the argument clearly would be stronger with a sample of 40 students who were equally representative. In general, the larger the sample the stronger the argument. However, as the size of the sample is increased, the increase in strength becomes smaller with each additional increase in the size of the sample. For example, an increase from 20 to 40 students produces a much greater increase in strength than an increase from 220 to 240. In practice, therefore, we can often work with relatively small samples, especially if the population is homogeneous and we are careful to ensure that our sample is representative.

When an inductive generalization is weak for either of these two reasons it violates the criterion of adequacy. The premises of the above argument are presumably acceptable and are clearly relevant, but if the sample is unrepresentative or too small then the premises will be inadequate to support the conclusion.

10.3 Statistical Syllogism

All statistical syllogisms have the following form:

Z per cent of all F's are G.

x is an F.

It is probable to the degree 0.Z, therefore, that x is G.

In this schema, *x* refers to a single individual. The phrase *It is probable to the degree 0.Z...* is the way statisticians normally express degrees of probability. It means the same as *There is a Z per cent chance that...*

Statistical syllogisms always start from a generalization and use it as the basis for determining the likelihood that it will apply to a particular individual case. Whereas inductive generalizations move from the particular to the general, statistical syllogisms move from the general to the particular. For example, if we want to predict how likely it is that a particular student at the University of X believes in God, we would start with the conclusion of our previous inductive generalization and develop the following statistical syllogism:

> *Sixty per cent of students at the University of X believe in God.*
> *Fred is a student at the University of X.*
> *It is probable to the degree .6, therefore, that Fred believes in God.*

To determine whether a statistical syllogism is weak, it is necessary to look beyond the premises for any other information that might be relevant. The question we need to ask is:

> Is there additional relevant information available concerning x that has not been included in the premises?

For example, if we know that Fred is a regular churchgoer, then it is likely that the chance that he believes in God is much higher than 60 per cent. Or if we know that Fred refuses to go to church even for family funerals or his friends' weddings, then it is likely that the chance that he believes in God is much less than 60 per cent. Or if we know that Fred is a history major *and* that only 40 per cent of history majors believe in God, then it is likely that the conclusion of our argument will be false. Whenever we use or assess a statistical syllogism it is important to ensure that no relevant information has been overlooked.

When a statistical syllogism leaves out relevant information we can usually charge it with violating the criterion of adequacy, since the missing information significantly weakens the argument. In some cases, however, leaving out relevant information will lead to the charge of violating the criterion of relevance. For example, if it is known that Fred has explicitly stated that he is a committed atheist, the appeal to the generalization about University of X students becomes quite irrelevant.

10.4 Induction By Confirmation

Induction can be used to provide support for a hypothesis. A hypothesis is a principle or statement that, if true, would explain the event(s) or situation(s) to which it applies; for example, that Third World poverty is caused by international monetary policies, or that excessive exposure to sunlight causes skin cancer. To test the truth of a hypothesis we follow a two-stage procedure. First, we deduce from the hypothesis a number of *observation statements*. An observation statement is an empirical prediction, or statement that under certain conditions a certain fact will be observed. By deducing observation statements from our hypothesis, we are claiming that if our hypothesis is true then we would expect to find that these empirical predictions are true. We then proceed to the second stage, and make observations to determine whether or not our empirical predictions turn out to be true. If our actual observations agree with the predicted observations, they inductively support the hypothesis from which the predictions were deduced. They provide *confirming instances* for the hypothesis.

The form of such arguments is:

If h then o.
o.
It is probable, therefore, that h.

In this schema, *h* stands for a hypothesis and *o* stands for an observation statement that is logically deducible from *h*. When, as is usual, we have several observation statements, the form would be:

If h then o_1, o_2, o_3, and o_4.
o_1.
o_2.
o_3.
o_4.
It is probable, therefore, that h.

Induction by confirmation is widely used in the sciences, especially in the physical and natural sciences. For example:

> If the theory of general relativity is true, then it follows that light rays passing near the sun will be bent.
> During the solar eclipse of 1919 it was observed that light rays passing near the sun were deflected.
> It is probable, therefore, that the general theory of relativity is true.

Induction by confirmation is also used in other contexts. It is often used for solving such mundane problems as discovering why a car won't start. It is used by doctors when diagnosing diseases. It is also used in criminal trials, where the evidence presented by the prosecution is intended to provide inductive support for the prosecutor's hypothesis that the accused is guilty.

There are two possible weaknesses in inductive arguments by confirmation, and hence there are two questions that need to be asked. The first is:

(1) Is the number of confirming instances relatively high?

One swallow does not a summer make, and one confirming instance of a hypothesis usually does very little to show that the hypothesis is true. It is therefore important to gather a large number of confirming instances before asserting that the hypothesis is probably true. How large this number should be depends upon several factors: the range of different kinds of confirming instances, the scope of the hypothesis (i.e., does it apply to a large or small range of phenomena?), and whether the hypothesis is consistent with other well-established hypotheses. In general, the larger the number of confirming instances the stronger the argument, and the more likely it is that the hypothesis is true. This means that if the number of confirming instances for some hypothesis is relatively small, the argument could be charged with violating the criterion of adequacy.

The second question that needs to be asked is:

(2) Are there any disconfirming instances?

A disconfirming instance arises when an observation statement that is predicted by the hypothesis is found to be false. Unlike the first weakness, which is a matter of degree, the presence of any disconfirming instances does not merely weaken the hypothesis, it refutes it altogether. Any hypothesis will be refuted by a single disconfirming instance. There is an asymmetry between confirming and disconfirming instances in the way that they affect the hypothesis. Each confirming instance adds a little strength to the hypothesis, whereas a single disconfirming instance conclusively refutes the hypothesis.

This asymmetry is important. To understand the reasons for it, we need to recall two of the argument forms discussed in Chapter 9, the valid argument form of denying the consequent and the formal fallacy of affirming the consequent. Since observation statements are logically deduced from the hypothesis, we have to treat *if h then o* as a truth-functional statement. A disconfirming instance, therefore, presents us with a formal argument of the form:

If h then o.
Not-o.
Therefore, not-h.

This is a valid argument because it has the form of denying the consequent. Any disconfirming instance, therefore, entails that the hypothesis is false. On the other hand, a confirming instance presents us with a formal argument of the form:

If h then o.
o.
Therefore, h.

This, however, has the form of Affirming the Consequent and thus is fallacious. Clearly, we cannot rely upon a single confirming instance to prove that a hypothesis is true. It is a mistake, however, to regard induction by confirmation as relying upon an invalid argument. Induction by confirmation is genuinely inductive in nature, as is indicated by the fact that its conclusion is claimed only to be *probably* true. Each confirming instance does add support to the hypothesis by making it more probable that the hypothesis is true, unless, of course, we have one or more disconfirming instances, in which case we must conclude that the hypothesis is false.

In practice, however, scientists do not usually give up a hypothesis merely because of a single disconfirming instance. If the hypothesis is one that seems very promising and fruitful, it is reasonable to look for some other explanation for a disconfirming instance. Perhaps one of the test tubes was dirty, or there were impurities in the acid, or a piece of equipment malfunctioned, or a laboratory assistant was distracted when taking measurements, or any of a hundred other possibilities. If some such explanation seems likely then it is reasonable not to reject the hypothesis. But if a plausible explanation is unavailable the hypothesis should be rejected, since the argument in support of it actually refutes it. Scientists usually refer to disconfirming instances as *negative results*. Although it is disappointing to obtain negative results from one's research it is important to report that fact to other scientists so that they will know that a particular hypothesis has been refuted.

Another way of saving a hypothesis for which there is a disconfirming instance is to revise the hypothesis. Often only a minor revision is needed to save a hypothesis. For example, a hypothesis put forward to explain how a particular disease is transmitted may be saved by adding the qualification ...*at temperatures between 0 and 100 degrees Celsius*. Of course, the original hypothesis has not been saved: the revised hypothesis is a different one, even though the difference is slight. Much scientific research consists of this kind of refinement in an attempt to discover hypotheses that can withstand testing, that is, for which there are a large number of confirming instances and no disconfirming instances.

The method of induction by confirmation should not be regarded as a description of the way in which scientific research is conducted, but as an account of a method of scientific reasoning. If it is regarded as a simple description of how scientists do research it is somewhat misleading. The method suggests that we must have a hypothesis *before* we can make the observations to test it. In fact, many scientists reverse this order. They gather data that they believe might be helpful in explaining some phenomenon, and then attempt to find the hypothesis that best explains the data. There is nothing wrong with proceeding in this way, although it needs to be noted that no scientist would ever set out to gather data without having at least a vague idea of the kind of hypothesis that will explain the data being gathered. But data by itself is scientifically meaningless; it explains nothing. Data becomes meaningful only when it is used to support or reject a hypothesis, and science can only explain phenomena when it can produce a hypothesis that is supported by the data. Thus, induction by confirmation, regarded as a method of reasoning, is still necessary to transform data into a scientific explanation.

10.5 Self-Test No. 16

Indicate the type of inductive argument being used, and assess the strength of the argument by describing any weaknesses.

1.   In order to discover whether people were satisfied with the recreational facilities provided by the City, a questionnaire was included with the tax bills that were mailed out last spring. The results showed that almost 80 per cent were satisfied with the current recreational facilities.

2.   The Ontario Minister of Tourism responded yesterday to recent charges by some resort operators that Ontario provides inadequate facilities for tourists. He claimed that the tourists themselves – about 80 per cent of them – stated that they were satisfied with the facilities provided for tourists, and cited a study conducted by the Ministry last summer, in which questionnaires were distributed to every car with non-Ontario licence plates leaving Ontario and entering the U.S. Approximately eighteen thousand questionnaires were returned. The results showed that 23 per cent were very satisfied and 56 per cent were satisfied with the facilities provided for tourists.

3.   The Career Placement Office predicts that 90 per cent of this year's graduates will find a job within three months of graduation. This is good news indeed for my roommate. He will be relieved to know that even though he will have only a general B.A. with a D average he still has a 90 per cent chance of getting a job.

4.   Recently the Philosophy Department surveyed all students registered in its introductory courses. One of the questions asked students whether they expected that a university education would improve their communication skills, and 88 per cent answered yes to this question. So it seems that 88 per cent of students at the university think that a university education will improve communication skills.

5.   For several years Alfred had been bothered by insomnia. He had a hunch that it was caused by drinking coffee during the evening, so he began keeping a record of when he drank coffee in the evening and whether or not he suffered insomnia that night. After a month he analyzed his records and discovered that on seventeen of the eighteen nights when he suffered insomnia he had drunk coffee after 8 p.m. and on eleven of the twelve nights when he did not suffer insomnia he had drunk no coffee at all. He concluded that it was the coffee that caused his insomnia.

6.   I recently read about a survey which showed that 90 per cent of Americans knew less about the Canadian political system than the average Canadian ten-year-old. Well, there's an American student in my Canadian politics course, and I don't know how he hopes to pass the course when he's that ignorant to begin with.

7.   Those of us who grew up in rural and small town Ontario in the 1940s and 1950s never met or heard of any local communists or even communist sympathizers. If any existed, and according to the press there were a few around, we all believed they must be spies and could be found only in Toronto, Ottawa, or Montreal. But now we are told that during this period one of the largest and most powerful trade unions in northern Ontario was controlled by communist sympathizers. Well, I for one simply don't believe it. I lived through that period and I should know.

8.   Last year both Frances and Rhonda spent six hours a day training with Jim Birkin and followed his special diet, and both made Canada's national swim team. This year I'm training just as hard with the same coach and following the same diet. So I bet I'll make the team.

9.   The Student Union conducted a telephone poll of students to see how much support there was for a fee increase to help pay for new athletic facilities. Every twentieth name in the student directory was telephoned on a weekend. The results showed that only 44 per cent supported the proposal.

10.   The defendant insists that he didn't intend to shoot his wife. But the only conclusion that fits the facts is that he did intend to kill her. If he intended to do it, then he would have purchased the gun ahead of time, which he did. He would have taken her to a secluded place, which he did. He would have arranged an alibi, which he did. He would have had a mo-

tive, which he does. All the evidence you have heard supports the conclusion that he intended to kill his wife, and you should therefore find him guilty of first-degree murder.

10.6 Questions for Discussion

1.   A few years ago, Ann Landers asked the women readers of her newspaper column to send her a card stating which they would prefer: "to be held close and treated tenderly," or to have sex. Of the ninety thousand people who replied, 72 per cent said they would prefer the former. She concluded that most women preferred being held close and treated tenderly to having sex. How strong is this inductive generalization?

2.   Fifty per cent of those who voted in the 1984 federal election voted for a Conservative candidate, presumably because they wanted a Conservative government. Many people concluded from this that 50 per cent of all Canadians wanted a Conservative government. Is this a reasonable conclusion?

3.   It is sometimes suggested that racism is caused by two types of bad inductive reasoning. First, it is argued that racial stereotypes are caused by weak inductive generalizations: racial stereotypes arise because people tend to notice individuals who stand out from the crowd, and then use this sample as the basis for their generalizations about race as a whole. But such a sample is necessarily unrepresentative since it is based only on those few individuals who stand out, that is, who are different. Second, it is argued that individual members of other races are discriminated against because of weak statistical syllogisms: all evidence that an individual does not fit the generalization is ignored. Is this a plausible explanation for racism?

4.   It is clearly unreasonable to argue as follows: *I have known three Irishmen in my life, and all were drunkards with violent tempers; therefore all Irishmen are drunkards with violent tempers.* Why then is it not equally unreasonable to argue as follows: *I have read three Harlequin Romance novels, and all had uninteresting characters and predictable plots; therefore all Harlequin Romance novels have uninteresting characters and predictable plots?*

5.   When medical treatment is unsuccessful and the patient dies or is permanently incapacitated, many people feel that the doctor must be guilty of negligence, and the patient or the family often launches a suit for medical

malpractice. Is this reasonable, given that the reasoning that lies behind all treatment decisions must be inductive in nature?

Chapter 11

Moral Reasoning

Moral reasoning – reasoning that leads to judgements about right and wrong, good and bad, fair and unfair – presents special difficulties. Much of what we have dealt with so far in this book is of only limited use when dealing with moral arguments. The primary difficulty is that the criteria we actually use to assess moral judgements are themselves moral in nature, at least in part. In fact, at first glance it seems that when we criticize the moral judgements of others we are doing nothing more than setting our moral standards in opposition to theirs. You think a progressive income tax is unfair and I think it is fair, and it seems that when we have finished berating each other for being hard-hearted or soft-headed there is nothing else we can say to one another. Certainly, it often seems that there is nothing *rational* that two people can say to each other when they have a moral disagreement. Some people conclude from this that moral judgements are essentially like judgements of taste: I like the taste of parsnips, you can't stand it. As they say, there's no accounting for tastes, and if moral judgements are merely matters of taste then there is no room for rational debate and discussion, and our critical thinking skills will be of no use to us. Is this a reasonable view?

11.1 Moral Judgements and Judgements of Taste

Moral judgements and judgements of taste are obviously similar in some respects. But the suggestion that they are essentially the same rests on a weak analogy, for there are major differences between them. First, their subject matters are quite different. Moral judgements are always about how people *ought* to be treated, either how we should treat others or how others should treat us. Judgements of taste, on the other hand, are always about the kinds of experiences we *like* or *dislike*. Some of these experiences may involve other people, such as playing hockey or having a party, but when judgements of taste involve others they do not involve judgements about how we *ought* to treat them. Judgements of taste, in other words, are nothing more than descriptions or expressions of our feelings, and imply nothing about how we ought to treat one another.

Second, almost everyone believes that moral judgements are capable of being justified, whereas almost no-one believes that judgements of taste can be justified. People may think you are pretty peculiar because you like parsnips, but it would never occur to anyone to suggest that you should be called upon to justify your liking for parsnips. If you were, what could you say? Only that, odd as it may seem, you really do like parsnips. You might add that you like them because of the way your mother used to cook them when you were a child; this does not, of course, justify your taste, it only explains it. In the end, all you can do is to reiterate that you just do like parsnips. Judgements of taste, in other words, are immune to demands for justification. With moral judgements, on the other hand, we always accept, and usually respond to, the demand for justification. I think a progressive income tax can be justified on the grounds that it redistributes wealth to those whose need is greatest, and also contributes to economic growth by increasing demand for goods and services. This justification may not persuade you to change your views, but it is clearly an attempt to provide a justification, that is, to provide reasons in support of my view.

Third, moral judgements, unlike judgements of taste, are always generalizable. What this means is that whenever we make a particular moral judgement (i.e., a judgement about what it is right or wrong for me or someone else to do in a particular set of circumstances), we are committed to making a similar moral judgement about what it would be right or wrong for others to do in similar situations. For example:

> Diane: *I don't see anything wrong with not paying Carl the twenty dollars I owe him.*
> Jean: *How can you say such a thing! How would you feel if someone refused to pay you money that they owed you?*

Jean's question presupposes that Diane's moral judgement can be generalized. Jean is in effect saying:

> *If it is morally acceptable for you not to repay Carl, then it must also be morally acceptable for someone who owes you money not to repay you.*

This is a way of making the point that there is a moral principle involved in Diane's judgement, and that the principle is one that could be applied against Diane in certain (perhaps hypothetical) situations. With judgements of taste, on the other hand, there is no analogous move. If I like Mozart, you might think that I should also like Haydn, but if I don't you cannot turn around and challenge my judgement that I like Mozart. I just do like Mozart and don't like Haydn, and that is all there is to the matter.

These three differences show that the analogy between moral judgements and judgements of taste is very weak. The second difference – that moral judgements call for some sort of justification – is crucially important because the only way to justify a moral judgement is by developing an argument, and arguments are, of course, always open to critical assessment. But what is a strong moral argument? What kinds of premises can we use to defend our moral conclusions? In other words, what premises can we appeal to that will be acceptable, relevant, and adequate?

11.2 Moral Justification

Before looking at the criteria for assessing moral arguments, we need to consider briefly the views of the radical sceptic. Radical sceptics hold that there are no criteria for moral justification at all, and that the belief that there are such criteria is an illusion that is explainable only by reference to some deep psychological need, or to our social and cultural history. (Those who claim that moral judgements are essentially matters of taste are usually radical sceptics.) Radical sceptics present us with a fundamental challenge, for they are in effect challenging us to prove our basic moral principles. The best refutation of this challenge would, of course, be a proof of some fundamental principle of morality, such as the principle that we should always seek to produce as much happiness as possible. If such a proof could be discovered radical sceptics would have to give up their scepticism. However, philosophers have failed to find such a proof despite more than two thousand years of searching. Each "proof" has, on reflection, turned out to be flawed in some way (usually because it begs the question), and thus is not sufficient to refute the radical sceptic. But the fact that we cannot refute radical scepticism does not force us to accept it. For just as no-one has been able to prove that radical scepticism is false, so radical sceptics have been unable to prove that it is true. The fact that philosphers have failed to find an acceptable proof of any objective moral principle does not prove that there cannot be such a principle. Nor does it prove that it is unreasonable to believe in such principles. In fact, the force of the radical sceptic's challenge relies upon the assumption that it is unreasonable to believe in any objective moral principle unless it can be proven rationally. But this assumption is certainly not an obvious truth, and is open to serious objection. There are many fundamental principles of mathematics and science, for example, that cannot be proven to be true, but it would be quite unreasonable to reject them just for this reason.

We thus find ourselves in a dilemma. The radical sceptic cannot prove that objective moral criteria do not exist, and those who believe in such criteria cannot prove that they do exist. The most reasonable response to this dilemma is to ignore it. If proofs are unattainable then we are free to choose between accepting and rejecting objective moral criteria. Ultimately, we must choose between these two views. But this is much more than a choice between two positions or theories: it is also a choice between two attitudes to life. The question we must ask is:

Do I want to lead a life in which moral considerations are important, or a life in which moral considerations carry no weight whatsoever?

To choose the former is to accept some objective moral criteria, to choose the latter is to reject all objective moral criteria and to live one's life entirely on the basis of the preferences of the moment. The fact that in practice virtually everyone chooses to accept some objective moral criteria, even though they do not always act on them, suggests (although it does not prove) that such a life satisfies a deep human need. The important point, however, is that such a choice is not an irrational choice. It may not be required by reason, but neither is it forbidden.

Once we take moral considerations seriously, there are two different types of moral criteria we can use as a basis for justification. Both criteria have long histories, and both are still embraced by almost everyone in virtually every society today. The two approaches represent two basic types of theories about ethics. Theories of the first type (called **deontological** theories) hold that the rightness or wrongness of an action is to be determined by appeal to an objective moral principle according to which actions of that type are right or wrong. The following are some principles that typically function in this way:

Thou shalt not commit adultery.

Never punish an innocent person.

Always tell the truth.

Everyone has the right to freedom of expression.

Theories of the second type (called **teleological** or **consequentialist** theories) hold that the rightness or wrongness of an action is to be determined by appeal to the goodness and badness of the consequences of all the actions open to the agent: the right action is the one which will have the best overall consequences.

Whenever we attempt to justify something we have done or intend to do, our justification inevitably rests upon one or other of these approaches. Either we appeal to some moral principle according to which our action is right, or we appeal to the consequences of our action and claim that they are better than the consequences of anything else we could have done, or we make both appeals together. For example, someone may justify a decision not to cheat on their income tax by appeal to the principle that one should tell the truth, or by appeal to the harmful consequences of cheating, or by both appeals at the same time. Every justification for an action will be of one or other of these types. (It should be noted that justifications are different from excuses, such as that we made a mistake, lost our temper, or were acting under duress. When we plead an excuse we are in effect denying that we are really responsible for the action, and hence do not need to provide any justification.) Once we accept the responsibility for an action and attempt to justify it, we inevitably appeal either to some specific moral principle or to the consequences of the action.

For our purposes we do not need to examine the details of particular theories. To do so would involve us in a number of issues that are of importance for a full understanding of ethics, but shed very little light upon moral reasoning. What we need is an understanding of how each type of approach gives rise to a method of moral justification, how each type can be assessed, and how the two types can come into conflict with one another.

11.3 Appeals to Principles of Right and Wrong

The initial step in justifying a particular moral judgement on the basis of an appeal to a principle of right and wrong is to articulate the principle involved. If we can find an appropriate moral principle, then we will have justified the particular moral judgement. This move is familiar to everyone. In the following examples the word *because* introduces the moral principles that are being appealed to.

> *He should not have killed his severely retarded daughter, because it is wrong to take an innocent life.*
> *It was wrong for the police to use coercion to try to get Martin to confess, because the police ought to obey the law.*
> *Ben Johnson should not have used steroids because cheating is wrong.*

This is also how Jean argued in the example used in section 11.1:

> *Diane should repay Carl the twenty dollars she owes him, because one ought to repay one's debts.*

If Diane accepts this principle she will be forced to accept the particular judgement. The principle thus justifies the judgement in the sense that anyone who accepts the principle must accept the particular judgement.

But conversely, if Diane rejects the principle she will have no reason to accept the particular judgement on which it is based. Does this mean that the justification has failed? Not necessarily. Obviously it has failed to persuade Diane, but this may be Diane's fault rather than the principle's. How, then, are we to defend the moral principles we invoke to justify our actions and judgements? What can Jean say to Diane to persuade her to accept the principle? The most powerful argument that can be used to defend particular moral principles derives from the feature of particular moral judgements we noted in section 11.1, namely, that they can be generalized. This feature reflects what is called the *generalization* principle:

> A right action is one that is entailed by a principle that is acceptable when applied generally, and a wrong action is one that is entailed by a principle that is unacceptable when applied generally.

When this principle is used to defend a particular moral principle, such as *one ought to repay one's debts*, the resulting argument is called a **generalization argument**. There is nothing mysterious about the generalization argument; it is very widely used by almost everyone, and was used earlier by Jean:

> Diane: *I don't see anything wrong with not paying Carl the twenty dollars I owe him.*
> Jean: *How can you say such a thing! How would you feel if someone refused to pay you money that they owed you?*

Whenever the question *How would you feel if everyone did that?* is used, the generalization argument is being invoked. The generalization argument is often expressed as the Golden Rule: *Do unto others as you would have them do unto you.* A more explicit rendering is: It is always wrong to treat others in a way that you would object to if others treated you that way and it is always right to treat others in the way that you demand others treat you.

How is the generalization argument assessed? What are its strengths and weaknesses? To answer these questions we have to examine how such arguments work in more detail. When Jean invokes the generalization argument in the above passage, she is in effect saying that Diane should agree that refusing to repay Carl is wrong because she, Diane, would not agree that others would be justified in using that principle as a reason for refusing to repay a debt to her. Jean is claiming that Diane's refusal to repay Carl must be based upon the principle that it is morally acceptable to refuse to repay one's debts. Since Diane has already implicitly accepted this principle, she can legitimately be challenged to defend it, not just in the particular application where she wants not to repay a debt, but in general. A general defense of the principle requires her to accept the application that others may make of the principle even when it is applied against her. How would she feel if someone refused to pay her money that they owed her?

This argument puts Diane in a bind. On the one hand, if she rejects the principle when others apply it against her then she cannot apply it against others. On the other hand, if she wants to apply it against others then she must allow others to apply it against her. If she tries to eat her cake and have it too, by accepting the principle when she wants to apply it against others and rejecting it when others apply it against her, she is a hypocrite. (It is in circumstances of this sort that the tu quoque argument (see section 7.4.2) can be used legitimately.) To avoid hypocrisy, Diane must choose between the two alternatives: either give up the principle and repay her debt to Carl, or accept the principle and allow others to renege on their debts to her.

The generalization argument does, however, leave room for a counter-argument that, if successful, would allow Diane to escape the dilemma Jean has tried to put her in. Diane might refuse to accept the principle Jean claims is implicit in her judgement. She might, for example, reply to Jean as follows:

> Look, I'm not basing my judgement on the principle that it is always morally accept-able for people to refuse to repay their debts. I accept the principle in general, but there is an exception to it: that it is morally acceptable to postpone repaying a debt if repaying it would cause personal hardship. Repaying Carl now would mean giving him my next week's grocery money. It is a pity, but he is going to have to wait for a few weeks.

Diane's reply shows that she does not accept Jean's generalization of her particular judgement. Diane is claiming that the principle underlying her judgement is different from the principle Jean has attributed to her. Note that Diane is not denying that she must appeal to some principle to defend her judgement; her claim is that Jean has appealed to the wrong principle.

If Jean still wants to challenge Diane's judgement, she has to focus on this new principle. She can argue that Diane faces a new dilemma: if she applies this principle against Carl she must allow other people to apply the principle against her, and if she is unwilling to allow others to apply it against her she cannot apply it against Carl. Unlike the first dilemma Jean posed, the second one is such that Diane could reasonably accept it when others apply it against her. She might respond as follows:

> But I am willing to allow others to apply the principle against me. When I lend money to someone, I do so on the basis that they should repay me only when they can afford to do so. If someone is never able to repay me I would regard it as a kind of donation to a worthy cause.

By acknowledging that she is prepared to allow others to use her moral principle against her, Diane has provided a plausible justification for her initial judgement.

What are Jean's options at this point? She has two. First, she can challenge the sincerity of Diane's claim that she thinks it would be morally right for others to refuse to repay a debt to her if they could not afford to do so. Does Diane really believe this or is she merely saying that she does? Jean might be able to point to another situation in which Diane had demanded repayment of a debt from someone who could not afford to repay her. Diane would then either have to admit she had been wrong to demand repayment (in which case she might be open to another charge of insincerity), or concede that she is now being hypocritical. The charge of insincerity is often difficult to sustain, for we have no direct access to the feelings and motives of others. Jean may suspect that Diane is being insincere, but be unable to find much good evidence to support her suspicions. Even Diane may have to admit that she cannot be sure whether she would be so ready to forgive someone who refused to repay a debt to her: perhaps she is deceiving herself about the kind of person she is. However, the fact that generalization arguments leave us open to possible charges of insincerity shows the importance of ensuring that we should not make such claims unless we really mean what we say.

Second, Jean may challenge Diane's version of the principle she is implicitly appealing to. For example:

But you cannot use that principle unless you make sure that the person from whom money is borrowed realizes that the debt will be repaid only when the borrower can afford to do so. Did Carl know that he wouldn't get his money back until you felt you could afford it?

If Carl knew that the debt would be repaid only when Diane could afford it then Diane can accept this new version of the principle, since it justifies her initial judgement and she can accept it when others apply it against her. On the other hand, if Carl did not know, then Diane faces the old dilemma: either she must accept that it is morally acceptable for others to mislead her when they are borrowing money from her, or she must concede that she is not morally justified in refusing to repay Carl.

The above example has been developed at considerable length because it illustrates the steps that may be involved in attempts to justify a particular moral judgement on the basis of the generalization argument. These steps can be summarized as follows:

(1) We appeal to some general moral principle according to which our particular moral judgement is correct.

(2) We defend the general moral principle by showing that we accept that

it would be morally right for others to follow it, even when it is applied against ourselves.

(3) The claims made in step (2) must be sincere; if challenged, we must be able to make a believable case for our sincerity.

(4) If we are unsuccessful in steps (2) or (3) we must go back to step (1) and look for another general moral principle that will allow us to carry out steps (2) and (3) successfully.

These steps show not only what we must do to develop an adequate generalization argument, but also the kind of challenges we may have to respond to, and how we can challenge a generalization argument put forward by another person. These challenges are, first, that the general moral principle invoked may not be acceptable because the person invoking it does not accept that others are morally entitled to use the principle against him or her (step (2)), and second, that the person's claim to accept the principle may be insincere (step (3)).

11.4 Self-Test No. 17

Suggest two different moral principles that, if accepted, would justify each of the following particular moral judgements:

1.   I refuse to vote for Robinson because he was convicted two years ago for tax evasion.

2.   I think what she did was wrong. I believe she should take her children and move back in with her husband as soon as possible, if he'll still take her back.

3.   I have no sympathy for him. He should have informed the police as soon as he realized they were selling illegal drugs, and if he had to go to court to give evidence at the trial then that's just too bad.

4.   How can you even think of handing in an essay that someone else has written?

5.   All those people who turn up in Canada claiming refugee status, like the boat people a few years ago, should be sent back to where they came from.

11.5 Questions for Discussion

Each of the following arguments appeals to a moral principle to justify a particular moral judgement. What kinds of questions should be asked to determine whether the reasoning is acceptable? If the reasoning is unacceptable, is there another principle that could justify the action or policy?

1. The School Board should ban the use of corporal punishment by teachers. Only parents have the right to inflict physical punishment on their children.

2. We would all agree to condemn someone who inflicted pain on a child simply to obtain pleasure. Everyone agrees that inflicting pain for pleasure is inherently evil, and our condemnation is especially strong when the pain is inflicted on those who have done nothing to deserve it. Those who eat meat can only do so at the cost of great pain and suffering being inflicted on farm animals, both in the way they are raised and in the way they are slaughtered. So there can be no justification for eating meat.

3. It was wrong for Warren to break his promise to Marilyn that she could use his car to drive to her sister's wedding. The fact that he wanted to use his car to visit his mother who was having an operation is no excuse. Promises ought to be kept.

4. The government was right to prosecute the Mohawk Warriors who were involved in the confrontation at Oka, since they clearly broke the law. A state is always entitled to punish those who break its laws.

5. Mrs. Robinson was entirely justified in not informing the police that her husband was involved in illegal arms sales to Iraq, even though she knew he was involved. When loyalty to one's family clashes with loyalty to the laws of one's country, one ought to prefer one's family.

11.6 Appeals To Consequences

Appeals to consequences are much easier to describe. They involve three steps.

First, we must identify the alternative actions open to us in the situation we face. Sometimes there may be only two alternatives: for example, to photocopy a library book illegally, or not to do so. Frequently, however, there are more than two alternatives: for example, to drink a lot, to drink a little, to drink nothing, or not to go to the party at all. There must always be at least two alternatives open to us. Moral decisions are made only when we face a choice: if there is no room for choice then no moral decision needs to be made. But when we are identifying the alternative actions open to us, it is important to ensure that we consider all the options. Failure to do so leaves us open to the charge of committing the fallacy of false dichotomy (see section 6.7.4).

Second, for each alternative we identify the consequences that, so far as we can tell, will result if we performed that action. The consequences for each alternative are then assessed to determine how much good and how much bad each will produce. For example, if we were considering visiting a sick friend in hospital, we would consider the good that would be produced (such as reducing the friend's boredom and preserving the friendship) as well as the bad effects (such as the money spent driving to and from the hospital and the time lost from other activities). It is important that *all* the consequences be assessed in this way. We should not exclude the long-term or indirect consequences, and we should not exclude the effects on any other person. We must consider the good and bad consequences for anyone, anywhere, at any time.

To make such assessments it is necessary to use some criterion of goodness (and badness). There are several possibilities: some philosophers have suggested pleasure (and pain), others have preferred benefit (and harm). Traditionally, the most common approach has been to use happiness (and unhappiness) as the criterion. There are difficulties with each of these, but we shall here use happiness since it comes closest to expressing the idea that most people seem to have in mind when they use this method of moral reasoning. The idea of happiness is a little vague, especially when dealing with borderline cases, and is notoriously difficult to define adequately. But most people are able to use the concept without being puzzled, and as long as we can put up with a little vagueness, it works reasonably well as a criterion.

The third step is to compare the net amount of good produced by each alternative and choose the alternative that produces the greatest net amount of good. The net amount of good is the total amount of good reduced by the total amount of bad. For example, if an action would produce an equal amount of good and bad, the net amount of good produced would be zero. There is, obviously, a difficulty in the idea of subtracting the amount of bad from the amount of good. It suggests that we could actually measure amounts of goodness and badness. This is clearly an absurd suggestion (although not so absurd that no-one has ever seriously proposed it). Fortunately, however, we do not have to measure quantities of goodness and badness in order for this approach to be feasible. If we take happiness as our criterion, we can usually make reasonable judgements about the net amount of happiness that an action will produce. Such judgements do not normally need to be precise: we need only as much precision as is necessary to enable us to make reasonable comparative judgements between the net amounts of happiness produced by the alternatives we are considering. For example, it is not difficult to show that getting drunk the night before a final examination will produce less net happiness than not getting drunk.

These three steps provide us with a method of justifying particular actions. They embody what is usually called the **principle of utility** or the **greatest happiness principle**, according to which we ought always to choose, from among the actions open to us, the action that will produce the greatest happiness of the greatest number of people affected by it. The fact that the appeal to consequences rests upon a principle such as this does not mean, however, that it is really an appeal to a principle of right and wrong like those considered in section 11.3. The principle of utility functions quite differently from principles of right and wrong. When we appeal to a principle of right and wrong to justify an action, it is the fact that the action is covered by the principle that justifies it. It is the nature of the act itself that brings it within the principle and makes it right. When we appeal to the principle of utility, on the other hand, the nature of the act itself is quite irrelevant: what counts are the consequences of the act. The fact that generalization arguments provide justifications for particular *judgements* whereas utilitarian arguments provide justifications for particular *actions* reflects this basic difference between the two approaches.

To illustrate how a utilitarian argument works, let us return to Diane and Jean. Had Jean wanted to challenge Diane on the basis of the principle of utility she would have proceeded quite differently. Instead of looking for a general moral principle that might apply to Diane's action, she would have examined the consequences of the actions open to Diane. If we assume that there are only two alternatives – repaying Carl the twenty dollars she owes him, and refusing to do so – Jean would compare the consequences of the two alternatives in the following manner:

Alternative 1: *Refusing to repay Carl.*
Good Consequences:

- Diane gets to keep the twenty dollars to spend on food.

- Diane avoids the embarrassment of having to sponge a few meals from her other friends.

- Diane's friends do not have to put up with her sponging a few meals.

Bad Consequences:

- Carl has twenty dollars less to spend on the things he wants.

- Carl feels a sense of grievance against Diane.

- Diane may lose Carl as a friend.

- Diane may get a reputation for being untrustworthy.

- Diane may find it much more difficult to borrow money the next time she needs to do so.

Alternative 2: *Repaying Carl.*
Good Consequences:

- Carl gets twenty dollars to spend on the things he wants.

- Diane preserves her friendship with Carl.

- Diane will gain or preserve her reputation as a trustworthy person.

- Diane will avoid having an argument with Jean.

Bad Consequences:

- Diane will have to sponge some meals from her friends.

- Diane may harbour a grudge against Jean for having pressured her into re-paying Carl.

This is merely a sketch of the kinds of consequences that will have to be examined. There could be many more. If, for example, Carl plans to donate the twenty dollars to Oxfam, then Jean will need to take account of the good that this would produce. And making reasonable estimates of how much happiness or unhappiness each of the consequences would produce will depend upon the particular facts of the situation, such as whether Carl is likely to complain to others about Diane's refusal to re-pay her debt.

Appeals to consequences can be criticized in two ways. The first way is quite straightforward. We may be able to argue that certain consequences have been overlooked. For example, someone who appeals to consequences in order to justify longer jail sentences for criminals may be challenged if the effects on the family of the criminal or the costs of building new prisons have been ignored. Such a criticism may not be sufficient to undermine the conclusion, but at the very least it will force a reconsideration of the calculation of the greatest net amount of good. Since the method of appealing to consequences requires us to take *all* the consequences into account, if we invoke this appeal but overlook some of the consequences, we can legitimately be challenged to rethink our conclusion. The second way in which appeals to consequences may be criticized is by challenging the assessment of the goodness or badness of a particular consequence. For example, a particular act may have the effect of making a person or group feel somewhat insecure, but it is not clear whether this should be regarded as a bad effect, and if so how bad it is. There are no easy answers to questions of this sort. They require careful thought as well as discussion with others whose feelings about the matter may be different from our own. In the end, our judgements should always be regarded as somewhat tentative.

11.7 Self-Test No. 18

Briefly outline some of the good and bad consequences of each of the following proposed actions or policies. Include only consequences that are good or bad solely on the basis of the happiness and unhappiness they produce. A consequence that is good or bad because it violates some moral principle should be excluded since it would not be part of a utilitarian's calculation.

1. Submitting an essay written by someone else.

2. Failing to declare five hundred dollars of income on one's income tax.

3. Providing a false alibi for a friend to prevent him from being charged with leaving the scene of an accident.

4. Legalizing the sale of marijuana.

5. Selling non-nuclear arms to right-wing rebel groups in Central America.

11.8 Questions for Discussion

Can a case be made for the following policies or actions solely on the basis that they produce the best consequences?

1. Legalizing the manufacture and sale of alcoholic products without any government regulation or control.

2. Making it illegal for doctors to charge their patients a fee in addition to the fee the doctor receives from medicare.

3. Banning all magazine, radio, and television advertising of alcoholic beverages.

4. Using laboratory animals in research that is aimed at finding a cure for AIDS.

5. U.S. President Bush's decision to launch an attack upon Iraq at the time of the Gulf War.

11.9 Rational Agreement

There can be no guarantee that the use of these two types of argument will produce actual agreement on moral issues. Each type of argument is rational on its own terms, but each allows for different moral conclusions to be drawn about the same situation by two different people. The problem with generalization arguments is that they cannot rule out the possibility that two different people, each of whom argues rationally, will come up with somewhat different general principles. The problem with utilitarian arguments is that they provide no rational way of resolving disputes over precisely how much happiness or unhappiness will be produced in particular cases. What is surprising, perhaps, is that within each approach there is usually substantial agreement in practice. Only rarely will two people reach opposite conclusions about whether promises ought to be kept on the basis of the generalization argument. And in most cases utilitarians will reach agreement on what is the best action.

One of the major causes of moral disagreement is the fact that we can appeal to both types of arguments. Virtually everyone recognizes that both embody an important form of moral reasoning; both carry moral weight. The problem is that, although they often support the same conclusions, sometimes they support opposing conclusions. The generalization argument may lead to the conclusion that an action is wrong, while the utilitarian argument may lead to the conclusion that the action is right. Many of the tough moral dilemmas we face are like this. And many controversial moral issues facing society (e.g., abortion, capital punishment, pornography) arise because the generalization argument tends to support one position while the utilitarian argument tends to support another.

Moral philosophers have long attempted to resolve the fundamental dispute between the two approaches, but this dispute, like the dispute with the radical sceptic, has failed to produce any generally accepted proof that one approach is superior to the other. In the absence of a conclusive proof it is probably best simply to recognize that both approaches are necessary, and that when they clash we have to make the best judgement we can and hope we will not regret it later. We must recognize that human life is inherently problematic, and that what is most important is not reaching provable moral conclusions but taking moral questions seriously and facing them as sensitively and honestly as we can. This may well be the most reasonable conclusion to reach: that the *way* we deal with moral issues is even more important than the moral decisions we make. This does not mean that the decisions themselves don't matter. It does mean that we should strive to develop maturity in our moral thinking. Moral maturity is important because moral decisions require more than rationality, and because we should not allow others to make our moral decisions for us.

11.10 Moral Maturity

We conclude this chapter with a brief description of moral maturity. The material in this section has been adapted from the pamphlet Ethical Discussion in the Classroom, written by the Ethics Research Group, Department of Philosophy, University of Guelph. Be warned, however, that it is not, or not entirely, an empirical description, nor is it simply a description of the way rational criteria apply to moral decision-making. It is both these, but it also incorporates an ethical ideal that may be open to challenge on moral grounds.

Moral maturity is best characterized by describing the qualities that we would expect a morally mature individual to exemplify. These are not necessary conditions, however, for an individual who is deficient in one or two respects could still be morally mature, although less so than someone who embodies them all. It should also be noted that it is an ideal: it is unlikely that anyone could live up to it all the time with regard to every moral decision. But it is a quality that is worth striving to achieve in our lives, and is widely recognized as such throughout Western culture.

The first three characteristics of moral maturity are implicit in what has been said earlier in this chapter, and need only be noted here.

1. Independence of judgement. We make or accept moral judgements only for reasons that we believe can withstand critical scrutiny, and never simply because we accept someone else's authority.

2. Justification by appeal to principles. We recognize that we must always be prepared to appeal to some general justificatory principle (either the greatest happiness principle or some specific moral principle) when called upon to justify our judgements.

3. Generalization of moral judgements. We recognize that what we think is right (or wrong) for one person to do in certain circumstances must be right (or wrong) for any other person to do in relevantly similar circumstances.

There are several other features of moral maturity we have not yet touched upon:

4. Consistency. The moral judgements we make should as far as possible be consistent. There are three ways in which consistency is important. First, our actions should be consistent with our judgements. If we believe it is wrong to cheat on our taxes, then it is immature to go ahead and cheat anyway. Second, there should be consistency between our judgements on different issues. If we believe that it is wrong for baseball players to assault one another during a game, but also believe that it is morally acceptable for hockey players to assault one another, we would attempt to remove the inconsistency either by changing one of our judgements, or by showing that the circumstances of the two sports are significantly different in a way that justifies treating them differently. Third, there should be consistency between the different principles we invoke. If we believe that euthanasia is morally acceptable but that capital punishment is not, we would recognize the apparent inconsistency between the deliberate taking of human life in the one case and the refusal to do so in the other, and would deal with this inconsistency either by changing one of our principles or showing that there is a morally significant difference between the two cases.

5. *Awareness of complexity.* Moral principles (such as *Love your neighbour as yourself, Respect all life, Keep your word, Be just*) typically need to be interpreted and balanced against one another when they are applied to specific concrete situations. How, precisely, are we to respect life? Who, exactly, is our neighbour? And how are respect for life and our neighbours to be balanced against one another when we are in a situation where it is difficult or impossible to do both? A morally mature individual recognizes these elements of complexity and does not pretend that an issue is simpler than it really is.

6. *Getting the facts straight.* A mature ethical judgement is adopted only after all the relevant facts have been taken into account. Since most of the moral issues we face pertain to complex situations, we should refuse to make moral judgements about them until we have gathered all the relevant facts. This is especially true of issues that arise because of developments in modern technology, such as the use of animals in medical research, surrogate motherhood, invasions of privacy by computers and electronic devices, technological aid to developing countries, and a host of similar issues. The very complexity of such moral issues means that we usually have to rely upon the advice of experts in these matters. But our reliance upon experts should be restricted to the factual domain. The moral decisions themselves should, of course, remain our own.

7. *Recognition of our fallibility.* The complexity of many moral issues and the difficulty of knowing that we have taken into account and properly understood the facts makes it hard to be sure that we have made the correct moral judgement on any specific issue, even when we have done our best. Moral maturity implies that we recognize that there is always

an element of personal judgement in our moral beliefs. No matter how confident we feel about a moral judgement we should always be open to the possibility that future reflection may lead us to revise it.

8. Tolerance. Moral decisions are never made in a vacuum. We are affected by the moral decisions of those around us, as they are by ours. If we want our judgements and our reasons for them to be respected by others, then we must respect the judgements and moral reasoning of others. We should therefore be tolerant of those with whom we disagree. Because of our fallibility, not only are we never in a position to claim that we must be right and those who disagree with us must be wrong, but we are always in the position of being able to learn from others, even those with whom we disagree, at least in cases where they exhibit the kind of moral maturity we strive to achieve for ourselves.

These characteristics represent an ideal that is often not fully realized in practice. When we face moral issues that are important to us personally, or that have generated public debate, we find all too often that emotions, bigotry, and prejudice tend to get in the way of reasonable and mature discussion. When ethical discussion falls too far short of the ideal it is extremely unlikely that it will lead either to moral insight or to a genuine resolution of the dispute. This is especially true when dealing with clashes between the utilitarian appeal to consequences and the appeal to moral principles.

11.11 Questions for Discussion

Identify the type of moral reasoning and any weaknesses involved in the following arguments.

1. I have no objection to erotic materials, but I think hard-core pornography should be banned because it legitimizes and encourages violence against women. There are many males in our society whose attitudes to women are deeply influenced by hard-core pornography. It encourages them to think that many women really want to be raped, and that inflicting violence and cruelty on women is both morally and socially acceptable.

   Hard-core pornography is often defended by an appeal to the right to freedom of expression. But surely no-one believes that freedom of expression has no limits. In fact, there are a number of limitations on freedom of expression that everyone accepts: there are the laws against libel and slander, for example, as well as the duty to keep certain information confidential. All I am advocating is that hard-core pornography be added to the list of types of things that cannot be defended by appeal to freedom of expression.

2.   I am opposed to all forms of censorship, including censorship of hard-core pornography. The right to freedom of expression is fundamental in our society, and it is important that it be defended whenever it is threatened. Once we start restricting freedom of expression because of some real or alleged harm we have started down the road to totalitarianism, where the government decides what we should be allowed to think. This is a question of fundamental human rights. If we don't like the way some people exercise their rights, we simply have to put up with it. I wouldn't have it any other way.

    Perhaps some pornography has harmful consequences – personally I find some of it quite disgusting – but even if it is sometimes harmful there is good reason to think that pornography also has beneficial consequences. It allows males to satisfy their sexual fantasies harmlessly in their imaginations. Otherwise they would have to inflict their fantasies upon women. Pornography therefore provides a harmless outlet for men with sick sexual fantasies. Perhaps we need more rather than less pornography to deter those males who now inflict violent and degrading treatment on women.

3   I believe that the law should be changed to permit euthanasia in certain cases. Specifically, I believe that terminally ill individuals who are mentally competent should be free to consent to having their life ended by a medical doctor. There are three reasons why I think this would be a good thing. First, it would make it possible for individuals who are suffering the ravages of some terminal disease to end their suffering in a manner of their own choosing. Second, it would allow these individuals to have the satisfaction of being able to choose to die at a time that they feel is appropriate for them. Third, by reducing the demand for medical services it would allow medical resources that are now devoted to the terminally ill to be used for other kinds of treatments and services that are not now available under Medicare.

4   The legalization of euthanasia is immoral even in strictly limited circumstances. The problem is that once you start euthanizing people there is no

morally significant stopping point. The current proposal is to permit euthanasia only for a terminally ill patient who, while competent, has given his or her prior consent. But now some people are calling for the legalization of euthanasia for those who are severely retarded if their family consents. But having started down this road, why stop here? What about elderly patients who are a burden to their families and who seem not to be enjoying life? What about children who suffer from severe physical handicaps? What about children or adults who are likely to be a permanent burden to society? There is only one moral reason for not employing euthanasia in these and similar cases, namely, that we place an intrinsic value on all human life. But if this is so then we have a compelling reason for not allowing euthanasia at all. In short, if there is a reason to stop euthanizing people at some point, then there is an equally strong reason not to start euthanizing people in the first place.

PART IV

APPLICATIONS

Chapter 12

Arguing Back

In debates and other argumentative contexts we are not usually content to remain passive and merely note the weaknesses in our opponents' arguments. Usually we want to argue back. We may want to help our opponents to see the truth (as we understand it). Or, if we do not know what the truth of the matter is, we may want to pursue the argument in hopes of increasing our understanding and perhaps getting closer to the truth. Or, we may simply want to persuade our opponents of the error of their ways because we don't want them to get away with weak arguments. Whatever the reason, we all want to be able to respond effectively to the arguments of our opponents. In this chapter we examine the main strategies of arguing back against an opponent or an opponent's position.

12.1 Explaining the Weakness

In Chapters 5 to 8 we examined the criteria a sound argument must satisfy, and the kinds of weaknesses arguments may be subject to. In Chapters 9 to 11 we examined certain specific types of arguments and their weaknesses. These chapters provide us with the basic ammunition for arguing back. When we detect a weakness in our opponents' arguments we can point it out, and hope that they see what is weak in their argument. Unfortunately, not everyone we are likely to debate with has studied critical thinking. If we accuse them of relying upon an unacceptable empirical premise or committing the post hoc fallacy, they may not know what we are talking about. If we are trying to convince an opponent who is not familiar with logical terminology, it is usually necessary to explain, and not merely name, the weakness.

A full explanation involves two stages. First, we need to explain the nature of the weakness being charged. It is usually best to begin by explaining the relevant criterion for a sound argument. If a fallacy is being charged it is best to name it only after the relevant criterion has been explained. The purpose of this part of the explanation is to ensure that our opponents understand what we are accusing them of. We should always ensure that our opponents understand the nature of a charge before we try to persuade them that the charge is correct. If an opponent disputes a charge we should immediately attempt to determine whether he or she fails to understand the charge, or understands it but believes we cannot back it up.

The second stage of a full explanation is backing up our charge. This involves reconstructing the argument, supplying missing premises, identifying the logical structure, and so on, in the way described in previous chapters. If done properly, our explanation should convince our opponents that their argument does indeed contain a weakness. An opponent who is unwilling to respond to a full explanation of a weakness in his or her argument is probably not interested in serious discussion, and we should (politely, of course) change the topic of conversation.

We should note here that sometimes it is difficult to decide whether a particular weakness results from violating the criterion of relevance or the criterion of adequacy. We have seen that sometimes an appeal to authority may be irrelevant (for example, when a strict proof is called for) and sometimes it may be relevant but inadequate. Appeals to ignorance are also sometimes difficult to classify. This can be a problem with other types of weak arguments as well. All we can do when faced with this problem is to make the best judgement we can as to which criterion will most clearly explain the weakness of the argument to our opponent.

12.2 Counter-examples

Fully explaining a weakness is a laborious method of arguing back. The method of counter-examples is a short-cut method that is easy to use and can sometimes be remarkably effective. Its use is limited, however, to arguments that rely upon a generalization in the premises that can be challenged as being unacceptable. The method consists simply of presenting an exception to the generalization that shows that it should not be relied upon in the way the original argument does. For example:

Mike: *You should try the wine cooler I just bought. It's really good. It is a new product, just put on the market by the producers, so it's bound to be better than their*

old ones.
Elaine: *Just like the new Coke, eh?*

Elaine attacks the missing premise of Mike's argument, that a new product is always better than existing products, by citing an example of a new product that was (or was commonly believed to be) inferior to the product it replaced.

Here is another example:

John: *I've decided to invest most of my savings in gold and gold-mine stocks. I read a book that came out a couple of months ago, written by a business professor at Harvard, and he strongly recommends gold as the best investment for the next few years.*
Peter: *A few years ago my cousin followed the advice in a book written by a business professor. She invested her life savings in an oil-exploration company and lost the bundle.*

Peter's counter-example responds to the missing premise in John's argument — that all business professors are good investment advisors. The counter-example shows that there are exceptions to this generalization. As long as John gets the point of the counter-example, this is a more effective method of challenging his appeal to authority than a detailed explanation of why his appeal has failed to meet the criteria for accepting an appeal to authority.

Unfortunately, the method of counter-examples usually allows our opponents an easy reply. Since most generalizations admit of some exceptions, an opponent can concede the counter-example but argue that, generally speaking, the generalization still holds. For example, Mike might argue that since most new products are better than existing ones, the new wine cooler is likely to be better than the old coolers. And John might claim that most business professors are likely to understand the investment market better than he does. If Mike and John respond in this way, we will either have to concede that our counter-examples have failed to show the weakness, or undertake the slower process of explaining the weakness.

Here are some examples of the use of counter-examples with differing degrees of effectiveness:

Fred: *I don't see that there is anything really wrong with an occasional extra-marital fling. Everybody needs some variety in their lives. It's like food. I mean, if we had to* eat the same thing for dinner every night we'd soon come to hate it.

Alice: *Does that mean you want to trade in the children for a couple of new teenagers?*

Son: *But, Dad, everybody I know is going to the rock concert. You say it might be dangerous, but it's not. How can it be dangerous if everybody else's parents are letting them go?*

Father: *What about that rock concert last summer where there was a riot and three teen-agers were killed? I'm sure their parents let them go because they thought it wouldn't be dangerous.*

Bruce: *I don't see anything wrong with the school board firing teachers whose moral standards are different from those of the community. After all, the members of the school board are democratically elected in free elections and represent the will of the people.*

Margaret: *That is exactly what they said in Nazi Germany. Don't forget that Hitler was democratically elected in a free election.*

12.3 Absurd Examples

A more effective way of displaying a fallacy is the method of absurd examples. It is similar to the method of counter-examples, but can be used against a broader range of weaknesses, often with devastating effectiveness. It involves constructing an argument that is parallel to the weak argument, but which has true or plausible premises and an obviously false or absurd conclusion. For example:

Bob: *As far as I'm concerned, people who are against teaching scientific creationism in the schools are communists. They are all atheists, after all, and all communists are atheists.*

Carol: *Don't be silly, Bob. That's like arguing that since all men have two eyes and all women have two eyes, all men are really women.*

Carol's reply shows the weakness in Bob's argument by challenging its structure. Both arguments have an identical structure:

All As are Bs.
All Cs are Bs.
Therefore, all As are Cs.

Carol is in effect saying to Bob that if his argument is a good one then so is hers; if he is going to believe that all opponents of scientific creation are communists, then he must also believe that all men are women. Since Bob is presumably unwilling to accept Carol's conclusion, he must either reject his own conclusion or develop another argument to support it.

To be effective, an absurd example must be closely similar to the original argument. The similarity must always involve an identical structure, but it often involves similarity of content as well. In general, the more closely an absurd example resembles the original argument the more effective it will be in showing a weakness. The above example relies on an absurd example with the same logical structure as the fallacious argument. Here is an example that relies mainly upon similarity of content:

> Walter: *I think the government should ban all pornographic publications. It really bothers me to think of all those people reading all that mindless stuff.*
> Will: *Great argument, Walt. And I think the government should ban the* Toronto Sun. *It really bothers me to think of all those people reading all that mindless stuff.*

Will's absurd example is structurally identical to Walter's argument, but its success as an absurd example depends not so much on this similarity as on the similarity of content.

The practical effectiveness of an absurd example depends on more than similarity of structure and content. To be effective the absurd example should use premises that are obviously true and uncontroversial, so that our opponent cannot reject it on the ground that it relies on unacceptable premises. Sometimes, we can get away with hypothetical premises. Will, for example, may not be bothered at all by the thought of people reading the *Sun*, but pretends to be in order to make his point. Of course, Walter might miss the point, and respond by arguing that Will is not really bothered by people reading the Toronto *Sun*, in which case Will's absurd example has failed in its purpose.

The main drawback to the absurd example method is that it is often difficult to invent a good absurd example on the spur of the moment. If we use a poor absurd example we give our opponents a plausible excuse to ignore the serious point we are trying to make, on the ground that we have missed the point of their argument. The greatest strength of the absurd example method, on the other hand, is that it places our opponents on the horns of a very awkward dilemma: either they must accept our absurd conclusion, or they must admit that their argument fails to support their conclusion.

Here are two more absurd example arguments:

Ed: *One of the primary responsibilities of parents is to provide their children with a sound moral education. Religion provides a solid foundation for morality. Therefore, any parent who cares about their children's moral education should give their children a religious upbringing.*

Jean: *Sorry, Ed, your argument is no good. It is just like the following argument: It is a responsibility of architects to design safe and sound buildings. Granite provides a solid foundation for a safe building. Therefore, any architect who wants to design safe buildings should design buildings with granite foundations.*

Ellen: *The main reason I think abortion is wrong is that you can't draw a sharp line between a fetus that is thirty-nine weeks old (i.e., one ready to be born) and one at any earlier stage of its development. Obviously, it would be wrong to kill a baby while its mother is in labour. But if it's alright to kill it at some earlier stage then there must be some point at which you can say, "Up to this point it was not a person, but at this point it becomes a person." But no-one can do this. Fetal development is absolutely gradual from beginning to end. So if you can't justify killing a fetus at the end of its development, you can't justify killing it at the beginning.*

Ethel: *There is something wrong with your argument. You are arguing as follows: You cannot draw a sharp line between when something is hot and when it isn't. When you boil water it starts out cold and gradually becomes hot. There is no point at which you can say, "Up to this point it is cold, but at this point it becomes hot." Bringing water to a boil is absolutely gradual from beginning to end. So if it is hot at the end of the process, then it must be hot at the beginning. So cold water is really hot.*

12.4 Counter-arguments

The final method of arguing back goes beyond the intent of the first three. They attempt to display the weakness of our opponent's argument not by attacking the conclusion directly, but by attacking the way the conclusion is defended. A counter-argument, on the other hand, attempts to show that our opponent's conclusion is false or problematic by constructing a different argument altogether to support a conclusion that is inconsistent with the original conclusion. For example:

Roy: *The state must retain the right to apply the death penalty in extreme cases. I believe that any person who commits cold-blooded, premeditated murder is unfit to remain a member of any civilized community. By their act of denying another's right to life they have renounced their own right to life, and the state is therefore entitled to put them to death.*

Dale: *The trouble with your position is that it brings the state down to the level of the murderer. If the right to life is so important, then don't you think the state ought to show how important it is by refusing to execute anyone, no matter how heinous his or her crime? The real question is whether you want to live in a society where the government from time to time kills some of its citizens.*

Notice that Dale makes no attempt to challenge any of Roy's premises and does not even suggest that Roy's conclusion does not follow from his premises. In fact, she is actually in partial agreement with one of Roy's premises: that there is a right to life. But she ignores Roy's argument and attempts instead to show that the state ought not to inflict the death penalty by appealing to a different set of premises. Every genuine counter-argument has this feature: it ignores the premises of the original argument and presents an independent set of reasons in support of a contrary conclusion.

Every weak argument is therefore open to a counter-argument. In fact, counter-arguments can often be developed against arguments whose weakness we are unable to identify. If we are presented with an argument whose conclusion we are reluctant to accept, there are two possible explanations for our reluctance: (a) the argument is weak, or (b) we are being irrational about the matter. If the argument really is weak, then we ought to be able to describe the weakness in such a way as to persuade our opponent. But if, as sometimes happens, we cannot do so, we would have to concede that our refusal to accept it may be irrational. In these circumstances it can be very useful to attempt to develop a counter-argument. If we can develop a plausible one then we have a good reason to believe that our opponent's argument is weak and that we are not being irrational.

In addition, a good counter-argument can often suggest what is weak about the original argument. In the above example, Dale's counter-argument does suggest a line of attack on Roy's argument. Roy appeals to the fact that murderers have denied the right to life of their victims as a reason for claiming that murderers have renounced their own right to life. Dale's argument relies on the premise that the right to life cannot be lost by anyone, which suggests a way of attacking this sub-argument: she could argue that it violates the criterion of adequacy. We do not as a rule hold that if A violates some right of B's that the state should deny A the same right; that if I, for example, violate your freedom of religion, the state should force me to become a Baptist. Consequently, Roy's sub-argument needs more support in order to be acceptable.

To develop good counter-arguments we have to be familiar with the subject matter under discussion, and we have to care about the issue as well. Counter-arguments cannot be developed merely as a reaction against an argument that looks weak. There are no logical rules for producing a good counter-argument. We have to be sceptical about our opponent's conclusion, which means we should have reasons for our scepticism. It is only on the basis of the reasons that lead us to be sceptical that we can develop a good counter-argument.

Counter-arguments are often found in debates over controversial issues. In fact, in controversial contexts we can most easily see the chief drawback to the method of counter-argument. We are all aware that in debates over controversial matters both sides often seem to pay no attention to the arguments of the other side. Both sides seem content to repeat, over and over again, their arguments (along with their slogans and, usually, a great deal of invective and frequent ad hominems), all the while ignoring the arguments of their opponents. To avoid such juvenile behaviour, we should use counter-arguments not as an excuse to stop thinking rationally about the issue, but as a useful tool for carrying forward a rational enquiry. Not only can they suggest weaknesses in our opponents' arguments, but they can give us a better understanding of the issue. A serious attempt to develop a counter-argument against a given argument, and then to examine the two as dispassionately as we can, will give us a deeper understanding of any complex issue.

12.5 Self-Test No. 19

I. Suggest a counter-example that shows the weakness in each of the following generalizations:

1.   Wealth always increases human happiness, since it removes one of the major barriers to achieving what we want out of life.

2. The function of law is to force people to do what they would otherwise choose not to do.

3. All humour is cruel: people never find anything funny unless it is at someone else's expense.

4. Women have still not been able to achieve real political power anywhere in the world.

5. Religion has always been a force for good in the world.

II. Suggest an absurd example that shows the weakness in each of the following arguments:

1. You might as well save your breath and go peddle your pamphlets somewhere else. I've been a Tory all my life. I was raised as a Tory by my father, and if it was good enough for him then it is good enough for me.

2. I don't think that taking things like pencils and paperclips from the company is really stealing because the company has never threatened to punish anyone for it.

3. If Jim had a steady job, then he'd be able to afford a new car; well, he has just bought a new car so he must have a steady job now.

4. You shouldn't eat any of that stuff. It's deadly. They've proven that it kills laboratory animals when they give them a steady diet of it.

5. My wife always gets my breakfast for me. She's been doing it every morning for fourteen years, so I'm positive she'll get my breakfast tomorrow.

12.6 Questions for Discussion

Suggest a plausible counter-argument against each of the following arguments.

1. The capitalist economic system is superior to any other system. Western civilization has advanced more since capitalism emerged in the late seventeenth century than in the previous two thousand years, and these advances could not have occurred except for the tremendous explosion of

productivity brought about by capitalism. It may not be perfect, but it is clearly superior to all its rivals.

2. Parliament committed a serious blunder in 1967 when it removed attempted suicide from the Criminal Code. Until then it had been a criminal offence for anyone to attempt to commit suicide. The value of the old law was not that it made it possible for the courts to punish those who were so disturbed or depressed that they wanted to end their lives. Its value was that it gave the police the right to apprehend someone who was threatening to take his or her own life. The way things are now, if the police find someone threatening suicide they cannot interfere, for the person is doing nothing illegal. And since most people who threaten suicide are really pleading for help, we should have a law that permits the police to interfere first and ask questions later.

3. Teachers in primary and secondary schools should avoid introducing any controversial political or ethical issues into the classroom. Such discussions tend to be divisive and to create friction among students. They lead many parents to feel that the school is subverting their authority as parents. And they allow teachers to abuse their authority and to impose their values upon their students.

4. Each year, *Maclean's* magazine publishes a ranking of Canadian universities. One of the criteria used is the grade average of students entering first year. This is an absurd criterion when used as a basis for determining the quality of a university. It is like determining the quality of a judge on the basis of the seriousness of the cases heard by him or her. The quality of a university should depend not on the quality of entering students, but on what happens to them after they arrive.

5. Most Western governments are willing to negotiate with terrorists to obtain the release of hostages or to achieve other goals. This is an ill-advised policy. What governments should do is to announce that their policy will always be to refuse to negotiate with terrorists under any circumstances, and then to adhere rigorously to this policy. They should inform all their citizens that this is their new policy and that those who travel abroad should not expect the government to negotiate for their release should they be taken hostage by terrorists. Once terrorist groups realized that a government was serious about its refusal to negotiate under any circumstances, they would realize that their terrorist acts were useless, or even

counter-productive. They would be forced to cease their terrorist acts, and fewer people would suffer as a result.

6.   Government spending on the arts is wasteful and should be abolished. If some particular artists or poets or singers are recognized as good by enough of the public they will be able to make a decent living by selling their books or giving concerts, in which case they don't need government hand-outs. But if they can't make a decent living it must be because not enough people think they are good enough to buy their books or go to their concerts. In this case, there is no justification for subsidizing artists who are regarded by Canadians as second best. So all support programs for the arts should be eliminated.

Chapter 13

Irrational Techniques of Persuasion

In this chapter we consider a variety of irrational devices that are commonly used as persuasive techniques. Several of these have already been touched on earlier, but are repeated here in order to give a more complete picture of these techniques. Some logicians treat these devices as fallacies, on the ground that they are used in attempts to persuade us of something, and thus at least pretend to supply a reason for us to accept it. However, if we treat them as fallacies we would be obliged to reconstruct an argument from the passages in which they occur, which is often difficult and usually violates the principle of charity. It is usually better to treat them not as arguments at all, but merely as irrational techniques of persuasion. In fact, their success frequently depends upon their *not* being used in an explicit argument, since once the argument is spelled out the weakness becomes glaringly obvious.

13.1 Loaded Terms

We saw in section 3.6 that many words have both a descriptive and an evaluative meaning. A group of rebels may be called freedom fighters or terrorists, or just plain rebels. All three terms have more or less the same descriptive meaning, but their evaluative meanings are quite different: *freedom fighter* has a positive evaluative meaning, *terrorist* has a negative evaluative meaning, while *rebel* has no (or a neutral) evaluative meaning. The first two of these — *freedom fighter* and *terrorist* — are frequently used as loaded terms. A **loaded term** is any term with a clear descriptive meaning and a positive or negative evaluative meaning, that is used in an attempt to persuade us to accept the evaluation conveyed by the term. Thus, anyone who wants to create support for a group of rebels can do so by always referring to them as freedom fighters, just as anyone who wants to create opposition to them can do so by always referring to them as terrorists.

Loaded terms are most effective in a context where the audience is not already committed to accepting or rejecting the evaluation carried by the loaded term, and where this question is *not* being discussed explicitly. In such situations people can more easily accept the loaded term because it sounds like it is a purely descriptive term. How many terrorists are there? How well armed are the terrorists? Do the terrorists have support from outside the country in which they operate? These are all empirical questions which do not explicitly raise the ethical question of whether or not the rebels should be supported. But after a discussion of such factual questions in which we become accustomed to referring to the rebels as terrorists, when the ethical question is finally raised we can easily find ourselves placed in a position where we *seem* to be committed to opposing the rebels. After all, terrorism *is* the kind of thing one ought to oppose, so the ethical question already seems to have been answered. In the same way, had we become accustomed to referring to the rebels as freedom fighters then, when the ethical question is finally raised, we *seem* to be committed to supporting the rebels. After all, freedom *is* the kind of thing one ought to support. In this way loaded terms can prevent us from making explicit value judgements, because the loaded term makes the judgement for us without our realizing it.

Advertisers are well aware of the fact that loaded terms can force value judgements upon the unwary. A company uses the slogan, *Seventy-five Years of Service to Canadians*; the fact that the company has been in business for seventy-five years means that it is not a fly-by-night outfit, but the phrase *Service to Canadians* suggests an affinity with service organizations such as the Red Cross. A blatant use of loaded terms sometimes occurs in naming certain products or even companies. A detergent is called *Joy* in an attempt to make us think we enjoy it. A car rental company is called *Budget* to suggest that it has low rates. But loaded terms are used in many contexts besides business. We are all aware of the impact of racist terms (e.g., *wop, kike, nigger, chink*) and of other derogatory terms (*pinko, fascist, nerd, shyster, egg-head, bleeding heart, yuppie, book-worm, jock*). Fortunately, most of these terms are so blatantly evaluative that they are unlikely to persuade anyone who is not already prone to accept the evaluation carried by them.

A loaded term must have both a clear evaluative meaning (positive or negative) and a fairly specific descriptive meaning. It is the *descriptive* adequacy of the use of the term that makes it possible to insinuate the evaluative meaning. Once we accept the descriptive adequacy of the term we are more likely to accept its evaluative meaning as well. It should be noted, however, that some evaluative terms, such as *good, evil, right*, and *wrong*, lack a descriptive meaning, and therefore cannot function as loaded terms. They are pure evaluative terms (i.e., they have no specific descriptive meaning) and thus can be used in almost any context, since there is no descriptive meaning to determine their correct use.

13.2 Vague Terms

In section 3.2.1 we distinguished vagueness from ambiguity on the basis that a vague sentence lacks a precise meaning, whereas an ambiguous sentence has two or more different but usually quite precise meanings. We noted that although vagueness is often acceptable it should sometimes be criticized: in particular, it should be criticized in contexts where greater precision is needed. The fact that a vague sentence lacks a precise meaning makes it possible for vague language to be quite misleading. A vague sentence has a large number of possible meanings, and often some of these possible meanings will make the sentence true while others will make it false. As a result we usually recognize that a vague sentence is true on at least one possible interpretation (i.e., that it is partly, or in some sense, true), and if we are not careful we can be led to think that it is also true on other interpretations, when in fact it is false. For example:

What I admired most about Ernest Hemingway was that he was larger than life.

The phrase *larger than life* is exceedingly vague. There are several different meanings we might give to it. It might mean that Hemingway was unconventional in his personal life. In this sense the claim would be true. On the other hand, it might mean that he was a creative genius, or that he gave us profound moral insight into the human condition. But on these interpretations the claim may well be false.

Vague language can thus be used to persuade us to accept something that is either false or problematic. This technique is much used by advertisers, politicians, and others who want to persuade us to do something that we would be reluctant to do if we thought carefully about it. It is commonly used in slogans of all sorts. For example:

Vote Jones – The People's Choice.

Coke Is The Real Thing.

Canadians want a leader who is human, who knows what it is to struggle, to have ups and downs, and who has compassion for the tribulations of ordinary people.

13.3 Loaded Questions

A question is not an argument and not even a statement, so it may be difficult to imagine how a question can be a technique of persuasion. Nevertheless, questions can sometimes suggest something in a way that may be persuasive. Sometimes the suggestion is explicitly contained in the question itself. For example:

Have you stopped beating your wife?

The form of the question requires a yes or no answer, but both answers involve the admission that you used to beat your wife. If you answer yes, you are admitting that you used to beat your wife, but no longer do so. If you answer no, you are admitting that you used to beat your wife and still do so. In either case you have admitted that you used to beat your wife. Such questions are called **complex questions** because they contain an assumption that both possible answers will confirm. Complex questions thus are a way of making a claim without appearing to do so. The only way to respond to a complex question containing a false assumption is to refuse to answer it in the form in which it has been asked, and to challenge the assumption directly.

Here are some more complex questions:

Is your sister still as moody as she used to be?

Are you opposed to the practice of broadcasting pornographic programs on television during prime time?

Has the U.S. lost its reputation as guardian of the free world?

Did the government lose the election because they were incompetent or because they were arrogant?

There are other more subtle ways in which questions can make suggestions. The context in which questions are asked normally suggests that the questioner believes that there is no obvious answer to the question. As a result, if someone asks a question that has an obvious answer the audience will tend to assume that the questioner has a plausible reason for believing that the obvious answer is false. Suppose a newspaper prints an article under the headline *Does The Premier Have A Secret Swiss Bank Account?* Even if the article makes no allegations, but merely describes how the reporter, despite a thorough investigation, failed to turn up any hard evidence that the Premier does have a secret Swiss bank account, the unwary reader will suspect that the newspaper had some grounds for asking the question. Simply by asking the question the article suggests that the Premier is the sort of politician who would do that sort of thing, and the fact that no proof was found may only show that the reporter has not found it yet.

Any allegation can be turned into a question, and even if the answer is no a suspicion that the allegation is true will remain. After all, if someone thought the question was worth asking, it is natural to assume there must have been some reason to think that the implied allegation might have been true, even if it turns out to be false. In some situations, the taint of suspicion will remain no matter how much evidence is produced to refute the implied allegation. Public figures are especially vulnerable to suspicions created through the adroit use of loaded questions, but the technique can be applied to anyone. For example:

Do you suppose he tries so hard to be macho because he is secretly afraid of impotence?

Was that essay really your own work, or did you crib it?

Is she just reacting emotionally to the situation, or has she actually sat down and thought it through?

Did you steal my Chemistry notes?

How long is it going to take before you learn to take some responsibility for your actions?

13.4 False Confidence

People are often willing to accept a claim if the speaker presents it with great confidence. The confidence can be conveyed both by the choice of words and by the manner in which they are expressed. If the speaker is genuinely confident of the truth of the claim then presenting it with confidence is quite appropriate. But if a questionable claim is presented with confidence the audience can be misled into thinking that it cannot seriously be questioned. For example:

> *I certainly don't want to suggest that all adopted children are miserable, but the fact is that a majority of adopted children do suffer from a serious problem of self-identity, and that the problem is most serious during their teenage years.*

Is this claim true? It is certainly plausible, but in the absence of solid empirical evidence one could just as plausibly claim that it is false. But if it is asserted in a confident tone of voice, and in a way that suggests that everyone who knows anything about adoption would know that it is true, most people will be inclined not to challenge the speaker. They will believe that it is probably true.

False confidence is different from deliberately telling a lie. Of course, if a lie is to be convincing the liar must tell it with confidence, so in a sense lying does require that the liar present false confidence. But we are here describing a different technique, one used by those who believe that what they are saying is true, but who want their audience to accept the claim without critical scrutiny. It is a way of suggesting, rather than saying, to the audience that there is no need to ask for the evidence. It suggests that anyone who did ask for evidence would only reveal their ignorance or naivety.

The effectiveness of false confidence in persuading an audience to accept a claim depends in large part upon the plausibility of the claim being made. No amount of false confidence would persuade most of us to accept a claim that flies in the face of common sense or is inconsistent with what we strongly believe to be true. For example:

> *Mongolian peasants use a method of predicting the sex of unborn children, that is accurate more than 95 per cent of the time. On a night when there is a full moon, the father spits into a cup of the mother's urine and leaves it on the doorstep of their hut overnight. If the spit is still floating the next morning the baby will be a boy.*

No matter how confidently such an assertion is made, most of us will refuse to believe the accuracy of this method of predicting the sex of unborn children. We have good reasons for believing that such a claim is inherently problematic, and are unlikely to accept it without strong evidence. But if the claim is one we think could well be true, and especially if we think the speaker just might know something we don't, we can be taken in by the speaker's confidence.

It is not clear why so many people seem willing to accept any plausible claim if the speaker presents it confidently. It may be out of a sense of politeness: not to accept the claim is to suggest that the speaker is ignorant or dishonest. It may be that many people are afraid they may be called upon to present evidence and arguments to defend their scepticism, which they may be unwilling or unable to do. Or it may be a naive belief that most people never seek deliberately to mislead others. Whatever the reason, false confidence can frequently be very effective in persuading people to accept something without supporting reasons.

13.5 Selectivity

Many judgements rest upon a complex body of evidence. Inductive generalizations, as we saw in section 10.2, rest upon a number of particular instances, and their strength depends upon these instances being a representative sample of the entire population; and since populations are not usually homogeneous we can be misled by an unrepresentative sample. This fact makes it possible for someone to create a misleading impression by bringing unrepresentative examples to our attention. Suppose, for example, we disapprove of the Canada Council's policy of giving grants to artists. Without presenting arguments against the policy, we can attempt to discredit it by looking for examples where the grants have been abused and mentioning them to anyone who will listen. We say nothing that is false, we make no claim that grants are always or usually abused, we present no arguments against the policy; we merely point out every abuse whenever we find one.

Presenting unrepresentative facts will mislead only when the audience is not aware of all the evidence. It may be that in 99 per cent of cases there is no abuse and that the policy is achieving its goal, but most people are unlikely to know this and will gain the impression that the grants are systematically abused. A rational response to such selectivity would be to ask for evidence that would show what percentage of grants are abused and how the abusers are dealt with, as well as to ask for evidence of the social and cultural benefits produced by the grants, for this is the kind of evidence we would need to pass judgement on the policy. But people who are deliberately selective in the facts they present usually want to avoid presenting such evidence, which is why they are usually careful to avoid even the appearance of presenting an argument. If they say, *Here is my evidence and here is my conclusion*, someone is sure to challenge the evidence, which will defeat the purpose of being selective.

The news media are frequently criticized for being selective in their approach to the news. Often the criticism is deserved, especially when the particular newspaper or television station has a strong political or ideological commitment. Stories that reflect favourably upon their cause are given prominence, and those that do not are ignored or relegated to the back pages.

Of course, if selectivity occurs in an argument the argument would violate the criterion of adequacy. Most often it would involve both of the weaknesses discussed in section 10.2.

13.6 Misleading Statistics

One of the more insidious types of selectivity involves the selective use of statistics. An extensive knowledge of statistics would be needed to be able to recognize the many different ways in which statistics can mislead, and we can here describe only a few of the more common types of misleading statistics.

It is often useful to know the average value of something. We may, for example, want to know the average grade for a course, the average grade of a student, the average wage paid by a company, the average rent for a one-bedroom apartment, or the average summer temperature in Australia. But averages can be quite misleading. Suppose we are told that the employees of a company earn an average of $500 per week. This is a quite respectable wage, and we would not have a great deal of sympathy if the employees complained of being seriously underpaid, since we would assume that most employees must be receiving around $500 per week. But this need not be so. Suppose the company has eleven employees who are paid as follows:

General manager:	$1,200
Sales manager:	1,000
Production manager:	1,000
Office manager:	900
Worker 1:	210
Worker 2:	210
Worker 3:	200
Worker 4:	200
Worker 5:	200
Worker 6:	200
Worker 7:	180
Total	5,500

The average weekly pay is $500, but no employee actually receives $500 per week or anything close to it. In such a case most people will be misled by references to the average wage.

To avoid such misleading averages, statisticians make use of two related concepts that help to give a more accurate picture than a simple average. The **median** is the middle point in the range: half the individual cases will be above it and half below it. In the above example, the median is $210. The **mode** is the particular value that occurs most frequently. In the above example, the mode is $200. The median and the mode are quite different from the simple average, or **mean**, as it is called by statisticians.

A second way in which statistics can mislead is when they are used to describe quantitative changes, such as increases or decreases in prices, productivity, crime rates, and so on. The problem lies in an ambiguity in the way such changes are described. If a merchant buys an item for $6 and sells it for $10, what, in percentage terms, is the merchant's profit? Calculated as a percentage of the merchant's *buying* price, the profit is 66.6 per cent. But calculated as a percentage of the *selling* price, the profit is only 40 per cent. Both methods of calculating the merchant's profit are legitimate, but they are different and mean different things. If we are told that the mark-up used by a merchant is 50 per cent, we can be misled unless we know which method is being used. Similar problems can arise in a variety of other contexts. If a landlord says the rent on a $600 apartment has increased only 25 per cent in the last five years, does this mean the rent went from $480 to $600 (because the rent has increased by 25 per cent of the original rent of $480) or from $450 to $600 (because the rent has increased by 25 per cent of $600 from the original rent of $450)? If a friend brags about having increased his or her semester average 10 per cent last semester, did it jump from 60 per cent to 70 per cent or from 60 per cent to 66 per cent? In each case, in order not to be misled we should ask, *Percentage of what?*

A third way in which statistical information can be misleading is when it is presented as a graph. Once again, the actual statistical information is not false: the problem is that it can easily be misunderstood if we do not pay careful attention to how it is being presented. The two graphs shown below present identical information about the increase in the price of a commodity over a one-year period.

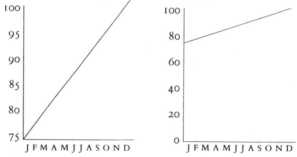

The graph on the left makes it appear that there has been a much more dramatic price increase than the graph on the right, even though both present *the same information.* The graph on the left suggests a greater increase because the bottom three-quarters of the graph has been cut off. The line looks different only because the vertical axis is drawn to a different scale. When interpreting any graph, we should always take into account the scale.

13.7 Humour

There is nothing wrong with using humour in a discussion. In fact, if a discussion starts to become boring a little humour can be a very good thing. Every good public speaker knows the value of a good joke or a witty comment. For example:

> You've heard of the definition of a philosopher as a blind person in a dark room searching for a black cat that isn't there? Well, a theologian is the person who finds the cat.

When I read what drama critics have to say about my work, I am reminded of Bren-
dan Behan's comment that critics are like eunuchs in a harem: they know how it's
done, they've seen it done every day, but they're unable to do it themselves.

There are, however, limits to the purposes for which humour can legitimately be used. In particular, it should not be used as a substitute for rational argument. In argumentative contexts, the use of humour is always
rationally irrelevant. When we use humour to divert attention from a
weakness in our argument, or to have some fun at the expense of our
opponents, nothing rational has been achieved. If our argument was
weak before we added some humour, it will be just as weak after.

The effectiveness of humour as a persuasive device depends, of
course, upon the views and prejudices of the audience. If the audience is
sympathetic to our opponent our attempts at humour may backfire, and
make us look mean and petty. If our jokes are too cruel they may create
sympathy for our opponent. And if the audience feels that it is also a tar-
get our humour may create hostility towards us.

But humour is not always used as a substitute for rational argument. It
can be used to make a rational argument more effective. For example:

Mr. Speaker, the Minister is still refusing to act on the unanimous recommendations of
his own officials as well as several independent experts regarding the leakage at the PCB
dump in my constituency. Everyone who has examined the situation agrees it constitutes
a serious health hazard to the twenty thousand people living nearby. But when asked by
a reporter yesterday what he was going to do about it, the Minister talked at great length
about consulting all the interested parties. This is a totally inadequate response. As
usual, the Minister's mouth is in high gear and his brain is in neutral.

In the face of unanimous recommendations regarding what to do about
a serious health hazard, the Minister's response certainly seems totally inadequate. The humour helps to make this point in a more effective
manner, even though it adds no logical or rational strength to the argument.

13.8 Red Herring

When responding to a criticism of some position we hold, it is often
tempting to ignore the criticism and launch a counter-attack on our opponent by raising a different issue altogether. When we do this we have

introduced a **red herring**. We are attempting to avoid a criticism by shifting the discussion to a new topic on which we can attack the critic. This device is regularly used by politicians when responding to attacks by opponents. For example:

> Opposition member: *Will the Minister tell the House why nothing has been done to clean up the mercury poisoning in the Kenora area, eighteen months after it was brought to his attention?*
>
> Minister: *The Honourable Member sounds like a broken record with his constant carping about health hazards. The fact is that my Ministry has been extremely successful in reducing, and in many cases eliminating, environmental pollution across this province. Our record is vastly better than the previous government's record.*

The Minister has clearly not responded to the question at all, but has attempted to shift the discussion to the government's record of pollution control in general to avoid having to answer the question that was asked.

It is important to realize that there is nothing wrong with attempting to shift a discussion from one topic to another. Many discussions ramble naturally from topic to topic; as we get tired of one topic we move on to something else that is more interesting. Shifting topics is only illegitimate when the shift is introduced in an attempt to avoid a criticism.

Here is another example of a red herring:

> *Critics of the automobile industry frequently claim that our cars are not as safe as they could be. One critic has even suggested that we are criminally negligent because of our failure to produce safe cars. What these critics so conveniently forget is that cars do not cause accidents. Accidents are caused by bad drivers. We co-operate with governments in promoting safe driving, and have taken numerous initiatives ourselves. We are not sure why our campaigns have been so ineffective. If we thought that spending more money on promoting safe driving would help we would gladly do so, but no-one knows what type of campaign would be most effective. This is where the critics could actually do some good, if they were to help us discover how to promote safe driving habits.*

13.9 Guilt By Association

One way of attacking an opponent or an opponent's position is by suggesting a similarity with another person or position that the audience regards in an unfavourable light. In a debate on the government's policy of attempting to create a sense of national unity, for example, someone might say:

So what you are really advocating is a system like they had in Nazi Germany where the Propaganda Ministry attempted to foster a national ideology.

Such a comment is an attempt to create the same kind of hostility towards the government's policy that people feel towards Nazi Germany. It suggests that the policy is a totalitarian or fascist idea that ought to be rejected out of hand.

Guilt by association involves a faulty analogy. In fact, the analogy is usually so faulty that if it were presented as a serious argument its weaknesses would be immediately apparent and the purpose of drawing the analogy would be defeated. Here are some more examples of attempts to establish guilt by association:

We should never forget that the politicians who gave us medicare in Canada borrowed the idea from the communists, who first introduced medicare in the 1920s.

So, you are driving a BMW now. I guess you will soon be sending your children to private schools, like all the other yuppies.

13.10 Persuasive Redefinition

An especially effective device for changing attitudes is what is called **persuasive redefinition**: the redefinition of a familiar term or phrase that has both a descriptive and an evaluative meaning in such a way as to change its descriptive meaning while keeping its evaluative meaning the same. Consider the term *poet*: the dictionary defines a poet as "a writer of verse, especially one possessing high powers of imagination, expression, etc." This is the term's descriptive meaning. It also has a strong positive evaluative meaning: to describe someone as a poet is normally to praise him or her. If we wanted to capitalize on this evaluative meaning we might try a persuasive redefinition that involves dropping the requirement that a poet actually has to write verse: *A poet is a person with a deep and vivid imagination.* Given this definition, we could describe someone as a poet (and hence praiseworthy) who has never actually written a poem. If we are challenged, we could claim that we are not using the word in its ordinary or vulgar sense, according to which anybody who can scribble a rhyme would count as a poet, but rather in the true sense of the term. The *essence* of being a poet, we might say, is having a deep and vivid imagination. In other words, we attempt to justify shifting the descriptive meaning by claiming that our new definition is superior because it is *truer*. In fact, of course, such definitions are not usually superior at all, but only different, and, if judged as reportive definitions, wildly inaccurate.

To be effective, a persuasive redefinition must not change the descriptive meaning too much, or else the audience will see the trick and not be fooled by it. If someone tried to redefine the term *intelligence* to mean the ability to use words of more than two syllables, no-one would take the attempt seriously. But where the change preserves some of the original descriptive meaning it may be harder to detect. A definition of intelligence as the ability to perform mental calculations quickly is closer to the original descriptive meaning and hence could be more successful as a persuasive redefinition. People who are good at doing mental calculations might well want to redefine intelligence in this way in order to attract the admiration that intelligence usually evokes.

Persuasive redefinitions are always stipulative, since the new descriptive meaning always differs from the original descriptive meaning to a certain extent. What distinguishes a persuasive definition from an ordinary stipulative definition is its purpose, for it always seeks to retain the original evaluative meaning. Most stipulative definitions are indifferent to the evaluative meaning of the term.

To illustrate the process of persuasive redefinition, let us consider an historical example. In the 1920s the term *fascist* came into use as a name for a political movement in Italy. It was strongly nationalistic and anti-communist, and placed great emphasis upon the role of a leader in expressing the spirit of the people and furthering the traditional values of the society. Similar movements in Germany and elsewhere also came to be referred to as fascist. Originally, the term lacked any clear evaluative meaning: people in many countries considered fascism as a serious political alternative, and many well-meaning people adopted a number of fascist views. The events of World War II, however, gave the term a strongly negative evaluative meaning. With the defeat of fascist regimes in Germany and Italy, one might have expected the term to fall into disuse. In fact, it has become an accepted part of our political vocabulary, probably because a number of influential political writers wanted to preserve it as a term of abuse. To do so, however, its original descriptive meaning had to be revised to take account of the fact that the original fascist movements no longer existed, and it now refers to any government with totalitarian or racist policies. The original descriptive meaning has largely, although not entirely, disappeared.

13.11 Self-Test No. 20

Identify the irrational techniques of persuasion used in the following passages.

1. So the city of Ottawa has launched an advertising campaign to attract tourists. It reminds me of the time when a Toronto newspaper had some kind of contest: first prize was a weekend in Ottawa, and second prize was a whole week in Ottawa.

2. We take great pride in our products. We've had over eighty years of experience making furniture and we've learned how to balance the highest standards of craftsmanship with a range of styles to suit the tastes of the modern consumer.

    And our customers agree. When people walk into our showrooms the words we hear most frequently are, *Ah, that's what I've been looking for!*

    Pardon us if we're smug. We are the best, and can't see why we shouldn't brag about it.

3. Frankly, I don't think it matters whether pornography is harmful to women or not. We live in a pluralistic society in which there are many different voices, all of which are entitled to be heard. Silencing opinions and points of view that some group doesn't agree with goes against what this country stands for.

4. What is Adam like? Well, he's kind of hard to describe. He's basically just a neat guy: lots of personality, sort of laid back, the kind of person you would like.

5. If you are one of the minority of wage earners over thirty who don't have the protection an RRSP provides, you should be asking yourself, *Why do I keep putting it off?*

6. Remember, the next time you're in the market for a new lawn-mower, try a Titan. They've got what it takes.

7. I'm fed up with those people who keep insisting that we shouldn't violate the rights of criminals. What I want to know is, what are they prepared to do for the victims of violent crimes?

8. He's not really a scientist. Sure, he has a Ph.D. in chemistry and works in a research laboratory, but all he does is try to find cheaper ways of making soaps and cosmetics. Real scientists are dedicated to making discoveries, take pride in what they are doing, and care deeply about the progress of the whole discipline. He is nothing more than a glorified lab technician.

9. There sure is a lot of talk these days about the free trade deal, and it's probably going to get a lot worse before it gets better. I don't know about you, but I'm having a helluva time figuring out who's right and who's wrong. You've got the union leaders bleating about the loss of jobs, and the business types telling us we're all going to get rich. I mean, who are you to believe? One thing I want to know is, is there any reason to think that this time Mulroney isn't just serving the interests of his tycoon friends in corporate boardrooms?

10. Did you see that, Doris? That car went right through the stop sign without even slowing down. And it was a woman driver too, just like the one that rear-ended Ken last month.

13.12 Questions for Discussion

Some, although not all, of the following passages present real arguments. However, all rely in part on one or more irrational techniques of persuasion to attempt to put their point across.

1. Religious cults are extremely dangerous, and we must do everything possible to warn people against them. They always prey upon the young, who are at that vulnerable age when they still retain their idealism but are beginning to learn that the world is a less moral place than it should be. Once they have ensnared a victim they completely take over his or her life. Cult members become slaves: they do exactly what they are told and any questioning or criticism is severely discouraged. They are forbidden all contact with their families and former friends. Their dependency is so complete that it is virtually impossible to rescue them without the risk of doing serious psychological damage.

2. Communism always presented itself as a scientific theory of history and politics, but the reality was that it was essentially a religion. Like religion, its claim to an objective basis was more apparent than real, and rested more upon faith than anything else. And it offered its adherents personal salvation: the assurance that they were right and that in the fullness of time they would be seen to have been right. It also offered an evil enemy that had to be opposed at every turn and whose ultimate overthrow would produce a new Jerusalem where at last the lion would lie down with the lamb.

3. For years many of us have regarded the NDP as an interesting and worthwhile third party. It has lots of ideas as to what the government should be doing, and some of those ideas are practical enough to deserve a hearing. And they're a decent bunch of chaps; they often take themselves too seriously, but basically they're honest and concerned people. But now that the polls suggest that they might actually win the next election, we have to ask whether the NDP has the competence – the ability to make tough economic decisions, for example – to govern a country as complex as Canada. How Canadians answer this question may well determine whether or not Canada will soon have its first socialist prime minister.

4. There can be no doubt whatever about the fundamental correctness of the government's fiscal and monetary policies, for we absolutely must get the deficit under control or else face economic disaster within ten years. There is, quite simply, no alternative to what the government is doing. Of course, the Opposition pretends that it has some magic wand that it can wave at the deficit and make it disappear. The reality, however, is that while the ship of state is in danger of sinking the Opposition has only a sardine can to bail with. It would be funny if it were not so tragic.

5. During the twentieth century, mankind, at least in the industrialized world, has achieved a standard of living that would have astonished people only a century ago. The average person today has more money, more comfort, and better health than ever before. He has a better job, his children are better educated, he travels more widely and more often, he has a better home with more possessions, and can retire at age fifty-five to enjoy another twenty-five years of comfortable living.

Chapter 14

Writing and Assessing Argumentative Essays

In this chapter we examine argumentative essays – sometimes called extended arguments – from two points of view: that of the author and that of the critic. Much of what is said here is a repetition or a common-sense extrapolation of material presented in earlier chapters. But it should prove helpful to draw this material together and expand upon it in order to indicate some of the special problems involved in dealing with argumentative essays.

The term *argumentative essay* refers to a written attempt to present a coherent discussion of a subject with a view to defending a specific thesis. The thesis of an argumentative essay is its main conclusion: it is usually a position or point of view, but may consist of a simple statement. The key phrase in the definition is *defending a specific thesis*. This is what makes an essay argumentative in nature, for any attempt to defend a conclusion requires premises. An argumentative essay can thus be regarded as an extended argument.

There are three elements in every essay: content, structure, and style. The content – the particular facts and ideas that form the subject matter – is different for each essay and is thus beyond the scope of our discussion. Questions about structure and style, on the other hand, tend to be the same for every argumentative essay regardless of content. We shall consider some of these questions first from the point of view of the author, and then from the point of view of the critic.

First, however, we need to address an aspect of good writing that is often overlooked. The goal of all writing is communication with an audience. This means we must know what audience we are writing for, and write for *that* audience. We must take the audience into account when deciding what we want to say and how we are going to say it. What is their level of education? How much political (moral, scientific, religious) sophistication do they possess? How much background information are they likely to have? What are their values likely to be? Answers to these and similar questions are relevant to many of the decisions we must make when writing. Writing a paper on capital punishment for a graduate seminar in criminology clearly requires a different approach from writing a column on the same subject for the Toronto *Sun*. When writing anything, we should *always* pay attention to the intended audience. An argumentative essay, obviously, is intended for an audience that is capable of being persuaded by arguments.

14.1 Writing Argumentative Essays: Structure

The largest structural feature of an essay consists of its division into three parts: the introduction, the body, and the conclusion. Next is the logical structure of the main argument of the essay, or what is sometimes called the macro-structure. Finally, there is the structural detail, or micro-structure – the structures of the sub-arguments of the essay and their relationship to each other and to the main argument. We shall deal with each of these structural features in turn.

The **introduction** is not merely a way of getting started: it has several specific purposes. These purposes are not so distinct from each other that they can be achieved in isolation, but each represents an important aspect of the introduction. (1) The introduction should always announce the subject matter, and should also mention any restrictions being placed on the topic. For example, if the topic is capital punishment but the essay considers only capital punishment in Canada, this fact should be stated. (2) It should establish a context for the discussion. The context may be the political aspect of the capital punishment debate in Canada, or current criminological research. (3) It should relate the essay to the views of others. These may be the views of the public, or the published work of scholars, or the views of lawyers and judges, or all three. (4) It should indicate what the essay hopes to contribute to the discussion. For example, *This essay attempts to show that there is no statistical basis for regarding the death penalty as an effective deterrent.*

These purposes are important not only because they tell the reader what to expect, but also because they are necessary aids for the reader in interpreting the essay. We have already seen how important it is to be able to appeal to the context and background when interpreting an argument and supplying missing premises and assumptions. The same is true of argumentative essays. If we want our readers to abide by the principle of charity we need to give them as much help as we can.

In the **body** of the essay the thesis is developed, elaborated, and defended. The body always consists of two elements. (1) It presents reasons and arguments to support the thesis. These reasons and arguments are the kind of specific arguments we have already considered in detail. They should, of course, be sound arguments. (2) It attempts to rebut objections. This second element requires us to anticipate the kind of objections we are likely to meet from our intended audience. We need to know which of our audience's beliefs we are challenging, and why they hold them. Once we know, we should address these concerns directly, for otherwise we may leave the audience with an easy way of discounting our arguments and ignoring our conclusion. They may be able to say, *Well, I see what you are driving at, but you don't really understand why we think differently about the matter, and you've given us no reason to give up our beliefs.*

Supporting reasons and rebuttals are closely related, since in practice most of the arguments that can be used to support a position either are themselves, or easily give rise to, arguments that can be used to rebut the standard objections from those who hold a rival position. But it is always useful in an argumentative essay to state explicitly our reasons for regarding the rival positions as untenable. We may think the weaknesses are too obvious to mention, but usually our opponents don't think they are obvious at all.

The body of an argumentative essay is the largest part of any essay and should embody some principle of organization. There is no one "right" organization here, only possible organizational structures that make coherent sense. It is common to present the arguments in support of our thesis first and then deal with the objections, but we could start by analyzing and criticizing the rival positions and use this discussion as a basis for developing the arguments in support of our thesis. Similarly, when presenting our arguments it makes sense to move from the easy and obvious ones to those that are more difficult and less obvious, or from the traditional ones to the more recent ones, or from the general to the specific.

The **conclusion** of an argumentative essay should present a brief summary of the main arguments and rebuttals and show how they support the main conclusion of the essay. It should also include a clear statement or restatement of the conclusion, and should note any significant restrictions or limitations that may apply. The primary purpose of the concluding section is to remind the reader of what we think our essay has (and has not) accomplished.

The **main argument** of an argumentative essay can best be understood by thinking of the essay as consisting of a single argument of the sort that could be presented in a few sentences. The thesis of the essay is the conclusion and the main reason or reasons are its supporting premises. The main argument can be regarded as a brief outline that can be diagrammed using the argument structures outlined in section 4.6. Usually the structure of the main argument can be represented by one of the three simple argument structures, although sometimes it may be somewhat more complex.

It is not always easy to distinguish the main argument from the sub-arguments of an essay. But it is important to make the attempt, for it is the main argument that contributes most to the clarity and strength of an argumentative essay. Before starting to write an essay we should have a clear understanding of the structure of its main argument, and should satisfy ourselves that it constitutes a sound argument. We should attempt to preserve this structure as we add the sub-arguments and the details of the micro-structure. Not only does this make for a better essay, it is of considerable help to the reader.

The **micro-structure** consists of the details that are necessary to explain and support the main argument. It includes the sub-arguments used to defend the premises of the main argument, explanations of key terms, rebuttals of objections, and clarifications of any difficult steps in the argument. Incorporating these elements into the tree diagram of the main argument would typically make it very complex, and is not usually necessary. But when writing we should always know precisely how they relate to the main argument.

14.2 Writing Argumentative Essays: Style

The most important criteria for style are clarity and coherence, and as long as they remain the over-riding criteria there is a great deal of room for individual variation. Aesthetic criteria are relevant, but elegant and beautifully crafted writing should never be allowed to interfere with clarity and coherence. The primary purpose of an argumentative essay is to persuade our audience of the correctness of our thesis, and anything that interferes with this purpose should be avoided.

When making decisions about style, we should bear in mind the intended audience. Will they be put off by a certain style? Will they understand references to other authors? Will they understand technical terminology? What kind of footnotes are expected? What kind of examples will best illustrate for them the points we want to make? Should humour be used, or is it likely to fall flat? These questions are important because much of the success of an argumentative essay in convincing the reader depends upon how they are answered.

There are several rules of good writing that are important when writing argumentative essays:

(1) Be brief. This means that we should be able to justify every word, phrase, sentence, paragraph, and section on the ground that they contribute to the overall purpose of the essay. The negative version of this rule is: avoid padding. Generally speaking, if it isn't necessary don't include it.

(2) Strive for simplicity. Simplicity is not the same as brevity. Simplicity is the avoidance of unnecessary complexity or obscurity. Often we can achieve simplicity by using fewer words: *Within the next ten years...* is better than *In the period between the present and ten years from the present...* Sometimes, however, simplicity may require more words, especially when we are dealing with a complex or technical topic. A complex point that could be expressed in a single sentence may require a paragraph to express simply and clearly. We should avoid long complex sentences unless the sentence structure is relatively simple. We should also use concrete rather than abstract terms wherever possible: *pet* rather than *companion animal*, and *touch* rather than *tactile sensation*. The passive voice should be used sparingly: *Most people regret that...* is better than *It is regretted by most people that...*

(3) Be specific. Using general terms instead of specific terms tends to obscure meaning, and to make the reader's task more difficult. If we are discussing criminals, we should not routinely refer to them as deviants. Criminals may be social deviants, but many deviants are not criminals, and when we use the term *deviants* we are in fact referring to both criminal and non-criminal deviants.

(4) Use examples judiciously. Examples are almost always helpful to the reader when presenting an abstract idea. But the example should be a good one; one good example is always better then several inappropriate ones. We should use more than one example only when we want to convey the range of application of an abstract idea or principle.

(5) Use quotations judiciously. If the topic requires us to talk about the views of a particular author, it is appropriate to present the author's views in his or her own words. But we should avoid quoting more than is necessary to establish the author's actual position. If the topic does not require us to talk about the views of a particular author, quotations should be used only when they contribute something to the essay. Quotations can be used to illustrate a point, to indicate the source of an idea, or to express in elegant or succinct language a point we wish to make. The danger in using quotations is that they can become a substitute for our own thinking, or can obscure the argument we are attempting to present.

(6) Always revise. We should never let anything we write reach its intended audience in an unrevised form. No-one can write a perfect first draft; every essay can be improved by careful revision. It is best to set aside the draft for a few days before revising it so that we can look at it with fresh eyes.

14.3 Assessing Argumentative Essays

Assessing an argumentative essay is in principle the same as assessing a short argument. The difference is merely one of complexity; there is a great deal more to keep track of when dealing with an argumentative essay. The rules for assessing arguments that were outlined in section 5.3 are still valid when used to assess argumentative essays but need to be applied somewhat differently. The major difference is that our assessment involves three phases: first, we conduct a provisional assessment of the main argument, second, we assess the sub-arguments, and third we make our final assessment of the essay as a whole.

First Phase. First, we need to identify the main argument of the essay. We do this by applying the first three rules to the essay as a whole.

(1) We identify the main conclusion, by asking what is the author's main thesis, or what is the position the essay is intended to defend. If the thesis is a complex one that cannot accurately be conveyed in a single sentence, we must look for or invent a summary statement of it. For example, to be fair to the author we may need to work out our own statement of the conclusion, such as: *Under present conditions (i.e., current political opinion, the uncertainties of economic theory, and trends in world trade) the government should increase interest rates in order to control inflation.* Only

when we have identified the main conclusion can we be sure that the essay constitutes an argument, that is, that it is an *argumentative* essay and not some other kind of essay. In doubtful cases, as always, we should use the principle of charity and any contextual clues to decide the question.

(2) We identify the premises by looking for the main reasons offered to support the conclusion. In an argumentative essay these premises will almost always be the conclusions of sub-arguments. If the essay is clearly written, with a clear structure, this task will be straightforward. Otherwise we will have to do some digging, especially if the conclusions of the sub-arguments have not been made explicit. The major difficulty is that we can be led astray by the sub-arguments. But if we have identified the main conclusion correctly we can avoid this difficulty by asking, *What are the main reasons the author presents as support for this conclusion?*

(3) Next, we identify the logical structure of the main argument of the essay. If we have correctly identified the premises and conclusion of the main argument, this step is quite straightforward and presents no special difficulties.

In the first phase of assessment, we provisionally apply Rules 4, 5, and 6, that is, we look to see whether the premises are acceptable, relevant, and adequate to support the conclusion. These rules must be applied provisionally at this point because we have not yet checked the sub-arguments, and the purpose of the sub-arguments is to defend the premises. But if we suspect that one or more premise is unacceptable, irrelevant, or inadequate, this provisional diagnosis tells us what to look for when we move to the second phase of assessment. Rule 7 (*Look for counter-arguments*) should be postponed until the final stage of assessment.

Second Phase. Now we can turn to the sub-arguments. When identifying sub-arguments, it is helpful to identify the other elements of the micro-structure of the essay. Examples, quotations, definitions, rhetorical questions, summaries, speculation, in short, anything that is not a premise or a conclusion of an argument, should be identified as such. This material is not to be ignored, but should be used to interpret both the main argument of the essay and the sub-arguments. In addition, when interpreting sub-arguments we should use the other arguments (including the main argument) as aids. The principle of charity is usually easy to follow when dealing with argumentative essays because we are given a great deal of supplementary material.

Each sub-argument should be assessed according to the normal rules for assessing arguments. The role of each sub-argument is to provide support for the premises of the main argument, so the conclusion of each sub-argument should be one of the premises of the main argument. A sub-argument may, however, contain its own sub-argument, in which case we should proceed as in the first phase: we should identify the sub-argument and make a tentative assessment of it before assessing the sub-sub-argument.

Third Phase. We are now in a position to assess the essay as a whole. First, we should check to see whether our interpretation of the main argument is supported by our interpretation of the sub-arguments. If it is not, we should amend it. Next, we assess the argument by applying Rules 4, 5, and 6. Our primary concern is with the main argument, but in order to decide whether it satisfies our three criteria we will have to examine the sub-arguments by applying our criteria to them, which will of course lead us to do the same to any sub-sub-arguments. Any weaknesses we find should now be easy to identify and describe. Finally, we should invoke Rule 7 and ask whether there are any significant counter-arguments that the essay fails to take into account.

14.4 Assessment of a Sample Argumentative Essay

To illustrate how argumentative essays should be assessed we will apply the steps outlined in 14.3 to an example. Our assessment is lengthy and thorough, not because this is necessary every time we assess an argumentative essay, but because it is important to understand what is involved in a full critical assessment. The following article has been created by drawing together a number of letters and editorials that appeared during a teachers' strike in Wellington County in 1985.

> (1) Most of us have come to accept the fact that every year, somewhere in Ontario, there will be yet another teachers' strike. In a bad year there may be half a dozen strikes; in a good year there may be only one or two. Teachers' strikes have become so commonplace that normally only the local media regard them as newsworthy unless they drag on for months or involve violence.
>
> (2) But, as anyone who has suffered through a strike knows, a strike that lasts for more than a week or two can be extremely disruptive, and a

lengthy strike can have a devastating effect upon many students, especially high school students. Some decide not to return to school after the strike and thus fail to complete their education. Others cannot keep up with the accelerated pace after the strike, and become discouraged and drop out. Others find that their grades have suffered and that they cannot gain admission to the college or university program of their choice. It is becoming increasingly obvious that giving teachers the legal right to strike was a serious mistake, and that the time has come to challenge that right.

(3) The fundamental dilemma we face is whether teachers are to be regarded as workers or as professionals. To understand this dilemma we need to look at the difference between workers and professionals. Workers are hired and trained by an employer to do a specific job whose details are determined by the employer: the nature and quality of the product, the materials and equipment used, the standard of workmanship, the hours of work, etc., are all determined by the employer. It is precisely because so much control lies with management that society recognizes that workers should have the right to strike, so that they can bargain effectively with their employers over pay and working conditions. Professionals, on the other hand, are not trained by their employers but by other professionals. Thus, when hired by an employer to do a specific job, they are expected and entitled to use their professional expertise to determine how they will do their work: they tell their employer how much time and what equipment and facilities they need to do their job properly. More importantly, they have professional obligations to society at large, and especially to their clients, regarding the quality of their work. It is precisely because they have a professional obligation to society and their clients that professionals should not have the right to strike. The right to strike is inconsistent with their obligations as professionals.

(4) So the question is: are teachers workers or professionals? The answer is obvious: teachers clearly fit the above description of professionals. Teachers have professional training and expertise. And they are responsible for most of what they do in the classroom: what is taught, how it is taught, how it is to be examined, and how it is to be graded. If we regarded teachers as workers, we would have to insist that these matters should be taken out of the hands of teachers on the ground that they are management prerogatives. This would be the height of absurdity.

(5) But – and this is the crux of the matter – if teachers are to be regarded as professionals then they must take their professional obligations seriously: they must recognize that their first obligation as teachers is to their students'

education, and they must refuse to use their students as pawns in their quarrels with school boards. In other words, as professionals teachers should give up their right to strike. It is a sad reflection upon the teaching profession that they cannot grasp that the right to strike is inconsistent with their professional status. They want to eat their cake and have it too.

(6) Teachers sometimes argue that they only strike to achieve improvements in the educational system and that the responsibility for strikes rests with school boards, which are more concerned with dollars than with the quality of education. They claim that the goal of every teachers' strike has been to improve the quality of education. Even higher salaries, they claim, will attract better people into the teaching profession, and thus benefit students. But where is the evidence to support such claims? The fact that the teachers themselves have not put forward such evidence suggests that there is none. Indeed, such claims seem to be little more than greed masquerading as benevolence, and should be rejected out of hand. Teachers who argue this way are a disgrace to what used to be an honourable profession, further proof that the teaching profession is now controlled by those who really do regard themselves merely as workers and who don't give a damn about the quality of their product.

(7) Surely the time has come to demand that the right to strike be taken away from teachers. The harmful effects of teachers' strikes are undeniable; the inconsistency between their professional status and their right to strike is clear; and the conclusion is inevitable.

First Phase. In the first phase we identify the main argument by applying the first three rules: we identify the conclusion, the main premises, and the structure of the main argument.

(1) What is the main conclusion? The final paragraph of the article presents a summary of the main argument and includes a statement of the main conclusion: *Surely the time has come to demand that the right to strike be taken away from teachers*. We shall restate it more briefly as *Teachers' right to strike should be taken away*. A check of the rest of the article ensures us that our interpretation is correct.

(2) What are the premises of the main argument? Paragraph 7 also includes a statement of two of the main premises. The first, which we will restate in the form it appears in the paragraph 2, is *Teachers' strikes can have a devastating effect upon many students*. The second, which we will restate in the form it appears in paragraph 5, is *As professionals, teachers should give up the right to strike*. A check of the article as a whole supports

our interpretation that these are two premises of the main argument. But we also find another premise in the rest of the article that is not included in paragraph 7. In paragraph 6 the author attempts to refute the claim made by some teachers that strikes achieve improvements in the educational system. If this claim is acceptable it would clearly support the teachers' right to strike, so the author's attack on this claim is needed to provide additional support for the main conclusion. Hence we need to add another premise of the main argument: *Teachers' strikes do not achieve improvements in the educational system.*

(3) What is the structure of the main argument? It is clear that each of the three premises we have identified is intended to offer independent support for the conclusion. This means that the main argument has a V structure.

As a result of the first phase of assessment we now have the following reconstruction and tree diagram of the main argument:

Main Argument:
P1. Teachers' strikes can have a devastating effect upon many students.
P2. As professionals, teachers should give up the right to strike.
P3. Teachers' strikes do not achieve improvements in the educational system.
C. Teachers' right to strike should be taken away.

We should now make a provisional assessment of the above argument. It is clear that *if* the three premises are true, then they are relevant and adequate to provide strong support for the conclusion. So the relevancy and adequacy criteria seem to be satisfied. But are the premises acceptable? This seems much less certain, so the question we should be most concerned about in the second phase of assessment is whether the premises are acceptable.

Second Phase. We now turn to the sub-arguments. There are three sub-arguments, one in support of each of the three premises of the main argument. The first sub-argument, which has P1 as its conclusion, is found in paragraph 2. Three reasons are offered in its support; they are stated below as premises P4, P5, and P6. It should be noted that they have been restated in order to express more accurately what seems to be the speaker's real meaning. These premises offer independent support for P1, which means that the first sub-argument has a V structure. Thus we have the following reconstruction and tree diagram:

First Sub-Argument:
P4. Some students do not to return to school after a long strike and thus fail to complete their education.
P5. After a long strike some students cannot keep up the accelerated pace at school, and become discouraged and drop out.
P6. After a long strike some students find that their grades have suffered and that they cannot gain admission to the college or university program of their choice.
P1. Teachers' strikes can have devastating effects upon many students.

The second sub-argument, which is found in paragraphs 3, 4, and 5, is much more complex than the first. What makes it complex is that it contains three sub-sub-arguments. We shall ignore these sub-sub-arguments for the moment. In paragraph 3 the author sets up an exclusive dichotomy between workers and professionals, and claims that workers should have the right to strike but that professionals should not. In paragraph 4 the author argues that teachers are professionals, and in paragraph 5 concludes that as professionals, teachers should give up the right to strike. This argument has a T structure, since the premises would all have to be true if they are to provide support for the conclusion. Thus, we have the following reconstruction and tree diagram for the second sub-argument:

Second Sub-Argument:

P7. Either teachers are workers or they are professionals.

P8. Workers should have the right to strike.

P9. Professionals should not have the right to strike.

P10. Teachers are professionals.

P2. As professionals, teachers should give up their right to strike.

We shall now briefly examine the three sub–sub–arguments. Their role is to provide support for premises P8, P9, and P10. They have the following reconstructions and tree diagrams:

First Sub–Sub–Argument:

P11. Workers are hired to do a specific job all of whose details are determined by the employer.

P12. Workers need to be able to bargain effectively with their employers over pay and working conditions.

P8. Workers should have the right to strike.

Second Sub–Sub–Argument:

P13. Professionals have obligations to society at large, and especially to their clients, regarding the quality of their work.

P14. Teachers should not use their students as pawns in their quarrels with school boards.

P9. Professionals should not have the right to strike.

Third Sub-Sub-Argument:

P15. Teachers have professional training and expertise.

P16. Teachers are responsible for most of what they do in the classroom.

P10. Teachers are professionals.

We now turn to the third sub-argument. It attempts to refute the claim that teachers' strikes have achieved improvements in the educational system, by presenting two reasons. First, it argues that there is no evidence to support such a claim, since if there were evidence teachers would have presented it, which they have not. This part of the sub-argument constitutes a sub-sub-argument. Second, it argues that the claim itself is simply based on greed. These two premises offer independent support for the conclusion. Thus we have the following reconstruction and tree diagram:

Third Sub-Argument:

P17. There is no evidence to support the claim that teachers' strikes achieve improvements in the educational system.

P18. The claim that teachers' strikes achieve improvements in the educational system is simply greed masquerading as benevolence.

P3. Teachers' strikes do not achieve improvements in the educational system.

The sub-sub-argument is intended to support P17. It has the following reconstruction and tree diagram:

Fourth Sub-Sub-Argument:

P19. If there were evidence to support the claim that teachers' strikes achieve improvements in the educational system, teachers would present it.

P20. Teachers have presented no evidence that strikes achieve improvements in the educational system.

P17. There is no evidence to support the claim that teachers' strikes achieve improvements in the educational system.

We can now present a complete reconstruction and tree diagram for the entire essay:

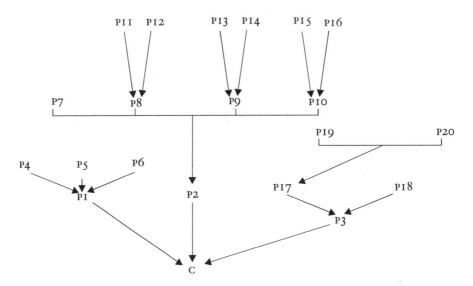

Third Phase. We are now in a position to assess the essay as a whole. We will consider each sub-argument in turn.

The conclusion of the first sub-argument (i.e., P1) rests on premises that are unsupported. Each premise could only be defended by an inductive generalization, but there is no indication that the author is aware of such evidence. Possibly the author is relying upon anecdotal evidence. But the absence of clear and specific evidence should make us cautious about accepting these premises. We cannot be sure that the premises are unacceptable, but we should at least regard their acceptability as questionable. On the other hand, the premises clearly are relevant, for they present the kind of evidence that would support the claim that lengthy teachers' strikes can have a devastating effect upon students. But are they adequate to support the conclusion? Each premise makes a claim about *some* students, and the vagueness of such claims makes them difficult to assess. Since the conclusion of the sub-argument is that strikes have a devastating effect upon *many* students, the premises must be regarded as inadequate. Had the conclusion been given in a weaker form, such as *Long teachers' strikes can have a harmful effect on some high-school students,* the premises of the sub-argument could be regarded as adequate, but such a conclusion would substantially weaken the main argument. The first sub-argument, therefore, must be regarded as quite weak since it only meets one of the three criteria for a sound argument.

The second sub-argument has several weaknesses. The first weakness arises in the sub-argument itself. It relies on a dichotomy: either teachers are workers who should have the right to strike, or they are professionals who ought to reject the right to strike. But there are two other possibilities: teachers are workers who should be denied the right to strike, or they are professionals who should have the right to strike. The latter possibility is the important one that the sub-argument overlooks. There are in fact some professional groups, such as doctors and nurses, whose right to strike is now widely, if not universally, accepted. Thus, the fact that teachers are professionals does not by itself show that teachers should not have the right to strike. In other words, the second sub-argument commits the fallacy of false dichotomy, and thus violates the criterion of acceptability.

But the sub-sub-arguments also have weaknesses, which we shall describe briefly. The first sub-sub-argument is designed to support one side of the false dichotomy, namely that workers should have the right to strike. The argument is weak, however, because its premises are inadequate, since they ignore the reasons that are commonly believed to justify denying the right to strike to workers in essential services. The second sub-sub-argument is weak because the fact that professionals have obligations to society at large and to their clients is not adequate to show that these obligations are more important than any other consideration. It is also weak because the premise that teachers should not use their students as pawns in their quarrels with school boards begs the question by assuming that it is wrong for teachers to strike. The third sub-sub-argument, on the other hand, is a strong argument, although its strength is insufficient to overcome the weaknesses in the sub-argument as a whole. These weaknesses are so serious that we must regard the second sub-argument as providing no support for the conclusion of the main argument.

The third sub-argument is also very weak. Its first premise, that there is no evidence to support the claim that teachers' strikes achieve improvements in the educational system, is defended by the fourth sub-sub-argument. This is a deductive argument that is valid because it has the form of denying the consequent. Since it is a valid argument we should accept its conclusion if we are prepared to accept its premises. It is reasonable to accept both premises, at least in the absence of contrary evidence, which means we should accept the conclusion. So the first premise of the sub-argument is acceptable. And it is clearly relevant. But it is also inadequate to support the conclusion, since it is an appeal to ignorance: the fact that there is no evidence to show that the teachers' claim is true, is used to support the conclusion that the claim is false. The second premise of the sub-argument, which asserts that the teachers' claim is simply greed masquerading as benevolence, is a clear ad hominem fallacy and thus irrelevant. So the third sub-argument relies upon one premise that is acceptable and relevant, but clearly inadequate, and one premise that is clearly irrelevant. It is therefore a very weak argument.

We can now provide an assessment of the main argument. As we have seen, none of the premises is well supported. All must therefore be regarded as unacceptable. However, we have encountered nothing in our assessment of the sub-arguments that would lead us to change our provisional assessment of the premises as being relevant and adequate. Nevertheless, the argument as a whole suffers from the fatal flaw that all its premises are unacceptable, so the fact that they are relevant and adequate does nothing to provide support for the conclusion that the teachers' right to strike should be taken away.

There is, however, something that can be salvaged from the argument. We noted that the first sub-argument would have been acceptable had its conclusion been *Long teachers' strikes can have a harmful effect on some high-school students*. We also noted that the fourth sub-sub-argument was a strong argument, so we should accept its conclusion that *There is no evidence to support the claim that teachers' strikes achieve improvements in the educational system*. Although these conclusions are obviously not adequate to support the argument's main conclusion, they do suggest areas where further research and study would be useful. If we could determine precisely how much harm is caused to students by lengthy strikes, and if we knew whether or not strikes did achieve improvements in the educational system, we would be much closer to being able to make a reasonable decision on whether the right to strike should be taken away from teachers.

And finally, we must ask whether there is a counter-argument against the main conclusion we should consider. In fact there is one that some teachers have used when faced with demands that their legal right to strike should be taken away. Before teachers were granted the legal right to strike, and when they wanted to put pressure on a school board to secure a better contract, they would all simultaneously submit letters of resignation. The right to submit a letter of resignation is quite different from the right to strike, since forbidding individuals from resigning their jobs would be a form of slavery. Since no school board could hope to hire enough teachers to fill the mass vacancies in the middle of a school year, the teachers were able to achieve the effect of a strike without actually calling a strike. So it could be argued that if the legal right to strike were taken away from teachers there would be no reduction in the number of "strikes," for the teachers would revert to their former practice of organizing mass resignations. The effect of this counter-argument is to show that the real issue is not the legal right of teachers to call strikes, but their actual withdrawal of services either through strikes, if they are legal, or by mass resignations, if strikes are illegal. And this issue would require a rather different argument from the one we have considered.

14.5 Question for Discussion

The following argumentative essay is compiled from several discussions and articles on politics and the news media in Canada. It is worth discussing not only as an exercise in critical thinking but also because it raises an important issue.

It is clear that the Canadian media make an essential contribution to the healthy functioning of our system of government. But this does not mean that there are no grounds for complaint. Politicians, of course, regularly complain that the media fail to present news the way the government wants, or give too much coverage to the opposition, or uncover scandals they would prefer to keep buried. There is probably some substance to such complaints, but it is inevitable that there will be honest disagreements about such editorial decisions, and in any case it is the price politicians must pay for living in a democratic society. But there is a much more serious problem with the media that must be addressed, namely, the way in which they treat all politicians as fair game for any kind of sensational and unjustified attack. Many commentators have expressed concern about the irresponsibility of the news media in their treatment of politicians of all parties.

No-one doubts that this kind of irresponsible journalism is very widespread. Scarcely a week goes by without the media smearing yet another politician. Reporters all seem to think of themselves as investigative reporters: if they don't dig out more dirt they reckon they aren't doing their jobs properly. Editors feel compelled not merely to publish all the dirt, but to display it as prominently as possible. What better story to feature on the front page than an accusation of political corruption; what better film clip for television than one showing a politician losing his or her composure under the relentless questioning of a reporter? The fact is that the media can make a politician appear guilty on the basis of an accusation, and can destroy a career on the basis of a few shreds of evidence that would never stand up in a court of law. Anyone who recognizes the importance of good government must view with alarm such irresponsible journalism.

We are all aware of the increase in recent years in public cynicism about politicians. Doubtless there are several factors that have contributed to this phenomenon. But one reason for it – a reason usually overlooked by the media – is the irresponsible political reporting of the news media. You cannot blame the public for its cynicism. Almost everything it knows about politicians it has learned from the news media, and since almost every story about politicians is negative it is little wonder that the public is so cynical. The media lead the public to expect that all politicians are unsavoury characters, and consequently the public has to a great extent lost its capacity to be shocked when a truly dishonest or incompetent politician is exposed. Increasingly, the public has come to think that there are only two classes of politicians: those who have been exposed as corrupt, and those who have not yet been exposed.

Every citizen – and this includes every journalist – has certain responsibilities. One is to ensure that as far as it is within our power we treat our fellow citizens fairly. Another responsibility we all have is not to deliberately pursue policies that we know will deter honest and honourable people from entering public life. The news media have shown themselves to be flagrantly irresponsible on both counts. They are persistently unfair to politicians, and by driving good people out of politics they ensure political mediocrity: what could be more reprehensible?

Journalists are usually quick to respond to such complaints by invoking the freedom of the press. But the quickness of their response leads them to miss the point altogether. Freedom of the press does not mean freedom from criticism; it means the right of the media to publish whatever they want without legal interference. This is not the issue. The issue is not whether they have the legal right to attack politicians, for clearly they do, but whether they are exercising that right in a responsible manner. The mindless way in which journalists invoke freedom of the press as a defence against all criticism is yet another indication of their irresponsibility.

Some cynical journalists invoke another self-serving justification. The kind of political coverage provided by the media, they say, is what the public wants. It sells newspapers and gives the TV networks high ratings. Don't blame us, they say, blame the public that demands that kind of stuff. What nonsense! If we take this argument seriously, then we should ask how journalists differ from pimps, porn merchants, and drug dealers. The answer should be obvious, even to journalists.

The fundamental problem is that the news media have great political power but are not accountable for the way they exercise that power. We cannot take away their power without destroying them. But we can, and should, insist that they take their responsibilities seriously and exercise their power in a responsible manner.

APPENDICES

Appendix I

Paradoxes and Puzzles

---

1. Logical Paradoxes

A logical paradox is any chain of reasoning that uses only meaningful and consistent premises and commits no logical errors, yet nevertheless produces contradictory conclusions. Such a result ought to be impossible, so when paradoxes arise they present a serious challenge to our assumptions. Are the premises really meaningful? Are they really consistent with one another? Is there a hidden weakness we have failed to detect? We know that something *must* be wrong with the argument: the challenge is to find it.

The paradoxes described below have all challenged philosophers and logicians, and continue to do so, since most of them have no generally agreed upon solution. The problem is that there are compelling reasons against rejecting any of the premises, and no-one has been able to provide a plausible account of a logical error that is being committed. They can, however, also be regarded as brain-teasers for which there is as yet no *right* answer.

(1) THE BARBER PARADOX

In a certain village there lives a barber who cuts the hair of all those, and only those, inhabitants who do not cut their own hair. Does he cut his own hair? If he does not then he is one of those who do not cut their own hair, in which case he does cut his own hair because he cuts the hair of all those who do not cut their own hair. If he does cut his own hair, then he is not one of those whose hair he cuts, because he cuts the hair only of those who do not cut their own hair. Thus, if he does then he doesn't, and if he doesn't then he does, which is a paradox.

This paradox, unlike those that follow, does have a solution. The first sentence makes a factual claim about the barber, namely, that he cuts the hair of all those and only those who do not cut their own hair. But why should we accept this factual claim? No-one has ever suggested that such a barber actually exists, and there is no reason why anyone would ever be tempted to make such a claim. In fact, as the paradox shows, such a barber could not exist. Any barber who set out to cut the hair of all those and only those who do not cut their own hair could not possibly succeed, not as long as he was an inhabitant of the village. The paradox only arises, then, because we have made a factual claim that could not possibly be true, and the solution to the paradox is simply not to make factual assertions of this sort. Perhaps the reason the factual claim looks plausible is because we forget that the barber is himself an inhabitant of the village. If he moved away so that he was no longer an inhabitant, and visited the village regularly to cut hair, then he could cut the hair of all those and only those inhabitants who do not cut their own hair. In this case the only way to discover whether or not he cuts his own hair would be to ask him.

(2) THE SURPRISE EXAMINATION

One Friday, a mathematics teacher announces to his class, *Next week there will be a test on quadratic equations. But I want the test to be a surprise when it comes, so I am not going to tell you which day it will be.* After the class, one of the students tells the teacher that he has figured out that there is not really going to be a test, at least not a surprise test. His reasoning is as follows:

> *The test cannot be given next Friday because if we got to Thursday afternoon without having the test we would know that it would be given the next day, and it would not be a surprise. So if it is to be a surprise then it cannot be given on Friday. But, since Friday is ruled out, then if we got to Wednesday afternoon without having the test we would know that it would be given the next day (i.e., on Thursday). But then it wouldn't be a surprise. So it cannot be given on Thursday. But, since both Friday and Thursday are ruled out, then if we got to Tuesday afternoon without having the test we would know that it would be given the next day (i.e., on Wednesday). But then it wouldn't be a surprise. So the test cannot be given on Wednesday. The same argument also rules out Tuesday and Monday, so I conclude that you will be unable to give a surprise test next week.*

What is wrong with the student's reasoning? The solution to the Bar-ber paradox won't work here, for the teacher's announcement certainly could be true. If no student was clever enough to recognize the paradox, the teacher could give the test on Tuesday, for example, and everyone would be surprised. Or, what is even more curious, the teacher could say to the student, *Your reasoning is impeccable*, and then give the test on Tuesday (or any other day), which would certainly surprise the student as well as the rest of the class.

(3) THE LIAR PARADOX

The liar paradox arises out of a feature of the following statement: *What I am now saying is a lie.* If what the speaker says is true, then it is a lie (i.e., it is false), and if what the speaker says is false, then it is not a lie (i.e., it is true.) If you don't see this, consider an alternative wording: *This state-ment is false.* It has the same feature; if it is true then it is false, and if it is false then it is true.

An old objection to this paradox is that the statement refers to itself, and this, it is held, explains why the paradox arises. But the paradox can easily be reformulated in such a way as to eliminate the self-reference. Consider the following statements:

(1) Statement (2) is true.
(2) Statement (1) is false.

Since every meaningful statement must be either true or false, and since both these statements are obviously meaningful, let us suppose that (1) is true. If it is true then (2) must be true (since that is what (1) says). But if (2) is true then (1) must be false (since that is what (2) says). Therefore, if (1) is true, it is false, which is absurd. Therefore, (1) cannot be true. So let us suppose then that (1) is false. If it is false then (2) must be false (since that is what the falsity of (1) means). But if (2) is false then (1) must be true (since that is what the falsity of (2) means). Therefore, if (1) is false, it is true, which is absurd. Therefore, (1) cannot be false. But we have already shown that it cannot be true. Therefore, (1) cannot be true and it cannot be false, which is absurd, unless it is a meaningless state-ment. But it is not meaningless. Hence, the paradox. Note that the same result emerges if we start with statement (2): it cannot be true and it can-not be false. (An interesting variation on the two-statement version of the liar paradox was seen on a T-shirt: on the front it said, *The statement on the back of this T-shirt is true*, and on the back it said, *The statement on the front of this T-shirt is false*.)

Once again, the solution that worked for the Barber paradox won't help us here. There is nothing suspect about either statement; anyone who has ever taken a true/false quiz will use both types of statements.

(4) THE LAW STUDENT PARADOX

In ancient Athens, a student wanted to study law with the noted teacher Protagoras, but could not afford the fee. Protagoras agreed to teach him on the condition that when he completed his studies and won his first case in court, he would pay the stipulated fee. The student, however, having completed his studies, decided not to practice law at all, and told Protagoras that according to their agreement he was under no obligation to pay him. Protagoras was most indignant, and sued the student for his fees. He presented the following argument to the judges:

> *If I win my case, then according to the judgement of the court the student ought to pay me the fee. But if the student wins, then according to our agreement he ought to pay me. In either case he ought to pay.*

The student, however, argued as follows:

> *If I win my case, then according to the judgement of the court I do not have to pay the fee. And if I lose my case, then according to our agreement I do not have to pay. In either case I do not have to pay.*

A practical solution to this paradox was once suggested by a lawyer. The judges should reject Protagoras' suit and rule that the student does not have to pay. Protagoras should then sue again, and this time the court would have to rule in his favour, since according to the agreement the student, having won his first case, would now be obliged to pay. But this practical solution does not resolve the logical paradox facing the judges at the first hearing.

(5) THE PARADOX OF OMNIPOTENCE

According to most religions, God is omnipotent. This means that there is nothing that God cannot do, if He chooses to do it. He can divide the Red Sea, cause plagues, and heal the sick. He could end disease or eliminate poverty if He chose to do so. (God's reasons for choosing not to do these things derive from His other attributes.) But could God create a stone that is too large for Him to lift? If you answer *yes* then you have admitted that the stone is too large for Him to lift, and hence that there is something God cannot do. If you answer *no* then you have also admitted that there is something God cannot do. In either case, it follows that God is not omnipotent.

This paradox can, of course, easily be resolved by merely denying that God is omnipotent, but this is something that most religious believers refuse to do, for they regard omnipotence as part of God's essential nature. For these people the paradox has to be dealt with somehow. One solution is to claim that it is part of God's nature not to be bound by the laws of logic, in which case God can both create a stone that is too large for Him to lift, and then lift it. After all, it is only the laws of logic that lead us to say that one cannot perform two contradictory acts. This solution, however, leaves us in a difficult situation, for if God is not bound by the laws of logic then since our understanding of anything requires us to follow the laws of logic there will be absolutely nothing about God that we can even begin to understand. Is there some better solution?

(6) ACHILLES AND THE TORTOISE

The tortoise has challenged Achilles to a race, but Achilles, being supremely confident that he can win, allows the tortoise to get a head start. After a few minutes, Achilles sets out to overtake the tortoise. But in order to overtake the tortoise, he will first have to cover the first half of the distance that separates them. Once he has done this, he will then have to cover the first half of the distance that now separates them. Once he has done this, he will then have to cover the first half of the distance that now separates them. And so on. He will always have to cover the first half of the remaining distance that separates them before he will be able to cover the second half. But, since any distance that separates them, no matter how small, contains a first half, Achilles will never be able to overtake the tortoise.

This is one of the paradoxes discovered by the ancient Greek mathematician Zeno. The paradox arises because of the assumption that every line is made up of an infinite number of points, for this means that every line, no matter how short, can be divided into two halves. This assumption lies at the basis of mathematics, and cannot be rejected without destroying virtually the whole of mathematics.

(7) THE PRISONERS DILEMMA

Al and Bob have been arrested and charged with several offenses relating to extortion and fraud, and are being held in prison without bail. When the prosecutor reviews the evidence, however, he realizes that although he has very strong evidence to support the less serious charges, the evidence to support the more serious charges is so weak that he is unlikely to get a conviction unless he can get at least one of them to testify against the other. He therefore approaches Al and Bob together and offers them a deal: if one of them agrees to plead guilty and testify against the other he will be given a suspended sentence and the other one will be given a sentence of six years; but if both plead guilty then, since neither will need to testify against the other, each will receive a sentence of four years; and if both plead not guilty each will receive a sentence of two years. As soon as the deal has been offered, Al and Bob are taken to separate cells so that they cannot communicate with one another, and told that they have twenty-four hours to decide whether or not to accept the deal. There is no bond of loyalty or trust between Al and Bob; they each correctly assume that the other will, like themselves, be motivated exclusively by self-interest. The dilemma arises when each attempts to decide, without the possibility of collaboration, whether it is in his self-interest to plead guilty. For example, Al's reasoning would be as follows:

If I plead guilty then I'll get either a suspended sentence (if Bob pleads not guilty) or a sentence of four years (if Bob pleads guilty.) If I plead not guilty then I'll get either two years (if Bob pleads not guilty) or six years (if Bob pleads guilty.) The choice is between zero and four years (if I plead guilty) and two and six years (if I plead not guilty.) So pleading guilty looks better than pleading not guilty. A better outcome would be for us both to plead not guilty (for then we would both get only two years), but if Bob thought I was going to plead not guilty he'd plead guilty like a shot in or-

der to get a suspended sentence, and then I'd end up with six years. And if I thought Bob was going to plead not guilty I'd plead guilty in order to get the suspended sentence. Since neither of us is going to let the other one get the suspended sentence we both have to plead guilty.

Of course, Bob's reasoning would lead him to the same conclusion. This is a paradoxical result, for Al and Bob would each be better off if both pleaded not guilty, since in that case they would each receive two-year sentences. By seeking only their own self-interest they each receive four years, whereas a better outcome (i.e., one that serves their interests even better) eludes them. Why should self-interest lead them to a solution that is not in their self-interest?

2. Puzzles

These are just for fun, although they do require the use of various critical thinking skills for their solution. The solutions are given in section 3 of this Appendix, but try them first before looking up the solutions.

(1) JEREMY AND HIS TWO GIRL FRIENDS

Jeremy is a rather weird fellow with two girlfriends whom he likes equally. Each Sunday afternoon he visits one of them, and in order to avoid having to decide which one to visit, he has hit upon a novel solution. Since both live on the same subway line, but in opposite directions from his subway station, he simply enters the station and takes the first train that comes in. If the northbound train arrives first he visits Nancy, and if the southbound train arrives first he visits Sarah. Since there is an equal number of northbound and southbound trains, Jeremy reasons that in the long run he will visit them with more or less equal frequency. But after a few months, he realizes that he is visiting Nancy four times more often than he is visiting Sarah. What is Jeremy's mistake?

(2) JONATHAN'S CLOCK

My uncle Jonathan used to teach logic at the University of Toronto. Like most logicians he was antisocial, and during the summer months he used to stay in a cabin in the woods a few miles north of Kapuskasing where he would write articles on logic. Once a week he would walk into Kapuskasing for supplies. He had no radio or television, and no watch, but there was a large wind-up clock in the cabin. I asked him how he could set the clock when he first arrived in the spring, since he didn't know what the time was. He said, *Oh, I just wait until I make my first trip into Kapuskasing, and figure it out from that.* I objected that he wouldn't know how long it takes to make the trip since he doesn't have a watch. *That's right,* he said, *but that's not a problem. And I don't have to lug that damn clock into Kapuskasing and back, either.* How did he figure out how to set the clock to the right time?

(3) ANNA'S ANTHROPOLOGICAL ADVENTURES, PART I

Anna was an anthropologist who was studying the inhabitants of an island in the South Pacific. The people were divided into two tribes: the Saints, who always told the truth, and the Sinners, who always lied. In all other respects, however, they were indistinguishable, a fact that would have created problems for Anna had she not taken a logic elective while at college. When she first arrived, for example, she was walking along a path through the jungle looking for the Saints' village when she came to a fork in the path. While she was wondering which way to go, she noticed a native nearby and, after a moment's reflection, put one question to the native. The answer allowed her to work out which fork to take. But since she didn't know whether the native was a Saint or a Sinner, she had to use her logical skills. What was the question?

(4) ANNA'S ANTHROPOLOGICAL ADVENTURES, PART II

When Anna had completed her anthropological research on the island of the Saints and Sinners and was about to leave, the two tribes decided to hold a celebration in Anna's honour on the evening before her departure. There were many speeches, some of which paid tribute to her wisdom and kindness, and some of which castigated her for her stupidity and cruelty. Anna, obviously, hoped that it was the Saints who gave the former sort of speech, and the Sinners who gave the latter sort. At the end, however, one chief stood up (Anna didn't know whether he was a Saint or a Sinner) and said, *Tomorrow you leave us to return to your homeland. All the members of my tribe earnestly hope that you will return to our island in the future for another visit.* He was immediately followed by the other chief, who said, *On behalf of all the members of my tribe, I say to you that you should go and never return to our island.* Anna quickly worked out whether they really wanted her to return. Did they, and how did Anna work it out?

(5) SAM AND THE SURGEON

Sam and his father had gone to a baseball game, and while driving home they were involved in a car accident. Sam's father was killed instantly, and Sam was critically injured. He was rushed to a nearby hospital where it was decided that he required immediate surgery. But when he was wheeled into the operating room, the surgeon took one look at him and said, *I can't operate on this patient. He is my son.* Sam was not adopted, and had no stepfathers or foster fathers, yet what the surgeon said was true. What is the explanation?

(6) THE WEEKLY POKER GAME

Allan, Bruce, Charles, David, and Edward are friends who meet every Tuesday evening to play poker. One of them is an accountant, one a barber, one a clergyman, one a doctor, and one an editor. The accountant's wife is Allan's sister, and Bruce's second wife is the doctor's sister. Bruce's first wife is now married to the barber. Edward and the doctor, who are brothers, are both secretly in love with the editor's wife. Charles is still unmarried. The only time they gave up their weekly poker game was when David tried to seduce the editor's wife and she complained to the doctor's wife, who told the editor. Things were a little tense for a few months, but after Allan and the doctor had a heart-to-heart talk with the editor, they agreed to start their weekly poker game again. What are the occupations of the five men?

(7) MIRANDA'S WILL

A few weeks after the death of Derwent's wealthy but eccentric aunt Miranda, the executor of her estate requested that Derwent come to his office. When Derwent arrived the executor explained that Miranda's will directed him to give Derwent three sealed envelopes – one white, one brown, and one green – along with a letter from his late aunt. The letter said:

Dear Derwent,

I've always thought that you were not too bright, but I am going to give you one last chance to prove me wrong. One of these three envelopes contains a cheque for one hundred thousand dollars, while the other two contain only blank pieces of paper. You get to pick one envelope, and if you fail to pick the one with the cheque, the money will be donated to the Home for Wayward Pets. On the front of each envelope is a clue, but at least one of these clues is false, and at least one of them is true. This information is sufficient to determine which envelope contains the cheque. If you cannot figure it out, it will prove that you are as stupid as I thought you were.

The clues on the envelopes were the following:

White: *The cheque is in this envelope.*
Brown: *The cheque is not in this envelope.*
Green: *The cheque is not in the brown envelope.*

Which envelope should Derwent pick?

3. Solutions to the Puzzles

(1) JEREMY AND HIS TWO GIRL FRIENDS

The crucial factor that Jeremy forgot to take into account is the spacing of the arrivals of the trains. Suppose that a northbound train arrives every ten minutes and a southbound train arrives every ten minutes. If they arrive alternately five minutes apart, then since Jeremy enters the station at random times he will get northbound and southbound trains with more or less equal frequency. But if the southbound train arrives two minutes after the northbound train and the next northbound train arrives eight minutes later, then he will tend to get a northbound train 80 per cent of the time, and he will visit Nancy four times more often than he visits Sarah.

(2) JONATHAN'S CLOCK

Before Jonathan leaves to walk into Kapuskasing he winds the clock and notes the time. He then walks at a steady pace until he reaches

Kapuskasing and notes the correct time on the clock at the bank. When he finishes his business in Kapuskasing, he notes the time on the bank clock and then retraces his steps back to his cabin at the same steady pace. When he reaches the cabin he then notes the time on his clock. He thus knows (a) how long his entire trip took (from the cabin clock) and (b) how long he spent in Kapuskasing (from the bank clock). He then subtracts (b) from (a) and divides the answer by two, and in this way knows how long it took him to walk back from Kapuskasing. He then adds this time to the time on the bank clock when he left Kapuskasing, and he can then set the cabin clock to the correct time. As long as he walked both ways at a steady pace his cabin clock should not be more than a few minutes out.

(3) ANNA'S ANTHROPOLOGICAL ADVENTURES, PART I

The question Anna must ask is, *Which fork leads to your village?* If the native is a Saint, then he will point to the path that leads to the Saint's village, since he always tells the truth. If the native is a Sinner, then he will point to the path that leads to the Saint's village, since he always tells lies. In either case he will have to point to the path to the Saint's village. Had Anna been looking for the Sinner's village, she would still have asked the same question, but instead of taking the path the native pointed to she would take the other path.

(4) ANNA'S ANTHROPOLOGICAL ADVENTURES, PART II

The first chief to speak must have been a Saint, because he said one thing (*Tomorrow you leave us to return to your homeland*) that you (and Anna) know to be true. So he wants Anna to return again. And, since the second chief had to be a Sinner, he must be lying and must therefore really want Anna to return. If you tried to approach this puzzle in the same way as number 3, you will have learned the importance of looking first for simple solutions, and trying more complicated solutions only when the simple ones fail.

(5) SAM AND THE SURGEON

This is not really a logical puzzle, but it does illustrate the importance of paying careful attention to our assumptions. If we make assumptions that are false, it is easy to be led to accept arguments that are blatantly invalid. The assumption in this case is a sexist one, for the surgeon was Sam's mother. Until very recently most people had difficulty solving this puzzle; as sexist assumptions disappear this "puzzle" should cease to be a puzzle.

(6) THE WEEKLY POKER GAME

Allan is the barber, Bruce is the editor, Charles is the clergyman, David is the doctor, and Edward is the accountant. The easiest way to solve puzzles of this sort is to draw up a matrix, or grid, which represents every possible combination of name and occupation.

Each statement gives information that can be used to eliminate possibilities. For example, *The editor's wife is Allan's sister* means that the editor is not Allan, so an X can be put in the Editor/Allen box. It is also helpful to note the marital status of each person beside the name and occupation. Once you have eliminated four possibilities in a row (or column) you will know the occupation of one of the men, and you will also be able to eliminate the other possibilities in the appropriate column or row.

	Allan	Bruce	Charles	David	Edward
Accountant					
Barber					
Clergyman					
Doctor					
Editor					

(7) MIRANDA'S WILL

The best strategy for solving this puzzle is to use the information given to eliminate possibilities. We know that at least one clue is true and at least one clue is false. (1) So let us consider the possibility that the white clue is true. If the white clue is true then the cheque must be in the white envelope, which means that the brown clue and the green clue are also true. But since at least one clue is false, this means that our assumption that the white clue is true must be false, that is, the white clue must be false. It also means that the cheque cannot be in the white envelope. This leaves three, but only three, other possibilities:

(2) the brown clue is true and the green clue is false.
(3) the green clue is true and the brown clue is false.
(4) both the brown and green clues are true.

(2) If the brown clue is true then the cheque must be in the green envelope, and if the green clue is false then the cheque must be in the brown envelope. But this is impossible, since the cheque cannot be in both envelopes, so this possibility is eliminated.

(3) If the green clue is true then the cheque must be in the green envelope, and if the brown clue is false then the cheque must be in the brown envelope. But this is impossible, since the cheque cannot be in both envelopes, so this possibility is also eliminated.

(4) If the brown clue is true then the cheque must be in the green envelope, and if the green clue is true then the cheque must be in the green envelope. And this is possible.

The last possibility is thus the only one that is consistent with the information given – that at least one clue is true and at least one is false. Therefore the cheque must be in the green envelope.

Appendix II

Answers To Self-Tests

The self-tests are designed not to test your comprehension of concepts and principles directly, but to test the critical thinking skills that are based on them. Most of the questions are quite straightforward. If you get more than one or two wrong answers in any test, you should review the preceding material in order to discover why you are having difficulty. Usually it will be because you have misunderstood some concept or principle, and not because of any difficulty in the questions themselves.

The fact that the questions are quite straightforward, however, creates a hazard that you should beware of. If you look up the answers without trying to work out an answer of your own, you will usually think-that the answer given is quite obvious. This may lead you to conclude that you do not need to do the self-tests. Resist this conclusion, for it is deceptive. The answers given here should all be obvious *after* you read them, but this does not mean that they would have been obvious *before* you read them.

It may be that some of these answers are not as plausible as others that might have been given. I hope this is not the case, but my hopes are no guarantee that I have not missed some better answers. If you are occasionally convinced that your answer is better than the one you find here, you may well be correct. If your critical thinking skills have been well developed by this book, your judgement should not lead you astray.

Self-Test No. 1

I.

1.   This is an argument.
       Premise: *You promised your parents you would go home.*
       Conclusion: *You should go home next weekend.*

2.	This is probably not an argument. However, it is possible, although unlikely, that the speaker means that a reason for going home would be to have a good time. On this interpretation, the passage would be an argument.

3.	This is an argument.
	Premise 1: *Ted won the Intercollegiate ten thousand metres last year.*
	Premise 2: *He has been training hard ever since.*
	Conclusion: *He should win the Intercollegiate ten thousand metres this year.*

4.	This is an argument.
	Premise 1: *The doctor told me that a second operation won't be necessary.*
	Premise 2: *I will be able to go home this Friday.*
	Conclusion: *I will be able to visit you next month.*

5.	This is not an argument. It is merely a description of an event.

6.	This is not an argument. It is merely a statement that is unsupported by any reasons or evidence.

7.	This is an argument.
	Premise: *The company's sales declined by 23 per cent in the last three months.*
	Conclusion: *The company was justified in laying off 250 assembly line workers.*

8.	This is not an argument. It is merely a claim.

9.	This is not an argument. It is merely a description.

10.	This is an argument, although the premises and conclusion need to be rewritten to make explicit what the argument implies.
	Premise 1: *Last year Alex and Doreen both took a full course load while working twenty hours a week.*
	Premise 2: *Last year Alex and Doreen both failed their semesters.*
	Premise 3: *You are taking a full course load while working twenty hours a week.*
	Conclusion: *You will fail your semester.*

II.

1. Sound. However, if you did not know that Guelph is in Ontario, or that Ontario is in Canada, you should have answered that it is merely a logically strong argument.

2. Merely logically strong. However, if you really thought that Guelph is larger than Vancouver, you should have answered that it is a sound argument.

3. Merely logically strong. Since you don't know who Jimmy, Jane, and June are, it would be incorrect to say that it is a sound argument.

4. Merely logically strong. Even if you knew that the first premise is true, since you don't know who Katherine is, it would be incorrect to say that the argument is sound.

5. Sound, assuming that hockey is Canada's national sport. Otherwise it is a merely logically strong argument.

6. Sound. However, if you did not know that both premises are true, you should have answered that it is merely a logically strong argument.

7. Merely logically strong. Since the context indicates that the word *cat* is being used in a very broad sense, the first premise is obviously false.

8. Sound. It is not necessary to know who the Prime Minister is in order to know that he or she is a human being.

9. Merely logically strong. You do not know who Robin is and thus do not know whether he or she is a winner. In addition, it is not true that everybody loves a winner: some people detest winners.

10. Sound. However, if you did not interpret *I* as referring to yourself, the correct answer would be that it is merely a logically strong argument.

Self-Test No. 2

1. Persuasive

2.   Descriptive

3.   Persuasive

4.   Emotive

5.   Descriptive

6.   Recreational

7.   Directive

8.   Performative

9.   Directive. Note, however, that although it appears to be addressed to all pedestrians, it is really a directive only for those pedestrians who want to cross the street.

10. Emotive and evocative. It is likely that the author has both purposes in mind.

Self-Test No. 3

1.   Too narrow, because the defining phrase (*the supreme legislative body of Canada*) applies only to the parliament of Canada, and excludes the parliaments of other countries.

2.   Too broad, because the defining phrase (*art form that uses words to communicate ideas and images*) includes other art forms that use words to communicate ideas and images, such as novels and plays.

3.   Too broad, because the defining phrase (*implement designed to remove snow*) includes other implements designed to remove snow, such as snow shovels and snow blowers. It is also circular, which would make the definition useless for anyone who does not know what snow is.

4.   Circular.

5.   Obscure. This definition would only be informative to someone who already has extensive knowledge of music theory.

6. Too broad, since the defining phrase includes several other devices that are used to fasten pages together, such as paper clips and binders. It is also too narrow, since the defining phrase excludes staplers that are designed for use in construction and for other industrial uses.

7. Too narrow, because the defining phrase excludes male nurses. It is also too broad, because it includes other health care professionals, such as doctors and chiropractors.

8. Too broad, since the defining phrase includes other kinds of one-storey buildings such as garages and shops.

9. Too broad, since the defining phrase also refers to other international organizations, such as the European Community, the Olympics, NATO, and the International Civil Aviation Organization.

10. Too broad, since the defining phrase also includes such competitive activities as operating a business, playing chess, and competing in music festivals, none of which are sports. It is also too narrow, since the defining phrase excludes such individual sports as sport fishing, surf boarding, and sky diving, that are not normally competitive.

Self-Test No. 4

1. There is a referential ambiguity here since it is unclear whether the term *his sisters* is being used collectively or distributively. If it is used distributively the sentence means that Billy gave two boxes of candy, one to each sister. If it is being used collectively the sentence means that Billy gave his sisters one box of candy to be shared between them.

2. There is a double ambiguity here. If *he* refers to a chicken then *chicken* is probably being used in its literal sense. But if *he* refers to a person then *chicken* is being used in its metaphorical sense to mean cowardly.

3. There is a grammatical ambiguity in this sentence. Literally, the sentence means that Melissa has nothing else in the world besides her one dress. If the location of the word *only* is changed to make the sentence read *Melissa has only one dress*, it means that although she may have many possessions, she has only one dress. This is the more likely meaning.

4. The term *general* is referentially ambiguous. It could refer to a local hospital, in which case the sentence means that the nurses won their strike with the hospital. Or it could refer to a specific military officer, in which case the sentence means that the officer was beaten by the nurses in some kind of contest or struggle.

5. If the term *conversational German* is being merely mentioned, then it refers to a textbook or a course, and the sentence means that it is a difficult book or course. If the term is being used, then the sentence means that it is difficult to learn how to speak conversational German.

6. The term *discipline* is referentially ambiguous. It could refer simply to corporal punishment, which is how some people use the term. But it could refer to a set of rules imposed by adults that children are expected to follow. It could also refer to self-discipline, that is, to a set of rules that children learn to develop for themselves. The meaning of the sentence is quite different depending upon which reference we choose.

7. Literally, the speaker has promised never to speak to the person again if he or she thinks it over and still decides to drop out of school. In most contexts, the principle of charity would require us to interpret the speaker as meaning ...*I won't say another word to you about dropping out of school*.

8. The term *instructors* is referentially ambiguous. If it is being used collectively the sentence means that the instructors, as a group, are free to choose whatever text they can all agree on. If the term is being used distributively, the sentence means that each instructor is free to choose whatever text he or she wishes.

9. The sentence is grammatically ambiguous. If *illegally* modifies *tested* the sentence means that the stores were illegally tested. If *illegally* modifies *sell* it means that the stores were illegally selling cigarettes.

10. This sentence is grammatically ambiguous. If *with a bright red hood* modifies *limousine* the sentence means that the limousine has a bright red hood. But if *with a bright red hood* modifies *arrived* the sentence means that she was wearing a bright red hood.

Self-Test No. 5

1. Analytic. If you know what a full deck of cards is you know that it must have fifty-two cards.

2. Analytic. Since a centimetre is defined as one-hundredth of a metre and millimetre is defined as one-thousandth of a metre, a centimetre must, by definition, be longer than a millimetre.

3. Synthetic. There is nothing about the meanings of the words in this sentence that guarantees its truth or falsity.

4. Synthetic. The truth or falsity of this sentence can only be determined by checking a reference book. The meaning of the sentence leaves its truth or falsity an open question.

5. Synthetic. As far as we know this is a true statement. But its truth is something we have learned, and is not determined by the meaning of the sentence.

6. Contradictory. The first clause in the sentence is contradicted by the last clause.

7. Synthetic. Assuming that the speaker correctly understands the meanings of the words in this sentence, he or she could only be proven wrong by sending him or her to the southern hemisphere with a compass.

8. Synthetic. Observations would be needed to determine the truth of this statement.

9. Synthetic, on both the literal and metaphorical interpretation. In both cases, the truth of the sentence could only be determined by investigating the facts.

10. On a literal interpretation this is an analytic statement. However, it would normally be used to mean something like *You should not adopt romantic or highly speculative interpretations of ordinary things,* which is synthetic.

Self-Test No. 6

1. The evaluative meaning is negative. Descriptively, *vicious competition* means that the usual aspects of competitiveness (such as wanting to be better than others, complaining when others do well, trying to place others at a disadvantage) are carried to extreme lengths. A good descriptive synonym would be *fierce*.

2. The evaluative meaning is negative. Descriptively, a *compulsively tidy person* is one who finds untidiness very annoying. A good descriptive synonym would be *extremely*.

3. The evaluative meaning is positive. Descriptively, *responsible student* means that Mark gets his homework done, submits his assignments on time, pays attention in class, follows the school rules, and so on. Perhaps the best descriptive synonym would be *obedient*, although this suggests that Mark always has to be told what to do, which is probably not part of the normal meaning of *responsible* in this context.

4. The evaluative meaning is negative, since a decline in moral standards means that they have changed for the worse. The descriptive meaning of *declined* in this context is that moral standards have changed. A good descriptive synonym is *changed*.

5. The evaluative meaning is negative. Descriptively, *greed* refers to a desire for money and material goods. A good descriptive equivalent would be *a desire for money and material goods*.

6. The evaluative meaning is negative, because it suggests that the budget reduction has been ruthless or excessive. Descriptively, *slashed* means reduced, and *reduced* is the best descriptive synonym.

7. The evaluative meaning is negative. *Very, extremely*, and *highly* all capture the descriptive meaning of *excessively* and would be good descriptive synonyms.

8. The evaluative meaning is negative. Descriptively, *suckered* means being persuaded to do something by underhanded or dishonest means. The best descriptive synonym is *persuaded*.

9. The evaluative meaning is positive since *mature* suggests the opposite of inexperienced. Descriptively, *mature years* means that he was middle aged or older. *Old age* would be the best descriptive synonym.

10. The evaluative meaning is negative, since referring to an adult women as a *girl* denigrates her. A better descriptive synonym is *secretary*.

Self-Test No. 7

1. A sufficient condition, since this is only one of several ways to bring down a fever. If interpreted as a necessary condition, it would mean that this is the only way of bringing down a fever, which is false.

2. The two conditions stated are jointly sufficient conditions for being required to withdraw from the university. If interpreted as a necessary condition for being required to withdraw, the statement would mean that this is the only way of being required to withdraw, which is false since one can be required to withdraw for other reasons, such as failing too many courses.

3. A necessary condition, since while no applicants will be admitted unless they meet the stated conditions, not every student who meets these conditions can expect to be admitted. If the sentence is interpreted as stating a sufficient condition it means that every student who meets these conditions will be admitted, which is a highly implausible interpretation.

4. Probably a necessary condition, since working hard throughout the term is not the only thing most students have to do to get an A average. If interpreted as a sufficient condition, it means that working hard will always produce an A average. This is an unlikely interpretation, since even students who work hard throughout the whole term would probably not get an A if they failed to hand in their term assignments.

5. A sufficient condition, since there are normally other defects that may lead to an essay's being returned ungraded, for example, if it is illegible or submitted late.

6. This statement gives both the necessary and sufficient conditions for winning the prize. If interpreted merely as a necessary condition it would mean that, although every winner would have the highest average, some

years the student with the highest average might not be awarded the prize. If interpreted merely as a sufficient condition it would mean that, although each year the student with the highest average would receive the prize, another student who failed to achieve the highest average might also receive the prize, perhaps with the money divided between them.

7. A necessary condition. If interpreted as a sufficient condition it would mean that every member of Parliament would become prime minister.

8. A necessary condition, since presumably if interest rates do not come down the confidence of the business community will not be restored. It might also be a sufficient condition, if reducing interest rates is the only thing necessary to restore confidence in the economy, but this would only make sense if it is assumed that all the other factors necessary to restore confidence (such as stable international markets, acceptable exchange rates, reasonable taxes) are already present and are unlikely to change.

9. A necessary condition, since good physical co-ordination is necessary for becoming a good skier. But it is not a sufficient condition, or else anyone with good physical co-ordination who had never skied before would already be a good skier, which is absurd.

10. A necessary condition. If it were a sufficient condition, it would mean that everyone with a Ph.D. would become a university professor, which is absurd.

Self-Test No. 8

1. Missing premise: *My car (van, truck, or motorcycle) doesn't have enough gas to drive you home.*

2. Missing premise: *Your car is flooded.*

3. Missing conclusion: *You should attend (or make an effort to attend) church at Easter.*

4. Missing premise: *Jennifer lives in Toronto and her sister does not.*

5. Missing premise: *Students who do not attend class regularly are likely to do poorly in the course.*

6. Missing conclusion: *Todd is a teenage rebel.*

7. Missing premise: *It won't be possible to repair my hearing aid.*

8. Missing premise: *School boards have a responsibility to achieve a low drop-out rate.*

9. Missing premise: *Students who work hard on an assignment deserve a high grade.*

10. Missing premise: *Animals deserve the same kind of legal protection as humans enjoy.*

Self-Test No. 9

1. This is not an argument, but an explanation. The speaker is offering an explanation for his or her stage fright.

2. This is not an argument. It is a description of an event, but it includes an explanation of David's behaviour (i.e., that David was upset at what he thought was his fault and felt responsible for Steven.)

3. This is an argument. It states a conclusion (*We'd better watch Gina closely for the next twenty-four hours*) and gives reasons to support it.

4. This is merely a general explanation of the form *X* may be caused by *a, b,* or *c.*

5. This is an explanation of why local taxes increase. By adding the comment *That is how the system works,* the speaker makes it clear that he or she is merely explaining the system.

6. This is a report of an argument. In a context where it was clear that the speaker approved of the Supreme Court's reasoning, it could legitimately be regarded as an argument.

7. This is an argument. The conclusion is *Never turn off your computer without following the exit procedure for your software program*. The reason given in support of this conclusion consists of an explanation of what the consequences will be if the exit procedure is not followed.

8. This is probably best interpreted as an argument with a missing conclusion: *You ought to refund the entire purchase price*. The advice received from the speaker's lawyer is the reason the speaker gives for this conclusion.

9. This is an argument. It includes an explanation of why the jury system allegedly works to the advantage of criminals, but this explanation is merely a premise used to support the conclusion that the jury system should be abolished.

10. This is probably best not interpreted as an argument. In most contexts it would likely be an explanation of why Americans fail to understand how Canadian political parties operate.

Self-Test No. 10

1. [Anyone who has brains and ambition will go far in this world.](P1) [Carla has certainly got plenty of both.](P2) <u>So she will go far.</u>

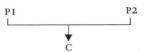

2. [I have never had any problems with the last four Fords I've bought,](P1) <u>so I don't think I'll have any problems this time.</u> Note that there is a missing premise in this argument: [A company that has made good products in the past is likely to continue to make good products.](MP2)

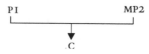

3. <u>The Blue Jays should win the American League pennant this year.</u> [They have solid depth in their pitching staff,](P1) [their hitting has been consistently good this year,](P2) [their coaching is excellent](P3), and [there is a good team spirit.](P4)

4. [A recent public opinion poll showed that more than two-thirds of Canadians believed that most politicians were dishonest.](P1) Clearly, <u>there is a crisis of confidence in Canadian politics.</u> There is a missing premise: [Widespread belief that most politicians are dishonest constitutes a crisis of confidence.](MP2)

5. <u>In the last thirty years there has been a tremendous increase in the university participation rate (i.e., the percentage of population in the eighteen-to twenty-two-year age group that attends university).</u> [In 1960, the participation rate in Canada was only 5 per cent.](P1) But [by 1990 the participation rate was over 15 per cent.](P2)

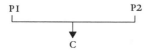

6. [Laura gets pretty good grades,](P1) [she is the best gymnast in the school,](P2) [she has a lot of friends,](P3) and [she organized the campaign last year which forced the school to start a recycling program.](P4) I think <u>she will probably win the election for president of the Students' Council.</u>

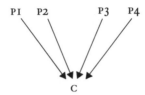

7. [If he tells his teacher he cheated he will be punished by the principal.](P1) But [if he doesn't tell his teacher he cheated he will be punished by his parents.](P2) One way or another he is going to be punished.

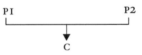

8. Since [angle CAB is 60 degrees,](P1) and [angle ACB is 40 degrees,](P2) then <u>angle ABC must be 80 degrees.</u> There are two missing premises in this argument: [Figure ABC is a triangle](MP3) and [The angles of a triangle always add up to 180 degrees.](MP4)

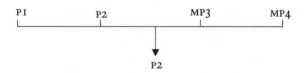

9. <u>Any reporter who says that good reporters never slant their stories but simply report the objective facts, must be either stupid or dishonest,</u> since [it is obvious that one cannot write anything without an element of inter-

pretation creeping in.](P1) There is a missing premise: [Someone who denies something that is obvious is either stupid or dishonest.](MP2)

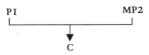

10. [That reporter is obviously not stupid.](P1) So <u>he must be dishonest.</u> There are two missing premises: [Any reporter who says that good reporters never slant their stories but simply report the objective facts, must be either stupid or dishonest](MP2) and [That reporter said that good reporters never slant their stories but simply report the objective facts.](MP3)

Self-Test No. 11

1. Empirical. Checking the facts about the most recent New Brunswick election will determine whether the statement is true.

2. Empirical. Checking the facts about my children's hopes regarding a white Christmas will determine whether the statement is true.

3. Non-empirical. No amount of checking empirical facts – either about St. Paul's Cathedral or about people's beliefs about it – will determine the truth or falsity of this statement. It is an evaluation.

4. Empirical. The empirical facts that will determine whether this statement is true or false are not easy to obtain, although scientists claim that there is clear and mounting evidence that it is true. But nothing other than empirical evidence could determine the truth or falsity of this claim. It is interesting to note that a conclusive empirical proof of the truth of this statement would only be possible when only one person remains alive.

5. Non-empirical. This is an analytic statement that states one of the defining conditions of a triangle. If you thought you could determine its truth value by measuring the angles of a triangle with a protractor, you would be treating this as an empirical statement. But as any mathematics teacher would tell you, doing this would not get you any marks on a mathematics examination.

6. Empirical. This statement should be interpreted as meaning something like *I am sure the Toronto Maple Leafs will not win the Stanley Cup this year*, and whether this prediction is true will be determined by what happens at the end of the season. Even if it is taken literally, however, it would still be an empirical statement whose truth would be determined by whether the speaker eats his or her hat if the team wins the Stanley Cup.

7. Empirical. This is a hypothetical statement, whose truth can only be determined by a complex analysis of a wide range of economic and political information.

8. Empirical. Despite the fact that the award is given to the best student in the school, this statement does not endorse the fact that Paula received the award. It is a simple statement of an empirical fact. In some contexts – for example, if cited as evidence that Paula is an excellent student – it could be interpreted as an evaluation.

9. Non-empirical. Although the statement includes the empirical claim that suicide rates are highest around Christmas, the primary purpose of the statement is most likely to make an evaluation of this fact.

10. Empirical. This is a claim about the effects of the policy of banning the sale of ivory. Its truth would be determined by an examination of the facts regarding the ivory market, and the decline in the illegal killing of elephants in Africa.

Self-Test No. 12

1. The conclusion of the argument is:
If we want economic prosperity for Canada, we ought to be looking for wars to get involved in.
The weakness in the argument is that the premise

Every nation that has fought a major war in this century emerged from the war economically stronger than it was before

is false. Many nations, such as Britain, the USSR, Vietnam, Japan, and Iran, among others, have suffered great economic losses as a result of wars they have been involved in. This is, or should be, a matter of common knowledge.

2. The conclusion of the argument is:

The government has no right to force me and others who think the way I do to pay the GST.

The argument commits the fallacy of equivocation. The word *governed* is used collectively in the first premise but distributively in the second premise.

3. The conclusion of the argument is:

There is nothing I can do about the fact that the outboard motor I bought last year turned out to be a real lemon.

The weakness of the argument is that it relies upon a false dichotomy in the premises. The speaker assumes that there are only two possibilities open to him or her: (1) sue the company, and (2) do nothing. But there are other things that could be done: for example, (3) write to the president of the company, asking for compensation, (4) make a public stink by writing letters to the press or mounting a sign on the boat that says *Evinrudes are Lemons.*

4. The conclusion of the argument is:

Only in democracies does the human spirit flourish.

The weakness in the argument is that it begs the question. Does the human spirit flourish only in democratic societies? Yes, says the author, because undemocratic societies prevent the human spirit from flourishing. The "evidence" is just another way of stating the conclusion.

5. The conclusion of the argument is:

He should be found not guilty.

This argument commits the fallacy of inconsistency. The lawyer cannot have it both ways: if either one of the two "compelling" reasons is true, then the other must be false. They cannot consistently be asserted together.

6. The conclusion of the argument is:

    People are much more interested in local issues than they are in provincial and national political issues.

    The weakness in the argument is that the premise is false. This is, or should be, common knowledge.

7. The conclusion of the argument is:

    Scientists should accept that biblical miracles actually occurred.

    The premises of the argument, however, use the word *miracle* in a quite different sense from the way the author uses it in the conclusion. The argument therefore commits the fallacy of equivocation.

8. The conclusion of the argument is:

    We should adopt a non-aligned foreign policy.

    The author, however, is presupposing that the two alternatives presented are the only possibilities. This is unacceptable, since it ignores the possibility of a foreign policy that does not rely upon the threat of nuclear annihilation but rejects a non-aligned foreign policy. The argument commits the fallacy of false dichotomy.

9. The conclusion of the argument is:

    Professor Smith's new course will be a great course.

    The weakness in the argument is that it fails to recognize the difference between being a member of a team that developed and taught a great course, and developing and teaching a course by oneself. What is true of the three professors as a team may not be true of them individually. Thus, the argument relies upon a fallacy of equivocation between the collective and distributive senses of the phrase *excellent teachers*.

10. The conclusion of the argument is:

    I am almost halfway through this book.

    The premise *There are thirteen chapters in this book* is false, as you could discover by checking the Table of Contents. Even though the conclusion is true, and the premise is relevant, the argument is weak.

Self-Test No. 13

1. There is no reason to think that the fact someone's father has been convicted for fraud means that the person is completely untrustworthy. The

premise is thus irrelevant. This is similar to an ad hominem, although it is personal qualities of the speaker's father that are being attacked rather than those of the speaker.

2. Unless one is prepared to argue that the popularity of a television show is a good indicator of the quality of the show, this argument commits an irrelevant appeal to popularity.

3. This is a legitimate appeal to authority, at least if presented by someone who knows who Gödel is and knows he meets the criteria for a reliable authority. If you did not know that Gödel meets these criteria, you should refuse to accept the appeal until you have reason to believe that the criteria are satisfied.

4. This argument commits the straw man fallacy. Evolutionary theory does not claim that humans are just monkeys with less hair, or that our ancestors were apes.

5. This argument commits the ad hominem fallacy. It attacks the views of feminists on the ground that feminists are selfish. It also commits the straw man fallacy, since feminists are characterized in a false way, that is, as a group that is seeking all the good jobs for women.

6. This argument appeals to *the wisdom of history* as the reason for condemning the view that mothers and fathers can be equal partners as head of the family unit. History is thus treated as a kind of authority on how the family should be organized. This is clearly an irrelevant appeal.

7. This is an example of the kind of irrelevant things we say when we are pressed to defend an irrational position. Obviously, the fact that Janine hates flying has nothing to do with whether or not the speaker is being silly.

8. This argument probably commits the straw man fallacy, since it is unlikely that the son actually believes, as his father claims he does, that everybody should be free to do whatever they want in life. Perhaps the son actually said what his father attributes to him, but in this case the father has violated the principle of charity, since the son probably meant something much more reasonable, namely, that everybody should be free to seek whatever career they want. The father's attempted rebuttal, of

course, is relevant only against the unreasonable interpretation of the son's beliefs.

9.   This argument commits the tu quoque fallacy, since it argues that the fact that anglophones treated francophones unfairly in the past is a good reason for the francophones to treat anglophones unfairly in the present. The only way to avoid the tu quoque charge would be to argue that revenge of this sort is morally justified.

10.   This argument is a blatant ad hominem. There is not even a pretence that the schoolteacher's charges against the principal have been investigated and found to be invalid on the basis of relevant evidence.

Self-Test No. 14

1.   This is a post hoc fallacy, since the only evidence offered to show that the nuclear power plant caused the miscarriage is that the miscarriage occurred after the plant was built. There may be a causal connection, but this argument does nothing to establish it.

2.   There is a very hasty conclusion to this argument. The conclusion makes a comparative judgement (*Indonesia has the worst record...*) while the premises merely give information about Indonesia.

3.   This argument probably commits the fallacy of common cause. Those who have not worked very hard during the term (a) tend to cram immediately before examinations, and (b) tend to get lower marks than the average. It is more likely that both (a) and (b) are caused by not working hard during the term, than that (a) causes (b).

4.   This is a slippery slope fallacy. The intermediate steps in the chain of predictions are only sketched, but even if they were spelled out in detail, the final predicted outcome (*complete loss of sovereignty*) would probably not be well supported. Without the intermediate steps being explicitly stated, the premises are clearly inadequate.

5.   There are two post hoc fallacies in this argument. (1) The stomach cramps started shortly after the fluoridation program was introduced; therefore, the fluoridation caused the cramps. (2) The stomach cramps disappeared

shortly after the speaker started drinking bottled water; therefore, the bottled water cured the cramps.

6. Perhaps there is no causal relationship whatever between high-school drop-out rates and the incidence of juvenile delinquency. However, there might be a common cause of the two phenomena: both might be caused by underlying social conditions. This is at least a plausible assertion. But if there is a common cause, it would not support the suggestion that increasing the drop-out rate will reduce juvenile delinquency.

7. The analogy that this argument relies upon is quite weak. There are several important relevant dissimilarities between giving clean needles to prison inmates and giving normal bullets to bank robbers: the former would not put the public at greater risk of harm, whereas the latter almost certainly would; the former would prevent the spread of a deadly disease, whereas the latter would not; the former is practicable, whereas the latter is not. Note that there is one important relevant similarity that gives the argument some strength: in both cases criminals are being assisted in committing crimes. This similarity, however, is not sufficient to outweigh the important dissimilarities. The premises are therefore not adequate to support the implied conclusion (that prison inmates should not be given clean needles).

8. The evidence cited by the politician is clearly inadequate to support the conclusion of the argument. There could be a number of plausible explanations for the fact that the politician has received no phone calls supporting the proposal: he or she may have a reputation for being unsympathetic to the poor; there may have been no publicity given to the proposal, so the voters may not know about it; and so on. The appeal to the absence of contrary evidence is illegitimate in this case.

9. To explain the weakness in this argument it needs to be reconstructed, for it contains a sub-argument. The reconstruction is:
P1. All the public opinion polls for the last year have shown that the government has a lower approval rating than either of the two opposition parties.
C1/P2. The Premier knows that the government is not going to be re-elected.
C2. The Premier will postpone calling an election until the last possible moment.
C1/P2 is not adequately supported by P1, since despite the polls it is possible that the Premier has not given up all hope of winning the election, and may believe that it is possible to increase the government's approval

rating before the election must be called. The strength of the sub-argument thus depends upon how much time is available before an election is required. The more time available to the Premier, the weaker is the first argument. It would have been better if, instead of C1/P2, the speaker had argued that the Premier is worried that the government may not be re-elected. C2, on the other hand, is better supported. However, it is still not a strong argument, since if the polls show an increase in the government's approval rating before the last possible moment, the Premier might call a snap election.

10. The weakness of this argument derives from the fact most people regard the right to hold demonstrations on public property as an important democratic right, one not to be restricted unless there is a very strong reason for doing so. Clearly, the author does not agree with this view, since he or she wants demonstrations banned simply because they are an inconvenience to some people. But the argument violates the criterion of adequacy because it fails to address the reasons most people have for tolerating the inconvenience of public demonstrations.

Self-Test No. 15

1. p = You buy a new coat.
   q = You won't be able to buy your textbooks for next term.
   r = Your grades will suffer.
   If p then q.
   If q then r.
   Therefore, if p then r.
   This is a chain argument, and thus is a valid argument.

2. p = Ellen violated the confidentiality of the committee.
   q = Ellen would have harmed herself more than anyone else.
   If p then q.
   Not-q.
   Therefore, not-p.
   This is a denial of the consequent, and thus is a valid argument.

3. p = I will have surgery.
   q = I will have a long program of physiotherapy.
   Either p or q.
   Not-p.

Therefore, q.

This is a disjunctive syllogism, and thus is a valid argument.

4.   p = It will rain during the game.

q = The team will lose.

If p then q.

Not-p.

Therefore, not-q.

This is a denial of the antecedent, and thus is fallacious.

5.   p = The Conservatives won more than 50 per cent of the votes in the 1989 election.

q = The Conservatives have a mandate to implement the free trade agreement.

If p then q.

Not-p.

Therefore, not-q.

This is a denial of the antecedent, and thus is fallacious.

6.   p = Chris wins the election.

q = Chris is well known to a lot of students.

If p then q.

Not-q.

Therefore, not-p.

This is a denial of the consequent, and thus is a valid argument.

7.   p = Chris is well known to a lot of students.

q = Chris wins the election.

If p then q.

Not-p.

Therefore, not-q.

This is a denial of the antecedent, and thus is fallacious.

Had we let p and q stand for the same statements as in question 6 the form of the argument would still be the same:

If q then p.

Not-q.

Therefore, not-p.

8.   p = Left-wing radicals are really committed to freedom of speech.

q = Left-wing radicals would defend freedom of speech whenever and wherever it comes under attack.

If p then q.

Not-q.

Therefore, not-p.

This is a denial of the consequent, and thus is a valid argument.

9.   p = This is question 5.

q = I am losing my mind.

If p then q.

Not-p.

Therefore, not-q.

This is a denial of the antecedent, and thus is fallacious.

10.   p = I have not lost my mind.

q = This is question 8.

If p then q.

q.

Therefore, p.

This is an affirmation of the consequent, and thus is fallacious. If we let p stand for *I have lost my mind* then we have the following form:

If not-p then q.

q.

Therefore, not-p.

This is still an affirmation of the consequent. By letting p stand for the negative statement it is easier to identify the form, but there is nothing wrong with using not-p instead of p as long as we do so consistently.

Self-Test No. 16

1.   This is an inductive generalization. There is no information on the number of questionnaires returned, so we cannot tell whether the sample is large enough. But the sample is not a representative one, for the responses will have come only from those who pay their municipal taxes directly, and this excludes all tenants and almost all young people. The argument is therefore quite weak. There is another possible weakness in the argument. Taxpayers were asked whether they were satisfied with the recreational facilities provided by the city at the same time as they were presented with their tax bills. It is likely that some people who were in fact not satisfied with the current facilities would state that they were satisfied

because they were unwilling to pay higher taxes for new facilities. This would also bias the sample, and further weaken the argument.

2. This is an inductive generalization. The sample is certainly large enough, but is clearly not representative, for several reasons. (a) Canadian tourists from other provinces are under-represented, since unless they were driving home through the United States they would not be included. (b) Overseas tourists are under-represented, since most of them travel by air. (c) American non-tourists such as business people, workers, and so on are included since they were given questionnaires and may have responded even though they were not tourists. The argument is therefore weak.

3. This is a statistical syllogism. It is a weak argument because some obviously relevant information is ignored: the roommate is taking a non-specialized program, it is in arts rather than in science or engineering, and he has only a D average. All these factors make it likely that his chances of finding a job within three months of graduation are somewhat less than 90 per cent.

4. This is an inductive generalization. If introductory philosophy is an elective and not a required course, it is possible that the sample may be unrepresentative, since the kind of students who choose introductory philosophy as an elective course may be more likely to expect a university education to improve their communication skills than those who would avoid philosophy as an elective. The sample in this case is self-selected, so it is difficult to know whether it might be unrepresentative.

5. This is induction by confirmation. It is not a scientifically sophisticated example, but is respectable nonetheless. Even though not all the observations support the hypothesis, it is likely that there is some connection between Alfred's insomnia and his coffee-drinking habits. The disconfirming instances can perhaps be explained as the result of unknowingly drinking decaffeinated coffee, or the presence of other factors.

6. This is a statistical syllogism. It is weak for two reasons. It ignores the fact that the American is sufficiently interested in Canadian politics to take a course in it. It also ignores the fact that he or she is, presumably, attending a Canadian university and thus is living in Canada. Both these factors

make it likely that he or she will know more about Canadian politics than the average American.

7. This is an inductive generalization. It is extremely weak, because the sample is far too small and clearly unrepresentative.

8. This passage is best interpreted as comprising two arguments. The first argument has a missing conclusion, (*Anyone who trains for six hours a day with Jim Birkin and follows his diet is likely to make the national swim team*), which also forms the premise of the second argument. The first argument is:
Last year Frances and Rhonda spent six hours a day training with Jim Birkin and followed his special diet, and made Canada's national swim team.
Therefore, anyone who trains for six hours a day with Jim Birkin and follows his diet is likely to make the national swim team.
This is a very weak inductive generalization. The sample is certainly too small, and probably biased as well. The second argument is:
Anyone who trains for six hours a day with Jim Birkin and follows his diet is likely to make the national swim team.
I am training for six hours a day with Jim Birkin and following his special diet.
Therefore, I am likely to make the national swim team.
This is a statistical syllogism. It is a strong argument as it stands, although there might be important and relevant information about the speaker that would lead us to revise this judgement. The possible strength of the second argument does not, however, compensate for the weakness of the first argument.

9. This is an inductive generalization. The sample is large enough, but it may be somewhat unrepresentative. Because the survey was conducted on a weekend the sample probably under-represents first-year students, who are much more likely to visit their families on weekends than senior students. And senior students are probably less likely to support a fee increase to pay for new athletic facilities that may not be ready until after they graduate. In addition, perhaps those who would be most likely to support new athletic facilities are less likely to be home on a weekend because they are out training or engaged in some sporting activity.

10. This is induction by confirmation. Four observation statements have been confirmed, and there are apparently no disconfirming instances. On the basis of the argument presented there is strong support for the conclusion. Of course, it may not be strong enough to meet the standard of proof that

the law requires in criminal trials, namely, that guilt must be proven beyond a reasonable doubt.

Self-Test No. 17

Note: The principles listed below are only some of those that could be invoked in an attempt to justify the particular moral judgement in question. Not all of them, of course, could be defended by an acceptable generalization argument.

1. No-one who has ever been convicted of a criminal offence should hold elected public office / Only those who have a reputation for honesty and integrity should hold public office / No-one with a criminal record should hold public office until at least five years after release from prison / No-one who has ever cheated the government should hold public office.

2. Married women should always obey their husbands / Married women should always obey their husbands except when doing so would violate either the law or the Ten Commandments / Women with children should always obey the father of their children as long as he is supporting the children / It is wrong for parents to separate or divorce when they have children under the age of twelve.

3. Citizens ought to inform the police whenever they become suspicious that a criminal offence may have been committed / Citizens of a democratic state ought to inform the police whenever they become suspicious that a criminal offence may have been committed / Citizens ought to inform the police whenever they become aware that a serious criminal offence has been committed / Citizens of a democratic state ought to inform the police when they become aware that a criminal offence has been committed, as long as they believe that the offence is morally wrong.

4. It is wrong to submit a plagiarized assignment in a course / It is wrong to submit a plagiarized assignment for credit in a course that counts towards one's degree requirements / It is always wrong to cheat / It is wrong to claim credit for work done by others.

5. Canada should give no special priority to refugees who wish to enter Canada / Canada should not accept refugees as immigrants / Prospective

immigrants who attempt to jump the queue should be permanently barred from entering Canada.

Self-Test No. 18

1. To avoid complexity, we will assume that you are the student in question, that you purchased the essay, and that if you had submitted your own work it probably would have received a failing grade. Here are some of the likely good consequences:

(a) The time you would have spent working on the essay could be spent on more pleasurable activities.

(b) You will get a higher grade than you would if you wrote the essay yourself.

(c) The person you purchased the essay from will have money to spend on something that will give him or her pleasure.

The bad consequences are more complex because we have to consider some effects that are possible, although not certain, as well as the effects if you are caught cheating. Notice that (b) and (c) constitute bad effects not because they involve further cheating (since from the utilitarian's point of view cheating as such is not bad) but because the further cheating may have its own bad effects:

(a) The money you paid for the essay cannot be spent on other things you want.

(b) Your action may have a bad effect on your character, since each time you cheat it becomes a little easier to cheat the next time, and this may contribute indirectly to further bad consequences.

(c) Your action may have a bad effect on your friends if they know you cheated, since they may be encouraged to cheat by your example, and this may lead indirectly to bad consequences.

(d) If you are caught, the bad consequences to yourself would be substantial: failure in the course, possible expulsion from university, bad reputation, inability to get letters of reference for job applications.

(e) If you are caught, the reputation of the university and the value of its degrees might be adversely affected.

(f) If you are caught, the instructor will feel annoyed and/or hurt, and may develop a more cynical and suspicious attitude to students generally.

2. The good consequences will consist primarily of whatever happiness results from the fact that you have more money to spend. If you use the

money to buy a new coat, then the merchant, the manufacturer, and their workers will gain some benefit. If you give the money to Oxfam then people who are starving will benefit. However, if you are caught and criminal charges are laid against you, there would also be the following good consequences:

(a) A lawyer would earn some money by defending you.

(b) Some people who might have been tempted to cheat on their income tax will probably be deterred by knowing that you were caught and prosecuted.

(c) Many people may feel a sense of satisfaction that a cheat has been caught and prosecuted.

The bad consequences will include whatever unhappiness results from the fact that you have more money to spend. If you use the money to buy illegal drugs then you may be contributing to your own addiction. If you use the money to invest in a company that makes hard-core pornography you may be contributing to violence against women. In addition, however, there are the following possible bad effects:

(a) The government has slightly less revenue, and there will be a very slight, but nonetheless measurable, increase in the government's deficit.

(b) Your action may have a bad effect on your character, since each time you cheat it becomes a little easier to cheat the next time, and this may contribute indirectly to further bad consequences.

(c) Your action may have a bad effect on your friends if they know you cheated, since they may be encouraged to cheat by your example, and this may lead indirectly to bad consequences.

(d) If you are caught, the bad consequences to yourself would be substantial: a fine, a criminal conviction, possible loss of your job, bad reputation.

(e) If you are caught, your family and perhaps your friends will be unhappy at your plight.

3. The good consequences will include the following:

(a) Your friend will avoid criminal charges.

(b) Your friend's insurance rates will not increase.

(c) Your friend will avoid gaining a reputation for being irresponsible.

(d) You will not lose your friend.

The bad consequences will include the following:

(a) Your friend may be encouraged to take risks while driving in the future.

(b) You may resent the fact that you had to commit a criminal offence to protect your friend.

(c) The victims of the accident will feel angry that someone got away with a crime.

(d) Your friend will not have to pay anything towards the costs of the accident, thus driving up insurance rates marginally.

4. The good consequences would include the following:

(a) Some people who would have been convicted of criminal offences will not be charged.

(b) The price would likely be reduced, thus reducing the amount of crime committed by those who steal and rob in order to get the money to buy marijuana.

(c) The government could tax marijuana and thus obtain much-needed revenue.

(d) The criminals who currently control much of the traffic in marijuana would be put out of business.

The bad consequences would include the following:

(a) More people would use marijuana, thus increasing the health risks.

(b) The new marijuana users would have less money to spend on other things.

(c) Such a policy would increase pressure to legalize all illegal drugs, which would lead to an increase in their use.

5. The most important set of consequences that must be considered when dealing with this question is the impact of the ultimate victory or defeat of right-wing rebel groups in Central America. We have to compare the general happiness of the people of Central America that would result if the rebels win the struggle, with the general happiness of the people that would result if the rebels lose the struggle. This question will depend upon a number of very controversial predictions concerning the kind of society that would evolve in each case. We cannot address these in any detail here, but they would force us to deal with such questions as:

What is the probability that a victory for the rebels would produce a small wealthy elite class with most ordinary people being in abject poverty? and

What is the probability that the defeat of the rebels would produce a Cuban-style dictatorship?

Each of these predictions would then be used as a basis for estimating the amount of happiness that would be produced for the people of Central America.

There is, however, another complicating factor that must be taken into account. This is the unhappiness that is caused by the armed struggle itself. It is possible that greater happiness would result from the victory of the rebels than by their defeat, but that when the suffering caused by the struggle itself is included our conclusion will have to be revised. If, for example, it is likely that the rebels can only win after a long and vicious war, but that if they do not receive arms from abroad they will suffer a quick defeat, then this additional suffering would have to be subtracted from the happiness that will result from a victory by the rebels.

In addition, we will have to also consider the consequences as they affect others outside of Central America. The good consequences would include the following:

(a) Employment for workers and profits for owners and investors in the arms industry.

(b) The sense of satisfaction that people with strong right-wing sympathies will feel that the struggle against communism is being sustained.

(c) The possible beneficial diplomatic effects elsewhere in the world.
The external bad consequences might include the following:

(a) Greater distrust from Third World countries towards the nation supplying the arms.

(b) Resentment from citizens within the supplying nation against their own government for violating the sovereignty of foreign countries.

(c) The possibility that relations between the superpowers may be destabilized, thus increasing the risk of nuclear war.

Self-Test No. 19

I.

1. There are many examples of wealthy people whose lives are obviously miserable (for example, through drug addiction or alcoholism). Others, such as Christina Onassis, Barbara Hutton, and Janis Joplin, have committed suicide.

2. This certainly applies to the criminal law, but there are important areas of law in which coercion is either absent or very remote. For example, some

laws lay down the conditions for making a valid will, and it is difficult to see how the function of these laws is coercive. Other examples of non-coercive laws: laws establishing courts, various aspects of constitutional law, and laws establishing the right of an individual to run for parliament.

3. The only real counter-example would consist of telling a joke that is not at the expense of someone else, such as a joke at one's own expense. To be effective, however, it needs to be funny.

4. The following women have become prime ministers of their countries: Margaret Thatcher, Golda Meir, Benazir Bhutto, Indira Gandhi, and Gro Harlem Brundtland. There have been numerous others.

5. The Spanish Inquisition, the Crusades, religious fanaticism in Northern Ireland, the Ayatollah Khomenei, Jim and Tammy Baker, and so on.

II.

1. Well, I've been a sex pervert all my life. I was raised as a sex pervert by my father, and if it was good enough for him then it is good enough for me.

2. I don't think that stealing my roommate's chemistry notes is really stealing, because he has never threatened to punish me for it.

3. And if Jim had found twenty thousand dollars lying in the street he'd be able to afford a new car; well, he has just bought a new car so he must have found twenty thousand dollars lying in the street.

4. Yes, and you shouldn't eat any salt either. It's deadly. They've proven that it kills laboratory animals when they give them a steady dose of it.

5. That's what my uncle said the day my aunt left him for good. Or, That's what the turkey said about the farmer the day before Thanksgiving.

Self-Test No. 20

1. Humour

2.   Vague terms: *the highest standards of craftsmanship* and *range of styles to suit the tastes of the modern consumer* have no clear meaning. False confidence: *We are the best...*

3.   If the speaker has been challenged to defend his or her earlier claim that pornography is not harmful to women, this would be a red herring. In some contexts, however, this attempt to change the topic might be legitimate.

4.   Vague terms: the entire passage is vague, but *neat guy, laid back,* and *lots of personality* are especially vague.

5.   Loaded question: The question assumes that we have been putting it off.

6.   Vague terms: *got what it takes.*

7.   If the speaker has been challenged to defend his or her earlier claim regarding how criminals should be treated, this would be a red herring. In other contexts, however, this statement might be legitimate.

8.   Persuasive redefinition: the term *scientist* is being redefined in a way that changes its normal descriptive meaning.

9.   Loaded question: the question *Is there any reason to think that this time Mulroney isn't just serving the interests of his tycoon friends in corporate boardrooms?* presupposes that normally Mulroney serves the interests of his tycoon friends. Loaded terms: *bleating, tycoon.*

10.   Selectivity: focuses attention on an unrepresentative sample of events.

Index